TEN

COMMENDATIONS

I am sure that like me you feel you know the Ten Commandments. On a good day you can remember them all and probably in the right order too. But until I had read this book I can now honestly say that I did not *really* know the Ten Commandments.

The book lends itself to being picked up and put down in short bursts. After all there are obviously ten distinct chapters. But you will not be able to put it down for too long, and J. John shows very clearly that the chapters are not exactly unrelated. For me it was '10 out of 10' for TEN!

Andy Reed, MP for Loughborough

J. John, showing how relevant the Ten Commandments are today, gives us Christian teaching at its very best, accessible and morally uplifting. His popular style and enthusiasm shows how the original message is just as important today as it has ever been.

Although Christians and Jews share common texts and yet interpret them differently, the aim of both our traditions is to make the world a better place and to help every individual find the way to live a full and a spiritual life. No one in the Christian world does this better than J. John. Even in those areas where Christian and Jewish interpretation differ, the message is positive and inspiring.

Rabbi Dr Jeremy Rosen

TEN

J. John

KINGSWAY PUBLICATIONS,
EASTBOURNE

First published 2000

Verses unmarked are the author's own translation.

ISBN 0 85476 874 2
Front cover design by Glenn Andrews.

10 11 12 Printing/Year 10 09 08 07

Published by
KINGSWAY COMMUNICATIONS LTD
Lottbridge Drove, Eastbourne BN23 6NT, England.
Email: books@kingsway.co.uk

Printed in the U.S.A.

I dedicate this book to
Tuana.
A friend on the journey.

Contents

Acknowledgements

You can't applaud with one hand. I am always grateful for the doors of opportunity – and for friends who oil the hinges. I would therefore like to acknowledge a number of people who have made this book possible. Especially Revd Chris Russell, not only my researcher, but a dear friend. Thank you for researching, reading, reflecting and ruminating. Chris, you are a treasured friend who answers whenever I call. Thank you also to Belinda Russell, for her professional perspective, input and advice on a number of issues.

I owe an incredible debt of gratitude to my dear friend and co-worker Paul Wilson. Thank you to my assistant Charlie Farmery who read and reread every chapter, and whose insights were invaluable.

Many thanks to my vicar, Dr Mark Stibbe – a wise and amusing friend. You have inspired, encouraged and provoked me to thought.

Special thanks to my dear friend Dr R. T. Kendall whose series of sermons on the Ten Commandments and book, *Just Grace*, were so illuminating and helpful. I recommend R. T.'s book.

I am indebted to Chris and Alison Walley for their astute reading, reflection and response to each chapter. Thank you for your time and effort.

I would also like to thank Dr Laura Schlessinger, Dr Ron Mehl and Dr Leonard Felder, whose teaching on the Ten Commandments stimulated my own thinking and enriched my understanding. I have also greatly benefited from Rabbi Jeffrey K. Salkin's very helpful teaching. Thank you to my friends Dr Chris Bignell and Dr Jane Bradnock (both medical doctors) for your helpful advice with several chapters.

To Gary Grant (Mr Entertainer), you are a true friend and a tonic. Thank you for your example in taking the fourth commandment seriously.

I would like to acknowledge and thank my trustees who supervise the work I undertake – Terry and Juanita Baker, Jamie Colman, Bob Fuller, Mike Shouler and Peter Wright. Thank you for your counsel, support and faith in God, who uses ordinary people like me.

The diamonds in my life are my three sons, Michael, Simeon and Benjamin – they challenge me not to be theoretical about the Ten Commandments, but to put them into practice. I feel privileged to have three sons entrusted to me by God, to be their soul support.

And to my partner, lover and best friend, Killy (my wife!), whose insights added an enormous amount to each chapter and whose warmth helps us to treasure each day.

Finally, to the true and living God – you are truly perfect, powerful and personal. You sustain us and guide us. You have blessed me with strength and purpose. Thank you for your promises. To you, Everlasting Eternal One, I am grateful.

J. John, AD 2000

Preface

This is a book on the Ten Commandments. Barely 300 words long in English, the Ten Commandments form the foundation of our legal system, are enshrined in the heart of our parliamentary structures and lie at the very core of Western civilization. In words so brief that they would make only a palm-size piece of text in a newspaper, this great arch of divine law encompasses family rights, property rights, the rights of the individual and even the rights of God. Someone once said that humans are such able creatures that they have made 32,647,389 laws and still haven't been able to improve on the Ten Commandments.

Most people in this country would probably admit that the Ten Commandments are important. Yet they are almost totally unknown. A recent survey of 1,200 people aged 15–35 found that most of those polled could name no more than two of the Ten Commandments – and they weren't too happy about some of the others when they were told about them! In speaking widely on the Ten Commandments I have been amazed at two things: the ignorance we have of them and the interest there is to know more about them.

The reason for the interest is, I think, pretty plain. When you look at almost all social trends, Britain is in deep decline. We are being confronted with a rise in crime, family breakdown, personal debt and drug abuse. We live in a generation that has lost its fixed standards. Our society isn't just a ship that has slipped loose from its moorings; it is a ship that has lost its compass and rudder too. For a society desperately adrift, the Ten Commandments offer us both a landmark and an anchorage.

Yet there is, I believe, another reason why there is an interest in the Ten Commandments today. I believe that these ancient rules are stamped – like the embossed numerals on a watch dial – onto the conscience of every man and woman. They are part of what we are as human beings, and when we hear them, we recognize them in our innermost beings.

I believe passionately that we need to recover the Ten Commandments for our society. The idea that God has rules for the way we live may sound uncomfortable and even off-putting to us today. Yet if there is a God who has made us and if he has spoken, then it makes a lot of sense to listen to what he has to say about how we run our lives. I come across many people who believe *in* God, but don't believe God; they believe in the Maker, but do not accept the Maker's instructions. That, of course, is nonsense. God himself is the source of the Ten Commandments, and because the basis of the Ten Commandments is the one who made the human race, *they work*.

I believe it's about time we started to take them seriously.

The Ten Commandments for the twenty-first century

At the start of a new century, though, there are those who would suggest that far from trying to recover the Ten

Commandments for our society, it is time to modify them. They say that the Ten Commandments are not simply unfamiliar, they are obsolete. A new world, they insist, needs a new ethic. But as to what sort of ethic, there is no agreement. Some have called for the development of a modern, secular – more twenty-first-century – set of Ten Commandments. Because this is the age of democracy and personal autonomy and few of us really wish to be pushed around by commanders or commandments, they suggest these might be renamed 'the Ten Suggestions'. We can imagine what they might look like; instead of ten firm, non-negotiable 'Thou shalt nots', there will be only one real negative: 'Do not drink and drive'. The rest would be gentle exhortations to punctuality, patience, tolerance, cheerfulness, doing your best, having a sense of fair play, keeping promises, caring for the environment and always, *always* putting the curtain inside the bath when you take a shower.

Others suggest that we do not even bother to modify the Commandments. We should just get rid of them. Why, they protest, should we burden modern men and women with the primitive code of a nomadic tribe that lived under skin tents in a desert? Yet the answer is that even amid vast changes, some things remain stubbornly unalterable. Switch the tents to flats and houses, transform the nomadic tribe to executives in business suits, alter the desert into a modern city and you will find that human nature stays exactly what it always was. Of course things have changed. The clicking abacus has become the sophisticated computer, the creaking ox-cart has become the supersonic jet, but fire is still fire, water is still water and humanity is still humanity. All our ancient literature, biblical or otherwise, shows that as far as ethics goes, humans have changed not the slightest in 4,000 years. We have the same vices as our ancestors. And we need the same rules.

No, the Ten Commandments are not obsolete, but they are *absolute*. They were not made for any particular period in history. They were made for human nature and therefore were commandments for all seasons, all centuries, all cultures. They are as universal and perpetual as honour and truth. No nation, least of all Britain, can survive apart from a moral base built on them.

There is a savage irony here. We have got rid of the Ten Commandments in the name of freedom, yet the price we have paid is our own liberty. We have pushed aside these old laws in order to have personal freedom. Yet in the resulting moral vacuum that is modern Britain we are no longer free to venture out at night, no longer happy to let our children play on the street and no longer able to have cars and homes without equipping them with alarms and hi-tech locks. In a particularly curious twist, we have come to accept a level of video surveillance of our actions in city centres that, until recently, was only applied to inmates of high-security prisons.

Law and liberty are not in opposition. In fact, law is at the heart of liberty. Laws do not restrict us; rather they free us to live in order and harmony. This is true for societies and it is true for individuals. St Augustine paraphrased the Christian law as 'Love God and do what you like'. Many people have gone for a different motto: 'Do what you like and soon after, rush to a psychoanalyst to find out why you no longer seem to like anything.'

We have come to realize that nothing is quite so enslaving as total freedom.

About this book

This book originated around ten years ago as *God's Top Ten*. Since then, as I have spoken and thought more about the subject of the Ten Commandments and my thinking has evolved and been challenged, it has been completely rewritten and much enlarged.

The Ten Commandments occur in two places in the Bible. In Exodus 20 we have an account of how they were given to Moses on Mount Sinai, and in Deuteronomy 5 we have them repeated in the introduction to the Jewish laws. They were given to the people of Israel on their way out of slavery in Egypt to the Promised Land around 1450 BC. I have not gone into the setting here or how they were given. If you want to know the background, any good Bible dictionary, encyclopaedia or study Bible will help (I have recommended some at the end of this book).

Of the Ten Commandments, numbers one to four deal with our behaviour towards God. Commandments five to nine deal with our behaviour towards other people, and the tenth commandment deals with our thoughts. For each commandment, I look at the issue it addresses, try and look at the heart of the problem and then present a series of suggestions as to how we can keep it in the twenty-first century.

I have chosen to start with the tenth commandment and end with the first. I have my reasons for, as it were, going from the outside in. The first commandment seems to me to be the glowing heart of the law, like some fiery star in the centre of a planetary system. For us in our culture today I think it is easier to spiral in slowly through the outer laws before we come face to face with the incandescent glow of the first commandment.

Let me also say here what this book is not. It is not some cold, analytical intellectual study on the Ten Commandments carefully drafted on a year's sabbatical in a quiet university cloister. What I have written here has been hammered out in almost countless seminars and speaking events before tens of thousands of people. I am aware that many I speak to, and many who read this, are struggling anxiously with issues of right and wrong. Some are coming to terms with the sombre implications of their moral failure. This book is not a philosophic thesis on military tactics; it is a blood-stained message from the front line. Yet isn't this how it should be? The Commandments were not given to be debated; they were given to be lived.

On this basis, there are lots of technical questions I have ducked. There is, for instance, very little here on the relationship of the sixth commandment ('You shall not murder') to warfare or capital punishment. You can't put everything in. I am also concerned about the great temptation we all have to occupy our minds with intriguing abstract problems that we do not face in order to duck dealing with the real ones that we do. For those who want to pursue matters further, there are a number of books recommended at the end of this book that may help you.

There are lots of quotes in this book and where I can I have tried to give due credit to their authors. The eighth commandment applies to words as well as things. However, in some cases they have been bouncing about in my brain (or my study) for so long that their sources have become worn away. For the unconscious use – or abuse – of any such material, I ask forgiveness.

Finally, let me also say a word about the quotations from the

Bible here. Most of the verses cited are from either the New International Version or the New Living Translation and the letters 'NIV' or 'NLT' therefore appear after the reference. However, having grown up as a Greek speaker, I have been unable to resist occasionally making my own translation of the New Testament where I felt the published versions didn't reflect the best meaning of the text.

J. John, 2000

The Ten Commandments

And God spoke all these words:

'I am the LORD your God, who brought you out of Egypt, out of the land of slavery.

'You shall have no other gods before me.

'You shall not make for yourself an idol in the form of anything in heaven above or on the earth beneath or in the waters below. You shall not bow down to them or worship them; for I, the LORD your God, am a jealous God, punishing the children for the sin of the fathers to the third and fourth generation of those who hate me, but showing love to a thousand generations of those who love me and keep my commandments.

'You shall not misuse the name of the LORD your God, for the LORD will not hold anyone guiltless who misuses his name.

'Remember the Sabbath day by keeping it holy. Six days you shall labour and do all your work, but the seventh day is a Sabbath to the LORD your God. On it you shall not do any work, neither you, nor your son or daughter, nor your manservant or maidservant, nor your animals, nor the alien within your gates. For in six days the LORD made the heavens and the earth, the sea, and all that is in them, but he rested on the seventh day. Therefore the LORD blessed the Sabbath day and made it holy.

'Honour your father and your mother, so that you may live long in the land the LORD your God is giving you.

'You shall not murder.

'You shall not commit adultery.

'You shall not steal.

'You shall not give false testimony against your neighbour.

'You shall not covet your neighbour's house. You shall not covet your neighbour's wife, or his manservant or maidservant, his ox or donkey, or anything that belongs to your neighbour.'

Exodus 20:1–17, NIV

COMMANDMENT 10

You shall not covet your neighbour's house. You shall not covet your neighbour's wife, or his manservant or maidservant, his ox or donkey, or anything that belongs to your neighbour.
(Exodus 20:17, NIV)

So what's the problem?

Coveting may not be a word that we use a lot today. Yet the concept of wanting what is not ours to have is well known. In fact, the problem that the tenth commandment addresses is so familiar that it is expressed in dozens of popular sayings and quips. Consider these:

- The closest to perfection a person comes is when they fill out a job application form.
- The biggest room in the world is the room for improvement.
- The grass is always greener on the other side of the fence.
- People live in one of two tents: content and discontent.
- However long you take agonizing over the menu deciding which sweet to have, when the next person's dessert arrives, you realize you have made the wrong choice.
- God made us a little lower than the angels, but most of us are concerned to climb a little higher than the Joneses.

- The average family ambition is to make as much money as they are spending.
- Our yearnings will always exceed our earnings.

Whether it is desserts, clothes, houses, salaries, talents, lifestyles or cars, we want what other people have. Each one of us has unique desires – we like different things, have different tastes and different priorities. It would be a boring world if we liked the same things. Yet while our desires might be different, what we all have in common with each other is this: we all want what we haven't got.

Not all desire is wrong, of course. We desire all sorts of things, in all sorts of ways. Some of our deepest desires are for good things: pleasure and joy, belonging and security, comfort and safety, excitement and adventure. We want to be well respected, to be looked up to, to be significant and loved; and to have some meaning in our lives. Those are all important things and things that we need from the moment we are born to the moment we die. Without any desire we would be little more than walking vegetables.

Yet what we aren't so aware of is that, from the moment we are born, our desires are being moulded by the world around us. Soon we start to believe that the fulfilment of those good desires to be loved, to be respected, to belong, is to be found by obtaining material things. We want to be content, but we think that the only way of achieving this is by acquiring things we don't already have. We have started coveting – having an illegitimate or wrongful desire for something that, for whatever reason, is not ours to have.

The result is the mess we are in. We are a nation of people who desire what we haven't got, whether it be fridges or food, bank balances or brains, wives or families, houses or lifestyles. We are never satisfied! We want more and more; we want to be better and richer. It is not surprising that in a desperate – but futile – attempt to satisfy the insatiable thirst that covetousness produces, our favourite national pastime is shopping.

But why start here? After all, you say, desire – even a wrong desire – is hardly a heinous crime. Aren't the other commands more important? We agree that people can, and should, be prosecuted for stealing or murder. But it is not against the law to covet. What's the big deal? What's wrong with a bit of dreaming, a bit of desiring?

It is true that nobody has ever been sent down for the crime of coveting. However, you don't have to look too closely to see the effect that wrong desires have on people's actions. We might not turn all our desires into actions, but all our actions are a result of our desires. For example, every act of theft starts with someone's desire to have something that they have no right to have. Every act of adultery begins with someone's desire for a person they are not married to. Once we recognize the place that desire has in our actions, we get to deal with what is underneath the surface. Starting this way round, we see the reasons that make us act in the way we do.

Covetousness might be unseen and impossible to legislate against, but its effects are seen everywhere, and they can be devastating. Many of the darker pages of human history have resulted from covetousness. Throughout history, rulers and nations have coveted the land, resources and wealth that belong to others. In their efforts to fulfil those wrong desires, they have caused hostility, invasion and war. Millions upon millions of men and women have died fighting for their country's covetous desires (often justified by such wonderful terms as 'maintaining natural justice', 'protecting legitimate territorial rights' or 'restoring historic boundaries'). Just as many have died defending their countries from covetous neighbours acting under similar fine phrases. Yet all these battles have originated because of the wrong desire rulers and peoples have had for power, control and wealth. Coveting is also one of the key factors in producing the global environmental crisis. Not only are there more people on the planet than ever before, but those people there are want more and more.

Covetousness also breeds exploitation and unrest within countries. At the end of 1999, there was a massive race to get the Millennium Dome finished for the 31st December deadline. This gave the key workers incredible power. In fact, it was reported that some of the electricians had threatened to strike if their demands for over £18,000 a week were not met. As a society, we find that we are soon outraged when we hear of the huge profits of, for example, railway companies, and the huge salary increases of their directors. Their greed, we say angrily, has taken money away from improving badly needed services. Yet so all-pervasive is covetousness that even our protesting becomes tinged with it. Behind our outrage against their greed lies a covetousness of our own.

What is more, coveting is not simply a matter of us having our own individual natural desires. That would be bad enough. The fact is that millions of pounds a week are poured into trying to enlarge and direct our desires. Encouraging coveting is a major national industry; we call it advertising. Americans, it is reported, spend more money on advertising than on all public institutions of education and I suspect the situation in Britain is probably similar. Once, advertisements might have been created with no goal other than the desire to inform the public; now though they clearly set out to manipulate existing desires and create new ones. Through advertising, the world and all its goods make a plea for space in our hearts. Whether we are sitting in front of our televisions, reading magazines or newspapers, or even just driving down the road, we cannot get away from being bombarded with subtle attempts to direct our desires. Adverts skilfully entice us to buy a nippier car, a slimmer phone, a more fragrant perfume or simply another type of tea. We read articles on the possessions and lifestyles of the rich and famous, we see programmes full of images of the bold and the beautiful, and we can't stop ourselves wanting what they've got and what they are. Advertisements create dissatisfaction. A car, house or hi-fi that we have been contented with for years suddenly, under the onslaught of advertisements, seems old and shabby and in need of urgent replacement.

This is what the tenth command tackles. Longing, wishing, craving, yearning, desiring – call it what we will – for what we want but cannot have. That is what coveting is all about.

Let's begin below the surface of our lives, in the place where it all starts – our hearts.

The heart of the matter

So why do we want all these things? Why is it a universal truth that men and women desire what they haven't got?

We all have desires that are God-given. For example, I believe that the desires to be loved and to feel worthwhile, to belong and to feel secure, are from God and are good. However, instead of trying to find fulfilment for them by going to our Creator God, the God who made our hearts and their desires, we go elsewhere. Let me give an example. I believe that the desire to feel significant is a good, God-given desire. Its real fulfilment lies ultimately in knowing that we are loved children of a heavenly Father. But for many people, the desire to feel significant shows itself in wearing the right clothes with the right label. With that label or designer name comes significance and we can believe (encouraged by advertising) that by wearing it this significance – and popularity and importance with it – is transferred to us. The right label gives our self-esteem a real boost. Or at least that's the thinking behind it. In seeking to fulfil our needs, we not only face in the wrong direction but are confused over what it is we actually do need. Why is this?

One person who succinctly explained the human dilemma, nearly 500 years ago, was the Christian leader Martin Luther. He said that our basic human problem is that our hearts are 'curved in on themselves'. His diagnosis holds today. The person we are most concerned about in the world is ourselves. All over our radio and TV airwaves at the moment, people are opening their hearts. If you listen to or watch *Oprah Winfrey*, *Ricki Lake*, *Kilroy*, *Talk Radio* and similar shows, what do people who open their hearts talk about all the time? *Themselves.* And if we were there behind the microphones, would we be different? I fear not. We are all self-obsessed. The root of covetousness is selfishness.

Early in the last century the question was raised in *The Times*: 'What is wrong with the world?' One writer wrote the following response:

> Dear Sir,
> I am.
> Yours faithfully,
> G. K. Chesterton

Why is this? Is it that when God made us we were deliberately constructed to be more concerned for ourselves than anyone else? Or is it some accidental design flaw with our species? Are we like those cars that you hear about that are recalled by the makers because they have some construction fault?

No, we can't blame God for it. At the beginning of the Bible, in Genesis 1, we're told that God made the world, and as it tells how he reviewed the world he had created, we read, 'God saw that it was *good* . . . God saw that it was *good* . . . God saw that it was *good*. . .' Man and woman too were made good; designed to enjoy the world, living together contentedly under God's rule.

Unfortunately, soon trouble came. We read in Genesis 2 how God gave humankind freedom to eat from any tree in the Garden of Eden. There was just the one restriction given: 'You must not eat from the tree of the knowledge of good and evil.' The Bible then describes how the devil, in the form of a serpent, tempted Adam and Eve to break this restriction. He suggested to Eve that eating the fruit would give the power to be 'like God'. The desire to covet – to want what was not hers to have – was sown in Eve's heart. It was an attractive offer. Imagine that: being like God and having all that power, all that authority. You would be able to make all the decisions in your life; you would not have to do what anyone else said; you would not have to live in the way that someone else told you. You would have total freedom.

It was too attractive an offer, and Eve and Adam took it up and disobeyed God. The result of their disobedience lives on with us today. What they did then, we continue to do. We too push God off the throne and plant ourselves firmly, immovably, there instead. We do what we want, we make our own decisions, we live as gods of our own lives, we love ourselves more than anything, or anyone, else.

The result is the tragedy of the human species. Our hearts were made to love God and to love others as we love ourselves. However, instead we choose to love only ourselves. As a result everyone else, God and the rest of the world, has to fall into place behind us. The effects of this total distortion of our relationships are massive.

Jesus' brother James wrote to a church that was going through difficulties: 'Those conflicts and disputes among you, where do they come from? Do they not come from your cravings at war within you? You want something and do not have it; so you commit murder. And you covet something and cannot have it; so you engage in disputes and conflicts' (James 4:1–2).

The heart of the human problem is simply the problem of the human heart. Our hearts have turned away from what God desires. Cut loose from God, we now desire all sorts of things, in all sorts of ways, that are bad for us. In the Old Testament God addresses his people saying, 'The heart is deceitful above all things and beyond cure. Who can understand it?' In the next verse God answers his own question: 'I, the LORD, search the heart and examine the mind . . .' (Jeremiah 17:9–10, NIV).

Over fifteen hundred years ago, a young man called Augustine, who had been brought up in a Christian home, rebelled against everything he had been brought up to believe in and did his bit of wild living. It wasn't long before he turned again to God and then was able to say, 'You have made our hearts, Lord, and they are restless until they find their rest in you.' We've all got restless hearts; it is the heart disease – or disease – that is universal. One of the most famous poets of the last century, T. S. Eliot said,

> The desert is not only in remote southern tropics,
> The desert is not only around the corner,
> The desert is squeezed in the tube train next to you,
> The desert is in the heart of your brother.
>
> (Choruses from *The Rock I*)

Recognizing the desert in our hearts, we try and pour water into it. Much of what we desire is a desperate misplaced attempt to try to irrigate our internal wasteland. This is the case in two specific areas: money and fame.

Money

We earn more now than we ever have; wages and the standard of living go up and up. Yet as they rise so do our expectations. We live at a time that seems more covetous for money than any other time in history. Today, those who set the trends in our society are earning extraordinary sums. To give just one recent example, in December 1999, after several months of hard bargaining, the 27-year-old Manchester United captain Roy Keane signed a four-year contract that will pay him around £50,000 a week. In the next four years it is conceivable he could earn £17 million. Roy Keane typifies today's heroes. With this kind of example, is it surprising that we are all wanting more and more?

Coveting today is made easier by easily available credit. Items that 50 years ago a family would have had to save up for can now be bought on instant credit, creating instant debts. 'Buy now, pay later' is the invitation, and '52 easy payments' is the slogan. I've never met an easy payment in my life! Nowadays, people can be divided into three groups: the 'haves', the 'have-nots' and the 'have-not-paid-for-what-they-haves'. Everything is faster in today's society – especially getting into debt.

The National Lottery typifies modern Britain's obsession with money. It has been estimated that 94 per cent of the adult population, nearly 43 million people, have played the lottery since it began in 1994. The average adult in the United Kingdom spends £3.32 a week on the lottery and each week as a nation we spend £82 million on lottery tickets. That comes to a staggering £4.3 billion a year. Even if we do not buy tickets, there can be very few of us who haven't spent just a couple of seconds wondering what we would do if, somehow, we did win.

The statistics, however, are devastating. The odds on winning are 13,983,816 to 1, and 99.9999 per cent of people who play lose money. Why then do we spend such billions on the lottery? When asked that question, psychologist Dr Mark Griffiths said, 'I think it is complicated.' Nonsense, Dr Griffiths! It is simple. We want money! We want to be richer people. We are convinced that more money will make our lives better. Yet one of the most significant figures about the lottery does not involve money or probabilities. It is that 90 per cent of all jackpot winners continue to play the lottery. Despite having won an average of £7 million it is not enough. If all that money had made them content and satisfied, why did they keep on playing? John D. Rockefeller, at one time the richest man in the world, had learned the grim answer. 'How much money does it take for a person to be really satisfied?' he was asked. His reply said it all: 'Just a little bit more.'

Money, even vast quantities of it, fails to refresh the desert of the human heart.

Fame

In addition to money, fame also offers the illusion of an answer to our deepest needs.

Surveys tell us that 70 per cent of all 18- to 24-year-olds define success in terms of wealth and career, and that nearly two-thirds of young people feel under pressure to succeed. The rat race is alive and well. It's just a pity that most people don't realize that the thing about the rat race is that even if you win it, you are still a rat.

We do not just covet money and things. We also covet life-styles; we want to be other people. We all have our heroes, but so many of us go further, desiring to have their kind of life. In the summer of 1999, a sample of British children were asked who they would like to be, and 86 per cent of them replied, 'Zoë Ball.' That summer saw Zoë Ball at the height of her career, anchoring the highly sought after breakfast show slot on Radio 1, voted 'The Most Desirable Woman in the Country' by a prominent men's magazine, regularly on the TV screens, and marrying Norman Cook, otherwise known as Fat Boy Slim, himself the most successful DJ in the country.

In our newsagents, a whole shelf of glossy magazines parade, in multi-page photo-spreads, the details of the lifestyles of the famous for us to goggle at. In doing this they pander to more than our curiosity. In our hearts we want to be like them, we want to be there in those photographs, we want to be receiving phone calls from other famous stars and invited to their parties and dinners. Surely fame, we tell ourselves, will answer all our deepest needs.

Yet we know, as with money, that fame's answer is an illusion. Star after star has said it. In an interview in September 1999, Zoë Ball herself said, 'I have a terrible fear of more talented people than me thinking I'm just a prat who does kids' TV.' The interview went on to describe how she craves normality and an everyday life. She is now taking an indefinite career break and states her ambition is to be one of those people who disappear from public life, only reappearing in years to come in the 'Where Are They Now?' sections of magazines.

Fame too, no matter how much we get of it, fails to permanently refresh the desert of the human heart.

Countering covetousness

So how do we respond? Shrug our shoulders and go and do a little shopping ourselves? Let me suggest several lines of defence against covetousness.

Beware and be realistic

Never ever underestimate the dangerous power of covetousness. The Bible is brutally honest about the effects of wrongful desire and the fact that it can run rampant in all of us. The classic case is that of David – great psalm-writer, noble warrior and excellent king who had, it might seem, everything he could want. Yet a single case of unchecked illicit desire almost destroyed his kingship and led to untold grief. The frank account in 2 Samuel 11 tells how one day David saw a woman bathing and, even though both of them were married, he desired her. From this act of covetousness things spiralled inexorably downwards in a tragic pattern of escalating sin. Acting on his desire, David sent for the woman, Bathsheba, and slept with her. She became pregnant and as Uriah, her husband, had been away for months at the war, this threatened David with a considerable scandal. David, desperate for a cover-up, sent for Uriah on the assumption that he would sleep with his wife and the baby could be passed off as his. However, as a man of duty and honour in a time of war, Uriah refused to go home to his wife. David, now in a real corner, was forced to get himself out of the mess by arranging for Uriah to be killed on the battlefield so that he could marry Bathsheba and legitimize the baby. Inevitably, the result was a disaster. David and Bathsheba were judged by God and the ensuing problems came to overshadow David's entire reign. David committed adultery, abused his position as lawgiver of Israel, lied and eventually murdered because he let his covetous desires for another man's wife overtake him. Desire in the heart leads to action. Breaking the tenth commandment resulted ultimately in David breaking the sixth, seventh and ninth commandments as well.

Not only is covetousness powerful, it is also subtle. In fact, it can enter into almost every area of life. The Bible talks a lot about coveting, not just of things and money but also of other people's gifts or responsibilities. Paul himself appears to have found coveting a particular problem (Romans 7:7–8). Covetousness, it seems, can easily turn followers away from Jesus and his words. In one of Jesus' most famous stories, the sower and the seed, he talks about how people do not allow God's word to work in their lives because they let the word become choked by the 'cares and riches and pleasures of this life' (Luke 8:14, NLT).

There is even a story in the Bible that tells how, in the days of the early church, a man called Simon so coveted the miraculous gifts of the Holy Spirit that the apostles had, that he tried to buy them with money (Acts 8:4–25).

We need to be aware that covetousness is powerful and subtle and can attack us in all sorts of ways. We need to be on our guard in every area of our lives.

See through the illusion

If we need to be on our guard about covetousness we also need to keep reminding ourselves that it is based on an illusion. Covetousness promises contentment and fulfilment. Yet few, if any, of the things we covet bring us either. Certainly neither riches nor fame deliver what they promise.

Ironically, this is something that, deep down, we know. In the case of money, the spectacular tales of quarrels, depression and suicides that have resulted from the big lottery wins are so widespread that some players dread winning. One recent winner refused to collect her £4 million jackpot money saying that she 'didn't want her life ruined'.

The limitations of material wealth have been well-stated by an anonymous poet:

> Money can buy medicine, but it cannot buy health.
> Money can buy a house, but not a home.
> Money can buy companionship, but not friendship.
> Money can buy entertainment, but not happiness.
> Money can buy food, but not an appetite.
> Money can buy a bed, but not sleep.
> Money can buy a crucifix, but not a saviour.

In the case of fame, we try and overlook the fact that those who are rich and famous often bemoan having desperately sad lives. The soap *EastEnders* regularly gets around 16 million viewers and in 1999 the highest ratings were for the episodes surrounding the departure of the character of Bianca. Patsy Palmer, the actress who played her part, was interviewed as she prepared to leave the high-profile soap. 'Several times', the article said, 'she referred to a metaphorical hole in her stomach. "You can't fill it up with drugs and you can't fill it up with drink and you can't fill it up with food."'

We need to remind ourselves of this: covetousness promises but fails to deliver. Not only that, but in fact it does the opposite. It traps. Covetousness is deceitful; it says that if you desire things, people, lifestyles or fame, once you get them you will be satisfied. Actually once you have got them, you still want more. 'Shop until you drop' becomes not so much a joke as a grim admission of the power of an inescapable compulsion. In 1851 the German philosopher Schopenhauer said that coveting 'is like sea water; the more we drink the thirstier we become'.

Someone has suggested shouting, 'Who are you kidding?' at adverts that come on the television. Certainly we need to be aware of what the underlying message is. And we most definitely need to be able to teach our children how the media generally – and adverts in particular – seek to manipulate our desires and confuse us over what we want and what we really need.

Above all, we need to remember that *things* are temporary. They are not real riches. In warning his followers about covetousness Jesus told a chilling story.

> A rich man had a fertile farm that produced fine crops. In fact, his barns were full to overflowing. So he said, 'I know! I'll tear down

> my barns and build bigger ones. Then I'll have room enough to store everything. And I'll sit back and say to myself, "My friend, you have enough stored away for years to come. Now take it easy! Eat and drink and be merry."' But God said to him, 'You fool! You will die this very night then who will get it all?' Yes, a person is a fool to store up earthly wealth but not have a rich relationship with God. (Luke 12:15–21, NLT)

Jesus pointed out how the man in this story had concluded that material possessions could satisfy all his needs. Suddenly, without warning, he was called to account and it was all taken from him.

Covetousness is a lie. We need to remember that.

Realize that fear feeds covetousness

It is easy to take covetousness as simply the product of greed or unchained desire. Yet I believe that the roots of covetousness are deeper. Strange as it may seem at first, I believe that one of the most fertile soils for covetousness is fear.

In today's world, fear is like the air we breathe; it's everywhere. We fear all sorts of things, some big, some small; some that are real threats and some that are not. Recent research shows that the number one worry people have is money. Either we worry we don't have enough or we worry about keeping what we do have.

When we face the future, we need to look to something for hope. Things, especially money, offer apparent security. In our fear, we focus our hopes and our confidence on things, not on God. We live as if it were all up to us; as if our survival depended on our own efforts. We take our life into our own hands, and in doing that find we have taken our life out of his.

Jesus points out the absurdity of the situation:

> Therefore I tell you, do not worry about your life, what you will eat or drink; or about your body, what you will wear. Is not life more important than food, and the body more important than clothes? Look at the birds of the air; they do not sow or reap or store away in barns, and yet your heavenly Father feeds them. Are you not much more valuable than they? (Matthew 6:25–26, NIV)

Jesus encourages people, time and time again, to trust in God, because he is faithful and true. If he looks after the birds, then of course he will look after those people who trust in him. Things provide only an illusion of security, not the reality.

Do you know which commandment is most frequently given by God to his people in the Bible? Interestingly enough, it is not one of the Ten Commandments at all. Instead, it is the command, 'Do not fear, do not be afraid.' Over 370 times God says to his people in various ways that they needn't fear. Why? Well, obviously, not because bad things don't and can't happen, but because he is the Lord, and they can trust him with their lives. As the Christian writer Dr Tom Wright says, this is the best news in the world because it's what we most need to hear – God addressing our fears and telling us we needn't be afraid because we can trust him.

If we knew God better, I believe we would be less tempted to be afraid. And that would cut at the very root of covetousness.

Cultivate contentment

What I have offered so far is largely negative advice about how to counter covetousness. But there is more to the tenth commandment than this. What I want to do now is to offer some positive advice about an alternative: contentment.

The old saying, 'The grass is always greener on the other side of the fence', isn't automatically true. The problem is that often we have been watering it. Maybe it's time we started watering our side of the fence. Let me offer you some tips for contentment.

Keep your heart in shape

The first way we find lasting contentment is by letting God, not the world, shape our desires. God wants us first to know that he desires us, and that we can trust him. Then if we will let him he will get to work on shaping our desires, so that what we will want is what he desires for us. The extraordinary thing is that God wants to do this. From the opening chapters of the Bible to the last, it is clear that God wants our love and our friendship. He wants to be close to us, not far away. The God of the Bible is neither remote from us nor wants some cold, mechanical relationship, as if we were just his little slaves or robots. He is a loving, caring, forgiving, kind and intimate God who will settle for nothing less than the closest of relationships with us. We need to return his love.

The first thing we must straighten out is the state of our hearts – something that no fitness regime or self-help programme can do. What we cannot do, God can. There is a wonderful promise made by God through the Old Testament prophet Ezekiel: 'I will give you a new heart and put a new spirit in you; I will remove from you your heart of stone and give you a heart of flesh' (Ezekiel 36:26, NIV).

This heart transplant is exactly what happens when we come to know Jesus. He removes from us our old hearts, curved in on themselves, self-obsessed and selfish. In their place, he gives us his own heart. It is an extraordinary exchange. He takes our messy, malfunctioning hearts and replaces them with his. If your heart feels tired and self-obsessed, might it not be evidence that you need that heart transplant? Whoever we are, wherever we are, we need to ask him to take our old hard heart from us and give us his heart instead.

We need to realize too that the only fulfilment of our desires, even those that are God-given ones, comes from God himself. Everything else is deception. In chapter 4 of John's Gospel, we read how Jesus once sat by a well with a woman and told her that he was the one who could give living water that would cause anyone who drank it never to thirst again. In saying that, Jesus was making the point that he alone is the one who satisfies our deepest needs. If you have become aware that you are thirsting for all sorts of things on offer in the world, it might suggest that you either haven't drunk deeply enough from him or you have never drunk from him at all.

The first secret of contentment is to have and maintain a friendship with God through Christ. We need to guard this friendship, protectively nurturing it and taking care that it grows and flourishes. That must be our number one priority.

Adopt an attitude of gratitude

As we have seen, coveting does not lead to contentment, only a dissatisfaction with what we already have. The philosopher Nietzsche said, 'We grow weary of those things that we most desire.' Yet we read repeatedly in the Bible that one of the qualities God desires his children to have is contentment. Listen to the apostle Paul, writing from prison: 'I have learned the secret of being content in any and every situation, whether well fed or hungry, whether living in plenty or want' (Philippians 4:12, NIV).

A major part of contentment is having a positive attitude to the situation we are in. That is not easy to do in our modern society, because coveting plays on our dissatisfaction. God, however, does not want an unhealthy complaining from us. Rather he seeks the opposite outlook – what we can call 'an attitude of gratitude'.

It is amazing to hear Paul (again from prison) saying that he can rejoice and then go on to tell his friends to 'rejoice in the Lord always!' (Philippians 4:4, NIV). How could he do this in such a miserable situation? One reason is because he knew that everything he had was a gift from God. One of the problems we have in the Western world is an assumption that we deserve everything, that it is owed to us and that we have a right to it. What we fail to see is that everything we have is a gift from God. We deserve nothing.

One of the basic attitudes God desires us to have is that of thanks and praise. This is another reason why coveting is so wrong; in such a frame of mind we believe that we will only be happy when we have something we do not now have. It takes our focus away from what we already have, to what we do not have. And as we will never have everything, it leaves us in a guaranteed permanent state of discontent. Instead of thinking longingly, 'I must have this,' we should have the attitude that says gratefully, 'Look at what I have already.' We need to live in thankfulness to God.

As a starter, think about all you have:

- You are alive.
- You live in a beautiful world.

- You live in one of the few very prosperous countries in the world.
- You have greater freedom and more security than the majority of people in the world.
- Almost certainly you have friends or family who care about you.
- Above all, God loves you and desires that you come to know him.

And that's just a start. Coveting makes us long for more; in contrast, thankfulness makes us able to see how much we already have. A man had no shoes and complained until he met a man who had no feet. Let's be grateful for what we have.

Be a wise steward

God, then, calls us to be thankful for what we have. However, he also calls us to responsibly manage what he has given us. And that is no light matter. God has entrusted humanity with the creation he has lovingly made, with each other, and with our own abilities and resources.

We need to remember that the things we want and set our hearts on are not ours by right. We have done nothing to deserve them. We cannot even keep them, as death strips us of all our possessions. At best, we are loaned our wealth for a little while. What we are loaned is God's and we are accountable for our use and abuse of his property.

Jesus made this point in a number of uncomfortable parables. Once, explaining how his disciples must be ready for his return, Jesus told the following story about a servant to whom the master had given the responsibility of managing his household and feeding his family.

> If the master returns and finds that the servant has done a good job, there will be a reward. I assure you, the master will put that servant in charge of all he owns. But if the servant thinks, 'My master won't be back for a while,' and begins oppressing the other servants, partying, and getting drunk – well, the master will return unannounced and unexpected. He will tear the servant apart and banish him with the unfaithful. The servant will be severely punished, for though he knew his duty, he refused to do it. But people who are not aware that they are doing wrong will be punished only lightly. Much is required from those to whom much is given, and much more is required from those to whom much more is given. (Luke 12:43–48, NLT)

'Much is required from those to whom much is given' is a sobering rebuke to covetousness. The more we have, the more we are responsible for. It is as if every possession we have comes with an invisible audit slip upon which God marks how we have used what has been given us. Having little has its merits!

This whole principle, that we are stewards not owners of what we have, has enormous implications that space does not allow me to draw out. But we in the wealthy West need to think much more about it. We have a higher standard of living than almost any other people who have ever lived and we control so much that happens across the planet. As a result, we have an enormous and daunting responsibility to be wise and responsible stewards. We have, quite literally, been given the earth.

Focus on relationships, not things

In the pursuit of riches, things and fame that covetousness produces, people can pay the price. In the race for prosperity, people are easily crushed in the rush. Children and families in particular can be sacrificed on the altar of overtime. Friends can fall by the wayside because of our desires for possessions or power.

God desires us to have high quality relationships, and coveting does no good to friendships. It takes away time and opportunity, it makes us competitors not friends, and it makes us envious and jealous of each other. God's call to us is to love people and use things. Covetousness inverts this disastrously so that we end up loving things and using people.

How are your relationships? Are any of them suffering because you covet, because you desire things that aren't yours? If someone looked at your priorities what impression would they get about your life? Would they think that relationships were your number one priority, or would they think it was money, or things, or becoming more prosperous and more comfortable?

The book of Proverbs in the Old Testament sums things up well: 'Better a little with the fear of the LORD than great wealth with turmoil. Better a meal of vegetables where there is love than a fattened calf with hatred' (Proverbs 15:16–17, NIV).

People matter. After all, they are eternal; things aren't.

Be a giver

Perhaps the best – and certainly the most drastic – antidote for coveting is to be generous with what we have. Instead of being concerned to amass things we should be concerned about giving them away.

I've talked a bit about the lottery as evidence of the grip that coveting has on this society of ours. One of the saddest things is that since the lottery began, giving to charity has gone down. In percentage terms, giving has actually been going down for the last 25 years in this country. It was never very good and now it's a lot worse. It seems that as we get wealthier, we get stingier. We might never have had it so good, but we make sure that other people don't share it with us. This seems to be a global trend. At the beginning of the year 2000 thc three richest people in the world together have more wealth than the poorest 47 countries put together. A total of 342 people have more money than half the world's population put together. We might not be in that 342, but we are rich by the standards of most of the world. Instead of grasping for more, we need to learn to give it away.

Jesus talked a great deal about giving. Why? Because giving is the antidote to materialism, and the infallible cure for covetousness. Jesus said, 'It is more blessed to give than to receive' (Acts 20:35, NIV). As the great Christian writer C. S. Lewis so succinctly said, 'Biblical charity is more than merely giving away that which we can afford to do without anyway.'

Let's do something for somebody who can never repay us. We need to live simply so that others can simply live. We need to learn again the gift of giving.

Evaluate your priorities

Complacency is very dangerous. It is a wise policy to check ourselves once in a while and make sure we haven't lost the things that money can't buy. Jesus himself said, 'Beware! Don't be greedy for what you don't have. Real life is not measured by how much we own' (Luke 12:15, NLT). We all need to make priorities. Remember, if you don't live by priorities, you will live by pressures.

Let me suggest some simple questions for you:

- What do you like to think about most?
- What do you like to talk about the most?
- What do you invest most of your time and energy in?
- What do you spend your money on?
- Is there anything you would find hard to give up to save your closest relationships?

Covetousness seems the least deadly of all the Ten Commandments. Of them all, it seems the most soft-centred, the one that we can most easily live with. That is why it is so perilous. They tell us that if you drop a frog into a saucepan of hot water it will leap out. But if you put a frog in a pan of cold water and increase the temperature slowly, the frog stays there until it is boiled alive. It seems that the frog cannot see a threat in the slow, but ultimately deadly, rise in temperature. Often I wonder if that's what our society is doing to us in this whole area of our desires. All around us the temperature is going up, yet we simply sit there, stunned and unprotesting, oblivious to our impending fate.

Let's take this commandment to heart and not get boiled alive.

COMMANDMENT 9

You shall not give false testimony against your neighbour.
(Exodus 20:16, NIV)

So what's the problem?

We are surrounded by words; from the TV and radio, through telephones, in books and newspapers, on e-mails, faxes, the Internet, Teletext and sometimes – but increasingly rarely – in good old-fashioned face-to-face conversation. Words are everywhere, words are vital, but all too frequently the words are not true.

In fact we now almost don't expect that words will be true. For example, it is hard to resist smiling in disbelief when we hear any of the following:

- 'The cheque's in the post.'
- 'I'll start my diet tomorrow.'
- 'We believe you can't buy cheaper elsewhere.'
- 'Give me your number and I'll call you back.'
- 'Money cheerfully refunded.'
- 'One size fits all.'
- 'This questionnaire will take just two minutes of your time.'
- 'Congratulations! You have already won a prize in our £50,000 draw.'

- 'Open wide – this won't hurt a bit.'
- 'I'm from the Inland Revenue and I'm here to help you.'

The loss of truth in the public world is well known and it seems that barely a week goes by without some major trial centring on claims and counter-claims of lying. President Bill Clinton saw his reputation shattered worldwide, because he lied live on national television, claiming he had not had improper sexual relations with Monica Lewinsky. Jeffrey Archer, the multi-millionaire author and politician, had to drop out of the election to be Mayor of London when it became public that he had asked one of his friends to lie for him in court. Former cabinet minister Jonathan Aitken spent the best part of a year in prison for lying under oath in court. And so on.

The public adopts an attitude of wearied moral outrage. 'Imagine such dishonesty going on!' we protest, but any surprise is simulated. After all, we have now reached the stage where we barely trust anyone in the public sphere to tell the truth.

The problem though is not just in the high-profile jobs. It is at all levels, and we have a thousand terms for it. Politicians are 'economical with the truth', statistics are 'massaged', signatures and dates are 'adjusted', expenses are 'inflated', our work experience is 'padded', alibis are 'invented', product defects are 'overlooked', excuses are 'manufactured', promised deadlines 'slide' and difficult issues are 'evaded'. In fact, when you think about it, we lie about lying.

We lie at work (about our hours, expenses, lunch breaks and who really did break the copier) and we lie at home ('No, really your hair looks lovely', 'I thought there was more in our account', 'I don't mind missing the rugby if you want to see your mum', 'Of course you aren't fat'). We lie to the taxman ('necessary expenses'), we lie to the doctor ('I do take regular exercise'), we lie to the bank ('a temporary shortfall') and we lie to the traffic police ('Speed restrictions? Sorry, I had no idea'). Lies are now everywhere.

In fact lies are so universal that some people would suggest that it is now quite impossible to tell 'the truth, the whole truth and nothing but the truth'. In the 1997 film *Liar, Liar* Jim Carey played a lawyer whose son makes a wish that one day, just for 24 hours, his dad will tell the truth. As his wish is fulfilled, the film shows the hilarious disruption that occurs when Carey is forced to tell the truth in his personal relationships, in his work, in his family and in the regular run-of-the-mill comings and goings of the day. He loses a court case, offends work colleagues, makes his secretary quit and his mother vows never to talk to him again. And that's just the result of a single day of telling the truth. Being honest, it seems, only results in trouble. Many people would agree.

The ninth commandment tackles the whole issue of truth and lies, particularly as they affect those about us. It is, however, more than a simple intellectual rule that truth is good and truth is right. It says, 'You shall not give false testimony *against your neighbour.*' In saying that, it points out that our use and abuse of truth affects our relationships with others. Lies are not simply wrong; lies hurt people.

Surely not! we protest. Lies are mostly harmless. But are they? The little white lie we told to shift the blame off us for the faulty product shifted it onto someone else instead; in getting ourselves off the hook, we put others on it. Adjusting our work record to make us look good makes someone else look worse. Someone, somewhere foots the bill for our creativity on our expenses sheet. Lies have price tags on them that someone has to pay.

Yet our love affair with the lie goes deeper. We love to hear the worst about others; we are a nation that delights to give, and receive, gossip. The most popular newspapers are the ones that dish out the grimiest dirt and spread the biggest rumours. It doesn't matter whether the tales are true. Are they tasty? We shake our heads in righteous revulsion over the latest tabloid sensations at breakfast time and then regurgitate them in the office at coffee break.

The cost of lying

The consequences of this almost universal atmosphere of untruth are very serious indeed. The financial costs are astonishing, with fraudulent claims cheating the social services of hundreds of millions, if not billions, of pounds a year. The losses to the Inland Revenue of the undeclared incomes of the 'Black Economy' are even larger. Insurance companies now assume that most claims involve some element of dishonesty. The response is even more costly as society spends more and more on trying to prevent fraud with investigative teams and double-checking mechanisms. And to cover the cost of both the fraud and the preventive measures, taxes stay high and insurance premiums rise.

There are other costs too. The issues of government are no longer about how things really are. They are about how things are seen to be. Spin-doctors are entrusted with massaging and manipulating the way that events and trends are received by the people. The result, ironically, is not that we now believe politicians all the time; it is that we now believe them none of the time. It is not surprising that the *X-Files*, with its slogan of 'Trust No-one' and its endless levels of conspiracy, deception and cover-up, has been so popular. The truth may be 'out there', but it certainly isn't down here.

There are other costs that are less easily calculated. This acid atmosphere of lies and cynicism affects all our relationships, whether they are at work or at home. Is it any coincidence that this epidemic of lying has also been a time of unprecedented breakdown of families and marriages? I think not. All our social relations are founded upon openness and trust, and where lying prevails neither can last long. In such a pervasive atmosphere of cynicism we refuse to believe anything that anybody says. Paranoia under such circumstances is not only acceptable, it is logical; the only person you can really trust is yourself. Maybe.

Is there any truth about truth?

If the concept of truth is sliding down the slippery slope, then it has to be said that many philosophers have helped to grease its progress. 'There is no truth,' say some of them. 'There is only what you think of as truth.' Instead of absolute truth, they propound that there are as many relative truths as there are people on the planet. On such a relativist view the only truth that there can be is something private, personal and individual. So what is true for you may not be true for me. There are no facts – only differing opinions. The only difference between truth and lies is your viewpoint. Everything hinges on where you stand and which way you look. Each person, it is argued, is entitled to his or her own opinion. And for each individual that opinion is perfectly valid.

Because of this relativist thinking the traditional concept of history is being challenged. No one can say what is the absolute truth. This is an increasingly widespread view. For instance, history is now widely seen to stand on shifting sand, with each generation and culture allowed to rewrite its past to suit its own purposes. Microsoft recently unveiled the latest version of its *Encarta Encyclopedia*. Technically it is an extraordinary achievement, but there are nine editions – American, British, French, German, Italian, Spanish, Dutch, Japanese, Brazilian – and in each one of these, history is apparently written to accord with the way those countries would like to see the past. One newspaper commented, 'He is already the richest man in the world, but now Bill Gates has taken on the task of rewriting history to keep his customers happy.' Microsoft's director of marketing was quoted as saying, 'If you look at the Battle of Waterloo in the English *Encarta* and the French *Encarta*, you get two very different versions of things, like, say, who won the battle.' The speed with which relativism has been adopted here has, no doubt, something to do with the marketing wisdom that people like to have their own prejudices reinforced. But if there is no absolute truth, then what's wrong with letting marketing wisdom decide what we say?

A parable, composed by a storyteller in the mid-eighteenth century, is widely used to justify the current attitudes to truth. A father has a magic ring that he must bequeath to one of his three sons. Since he loves them all equally and does not want them to accuse him of favouritism, he makes two imitation rings so they can all have one. The result is that each son thinks his own ring is magic and that the others are not. They have an argument in front of a wise man called Nathan, who says, 'Let each one think his own ring true and in the meantime show forth gentleness and heartfelt tolerance.' The heart-warming message is that the only thing that matters is that you believe that your own ring is true and you are tolerant. Yet a moment's thought shows the fallacy of the whole story. The fact remains that however much tolerance and gentleness is produced, only one ring is magic.

It is significant that science, engineering and medicine have remained entirely immune to the charms of relativism. Scientific theories are proved true on the basis of experiments, not simply because we wish them to be true. We are given medicines because they have been demonstrated to work, not because of the pious hopes of doctors. And, thankfully, engineers rely on more than wishful thinking when it comes to assembling aircraft.

There is truth. And where there is truth there can be lies.

The heart of the matter

The Bible pulls no punches about lying. God is *truth*, it says, but men and women naturally prefer lies, and their reaction to Jesus demonstrates it.

The God of truth

The Bible tells us about God's character, and at the very centre of it lies truth. God is true – there is nothing false in him. Throughout the Bible, we see the contrast between light and darkness, goodness and evil, right and wrong, love and hatred, truth and lies. The Bible teaches that it is not just that God possesses the characteristics of light, goodness, love and truth. God *is* light, goodness, love and truth.

Several times the Bible speaks of God being 'the God of

truth'. This means that God is true in all he does and is. He is true to his word, true to his character, true to his nature. This is something unfamiliar to us. We are inconsistent and our good character may often only be skin deep. It is common to hear in a courtroom some sad statement like 'I don't know what came over him. It is most unlike him', or 'She acted completely out of character'. In contrast, you can never look at one of God's actions and say, 'That's so unlike him.' He is always true to himself; he is completely, utterly, consistently and wonderfully true. It is interesting that Jesus (in John 8:44) terms the devil the 'father of lies' as if to point out the contrast with his heavenly Father.

We know that God is truth, not just because the Bible says so, but because in Jesus we have seen God. And in Jesus we see a man who – unlike any other who has ever lived before or since – never lies or misleads. On earth, this man practised what he preached. He told his followers to turn the other cheek, and when he was brutally beaten he did exactly that. He told his followers to forgive those who persecuted them, and when his executioners drove nails into his wrists he did just that – he prayed for their forgiveness. Jesus spoke about a God of love who accepted sinners and he showed it in his life. He spoke about a God of life who was stronger than death and he rose from the grave himself. This man shows us the truth of God. Now in heaven, Jesus has not changed. He is still the truth personified.

Not only do we need to accept that God is truth, we need to accept that he hears and sees our words. Our law courts spend much of their time trying to find out the truth of events; God already knows them. There is nothing hidden before him; every word, every action, every thought is done before him.

He knows the truth of everything about our lives, the world and us. One of the terrifying things Jesus said is that 'everything that is hidden or secret will eventually be brought to light and made plain to all' (Luke 8:18, NLT). One day, we are promised (or threatened), the complete truth will be made known.

In an age when people regularly talk of an 'eleventh commandment' as being 'Thou shalt not be found out', this is very challenging. Many people only show any tendency to acknowledgement of wrong and apology after their wrongdoing has been publicly exposed. The reason why is quite simple: they think they have got away with it. There is a belief that once something is forgotten, it never happened. God tells us that it is otherwise. It is not a question of whether we will be found out or not. We have already been found out by God. One day everybody else will find out too.

People of lies

If God is a God of truth, it is unfortunately the case that we are a people of lies. We may not lie all the time about everything, but we prefer to modify the truth far more frequently than we care to admit.

There are many different ways of lying. The most blatant form is, of course, the 'total lie': the complete and utter fabrication. Here someone states that what did happen, didn't, or alternatively what didn't, did. They say 'I was never there' when they were present all the time or 'I saw it all' when they were miles away. Many people would totally reject this most obvious form of lying. Yet there are more subtle ways to lie. There can be, for instance, the 'lie of silence' when we fail to mention a significant fact. So when the boss comes in wanting to know who left the office door unlocked and we know it was us, our failure to admit it is a lie.

Then there is the 'lie of the misleading hint'. Here we don't actually state the lie; we just assemble the pieces and let someone else put it together. So as the blame for leaving the office door open threatens us, we casually mention in a meaningful tone that the new secretary has been 'very preoccupied lately' and that 'they left in a hurry last night'. We tell ourselves that it is not a proper lie; we didn't actually *say* 'the secretary did it'. Yet the reality is that we have wrongly pointed the finger at someone else. In fact, when we look carefully at what we say when we are under pressure it is surprising and alarming how much of what we say falls short of being the total truth. We can lie about our lying.

Why do we lie? One reason for this is that we 'lie to deny'. We use lies to cover up who we really are and what our problems genuinely are. The other day in a national newspaper I read of a man who had written off his car and injured himself in an accident. It turned out that he was six times over the legal limit. However, rather than face up to this and admit his own responsibility, he had decided to take the owner of the pub where he had been drinking to court, claiming that as he had sold him all the drink, he was responsible. We might find such cases amusing, but we all do similar things.

We prefer almost anything to admitting that we are guilty. In order to deny our accountability we accumulate all sorts of explanations and excuses for our shortcomings. We say they are due to 'my parents', 'my school', 'my genes', 'my hormones'. Of course, we are all, to a greater or lesser extent, products of our environment and background, and some people have been through the most appalling circumstances and we need to take account of that. Yet we need to think carefully before we blame what we are on others. By doing that we are portraying ourselves as the helpless victims of events and are denying that we have the freedom and the potential to rise above our backgrounds and difficulties. Here, Christians are enormously helped by our knowledge that our Father God knows and understands what we have been through and has also given us his Holy Spirit to help us overcome our past.

We do need to realise that telling the truth is not always easy. After all, if you work or live in an environment in which unfair accusations and criticisms are frequently thrown around, then you need to defend yourself. The problem is that while engaging in that legitimate defence, it is all too easy to push the truth just a little bit too far. Most lies do not begin life as lies; they are born as slight deviations of the truth. We need to be aware that there are pressures which, if we let them, will twist our words.

The real danger in lying comes in the way that it deceives us about who we are. The worst lie you can tell is one to yourself. It is in this area of self-deception that the heart of lying occurs. I believe that the power of the temptation to lie comes precisely because we want to protect ourselves from the truth that shows us what we really are, rather than what we think we are. The Bible repeatedly compares truth and falsehood with light and darkness. To face the truth is the moral equivalent of walking out of pitch darkness into dazzling sunlight. Jesus himself puts it bluntly as he speaks of his own ministry. 'Their judgment is based on this fact: The light from heaven came into the world, but they loved the darkness more than the light, for their actions were evil' (John 3:19, NLT). Blinded by the light we desperately look for any excuse.

Where does this universal temptation to evade responsibility come from? It is fascinating to see how early on in human history such sentiments can be found. In the last chapter I described how the book of Genesis tells how Adam and Eve were tempted into coveting God's position and his authority. If we jump a few verses on, we can see what happened just after they had disobeyed God.

> Then the man and his wife heard the sound of the LORD God as he was walking in the garden in the cool of the day, and they hid from the LORD God among the trees of the garden. But the LORD God called to the man, 'Where are you?'
>
> He answered, 'I heard you in the garden, and I was afraid because I was naked; so I hid.'
>
> And he said, 'Who told you that you were naked? Have you eaten from the tree from which I commanded you not to eat?'
>
> The man said, 'The woman you put here with me – she gave me some fruit from the tree, and I ate it.'
>
> Then the LORD God said to the woman, 'What is this you have done?'
>
> The woman said, 'The serpent deceived me, and I ate.' (Genesis 3:8–13, NIV)

This story illustrates the heart of the problem of humanity. Adam and Eve have done something wrong so they hide – trying to get away from the consequences of what they've done. When God asks the man if he has done the one thing he had been instructed not to do, instead of owning up, Adam tries to pin the blame on Eve: 'the woman you put here with me'. Rather than take responsibility himself for his own actions he blames *her*. There is even a broad hint that, as God put the woman in the garden, *he* must take some of the blame. Then, as the questioning shifts to the woman, she doesn't take responsibility either but blames the serpent – it was *his* fault. Now in some ways neither Adam nor Eve was lying, but neither were they telling the truth. What they obviously failed to do was admit their fault and their guilt. And so there, in the very first breaking of a command given by God, it all starts – the great human characteristic of trying to duck responsibility. Blame it on someone else, something else, anything else.

If we have any doubt that our species is fatally flawed in this area of truth, then what happened to Jesus should make us think again.

The confrontation of truth and lies

I have said that if we want to know what God is like we need to study Jesus. In Jesus' life we see God. But as we read the accounts of his life in the Gospels, we see not only the truth about God, but also the truth about human beings. At Jesus' trial and crucifixion we are shown plainly that we as human beings dislike the truth and we refuse to face up to our own responsibility.

The story of the trial of Jesus shows us what we do when we get our hands on God. A hastily convened assembly of the religious authorities summoned the arrested Jesus. They wanted to get rid of him and wanted to pass a suitable sentence on him. But to do that, they needed charges of wrongdoing. It was not easy trying to pin a charge of wrongdoing on Jesus, the Son of God! The way they achieved it was the only way possible; they lied. False allegations flew across the chamber about things he had said and about the claims he had made. We read that 'many false witnesses came forward' (Matthew 26:59, NIV) and that Jesus' words were misreported and twisted. When confronted with the one human being who was completely true – who was in fact *the* truth – human beings told lies about him.

Shortly after this, Jesus was summoned before the Roman Governor Pontius Pilate, a man who had the power of life and death over him. All four Gospel writers indicate that Pilate was unnerved by Jesus, who refused either to answer his questions or plead for his life. At one point, responding to Pilate's question as to whether he was a king, Jesus said, '"For this reason I was born, and for this reason I came into the world, to testify to the truth. Everyone on the side of truth listens to me." "What is truth?" Pilate asked' (John 18:37–38, NIV).

Pilate's pathetic question echoes down through the ages to us. Jesus, the one who was, by his own admission, 'the way, the truth and the life', is just in front of him, staring him in the eyes. Yet Pilate is so blinded by lies that he cannot recognize the truth when it is standing an arm's length away from him.

I often have people say to me, 'If only Jesus came now, then I'd believe.' Nonsense! If he came today we would do exactly what they did with him then. First we'd try to change his views, then we'd try to silence him and finally, when that failed, we'd kill him. Jesus wasn't executed by moronic, unbalanced lunatics, but by educated, sophisticated and even religious people who simply wanted to preserve the system, keep the status quo and avoid trouble. The people who had Jesus executed were perfectly ordinary human beings. That's the scary thing.

There is a story about a man who was in court on a charge. At the start of the trial he pleaded not guilty but, at the end of the first day, he asked the judge if he could change his plea to 'guilty'. 'Why didn't you say that earlier?' came the question from the judge. 'Well, if you'll excuse me, your honour, I didn't realize I was guilty until I heard all the evidence.' This is, if you like, what Jesus' death does to us: it shows us what we are really like – it tells us about ourselves. What it says is simple: when we are faced with truth we want to kill it.

We also see, in the whole sorry business of the trial of Jesus, our habit of refusing to take responsibility. Pilate, of course, famously washed his hands, as if shedding blame for a judicial murder was as easy as a trip to the bathroom. 'It's not my fault,' he said, in effect. 'Don't blame me.' We have said the same ever since.

Yet if at the trial and the crucifixion humanity tries to deny responsibility, we see on God's side something else all together. On the cross, God in Jesus takes responsibility for the bad things we have done. The one innocent party in the history of the human race becomes guilty so that we might be spared guilt. It is the exact opposite of our actions. Pilate washes his hands, desperately trying to cleanse them of his own guilt, while Jesus extends his hands to take on the guilt of others. As the Old Testament prophet Isaiah predicted centuries earlier, 'All of us have strayed away like sheep. We have left God's paths to follow our own. Yet the Lord laid on him all the guilt and sins of us all' (Isaiah 53:6, NLT).

We might not want to take responsibility for our sins, but Jesus does.

Fighting lies

I want to turn now to the practicalities of how we combat our tendency to lie. As with the previous commandment I want to start with some suggestions on how to deal with the sin itself and then I want to move on to some ways in which we can positively affirm truth.

Beware the power of the tongue

First, we need to realize that words have more power than we give them credit for. A preacher got up into the pulpit one Sunday morning with a big sack in his hand. 'In this bag,' he told the congregation, 'I have the most dangerous thing in the world.' He put his hand into the sack and pulled out a sword. He swung it round his head, chopped the air with it and talked about all the terrible things that you could do with swords. Then he said, 'But the most dangerous thing in the world is not a sword.' He put the sword down. He reached into the bag again and pulled out a pistol. He pointed it at the ceiling and talked about the awful things you could do with guns, but then he said, 'Guns are not the most dangerous thing in the world,' and he put the gun down. Finally, he reached inside the bag and pulled out what looked like a long bit of red, fleshy meat. He held out the repulsive object for people to see. 'This, my friends,' he said solemnly, 'is the most dangerous thing in the world. The tongue.'

Jesus' brother James seems to have the same opinion. He tells us in the Bible that the tongue is 'a restless evil, full of deadly poison' (James 3:8, NIV). Elsewhere he says that the tongue is like the rudder of a ship in that, though tiny, it steers the course and sets the direction.

Our tongues take up less than 0.045 per cent of our body weight, but they can be both our greatest asset and our most destructive possession. Aesop, the famous teller of fables, was asked one day what was the most powerful thing in the world. 'The tongue,' he replied. 'And what is the most harmful thing in the world?' he was asked. Once more he replied, 'The tongue.' It has been said that the tongue is the only tool that grows sharper with constant use.

The fact that words are so easily spoken also means that they can spread quickly. And in spreading they become irretrievable; once spoken we cannot take them back. There is a story of a man in the Middle Ages who confessed to a monk that he had sinned because he had been spreading rumours about someone in the local community. What should he do? The monk told him to go and put a feather on every doorstep in the community. The man rushed away, fulfilled his penance as quickly as possible, and returned to the monk. To his surprise, the monk now told him to go back and pick up all the feathers. The man protested that by now they would have been blown by the wind and would be miles away. That, the monk said, was exactly what had happened with his careless and malicious words. It is not just true of rumours; it is true of all words.

We all know the power of the tongue; we have all, at some time, been wounded by harsh and cruel words. If we knew how potentially damaging our words were, we would not be so quick to speak. As one proverb goes, 'Don't talk unless you can improve the silence.' During the Second World War there was a poster that warned, 'Careless talk costs lives.' That's something that is not just true in wartime – it is also true in peace.

As the remark goes, there must be a reason why God made us with two ears but only one mouth. When we do talk, we need to make sure that we do so well and truthfully.

Remember the price of lying

I have already talked about the general costs of lying, particularly to society. It is good to remind ourselves of the cost of lying to us as individuals.

Even at the simplest level, lying poses problems. Telling lies often gets us in more hot water than if we had told the truth.

A lie may take care of the present, but it stores up trouble for the future. For one thing, you have to remember what it was that you actually said. As Abraham Lincoln put it, 'No one has a good enough memory to be a successful liar.'

Lies also have an extraordinary habit of growing. As Martin Luther said centuries ago, 'Lies are like a snowball – as they roll, the bigger they get.' To cover up a little lie we need another and then another. Of course the more lies we tell, the greater is the danger that the whole web of deceit may start to unravel.

Lies also affect the liar. They corrode our sense of who we are and what reality is. In many lives today the line between truth and fiction has dissolved. Many people would echo the sentiments of Bette Middler, the larger-than-life American actress who confessed, 'I never know how much of what I say is true.'

The liar ends up unable to trust others. This acid atmosphere of lies and cynicism affects all their relationships. 'If I lie,' they say to themselves, 'perhaps I am lied to?' The liar finds it hard to know what to believe about their friends, their family or even their lovers. Is she telling the truth? Is he? Can I trust them? Is *everything* lies and illusions, masks and pretences?

Ultimately the liar no longer knows who they are themselves. Fitting in and becoming part of the scene is so important today that people become like chameleons, changing their personalities, experiences and beliefs to suit the setting they find themselves in. I remember hearing the story of a very high-profile person who was very nervous before a major event. 'Don't worry,' someone reassured the star. 'Just be yourself.' 'The trouble is,' came the bleak answer, 'I don't know who I am.'

A more serious problem is that by lying we start to destroy our ability to detect what is wrong in our own lives. The Bible teaches that the only way we can come to know God is by admitting our wrong attitudes and actions, and by repenting of them. But if we have fabricated our lives, if we no longer know who we are, then we become blinded to the fact that we need to repent. Having the habit of lying about who we are is like disabling the warning signals on a car. It gives a comforting illusion that there are no problems, but it also prevents us being warned that we may need to take serious corrective action.

Shun gossip

Earl Wilson once said, 'Gossip is when you hear something you like about someone you don't.' Gossip is repeating private information to someone who is neither part of the problem nor part of the solution. Gossip falls under the ninth commandment because its words are always against our neighbour and are often false. In fact one of the characteristics of gossip is that whether or not it is true isn't an issue. We tell a bit of gossip because it is a juicy tale, not because it is true. This commandment speaks against a love for gossip and intrigue about others.

The book of Proverbs talks a lot about gossip: 'Without wood a fire goes out; without gossip a quarrel dies down'; 'The words of a gossip are like choice morsels; they go down to a person's inmost parts' (Proverbs 26:20, 22, NIV).

No doubt we could all name gossips, but I'm sure we would never think of ourselves as such. *We* are simply interested in being kept well informed about what's going on. Of course we do sometimes say things that begin with 'I shouldn't say this to you, but . . .', 'Have you heard about . . .?' or 'I am really worried about him; do you know that the other day . . ?'.

We need to realize how hurtful and damaging gossiping can be. As I mentioned in talking about the power of our words, gossip can travel as fast and as easily as feathers in a breeze. In fact rumours and tales are worse than feathers, for unlike them they multiply in number and size as they travel.

We need to be people who do not gossip. There are various guidelines for helping us here. One thing we can do is monitor what we are saying. We might ask ourselves whether what we are about to say includes anything that might be termed gossip. If it does, we should avoid it. Another guideline is to ask ourselves, when tempted to pass on some intriguing but damaging tale: 'If this was written down would I be able to sign it?' If we are not willing to put our name to a story, then we shouldn't share it. This, of course, brings us back to the fact that the ninth commandment addresses our capacity to tell lies. Yet another guideline is to ask how we would feel if the person concerned could hear us talking that way about them.

Yet I believe we need to go further. We need to be not only those who do not gossip, but also those who stop gossip. In fact we mustn't sit quietly by as the tales flow round us, sucking up the gossip like a vacuum cleaner. We need to challenge the speaker: 'Are you sure?', 'Have you checked this out?', 'Mightn't there be another, less harmful, interpretation?' We might even say bluntly, 'If you don't mind, I'd rather we didn't talk about this.' Even if people may be surprised or put out when we say such things, to become known as those who don't give – or receive – gossip, is to earn respect.

It may be helpful to remember two things. First, gossips are never trusted, because they break confidences. We all know that the one who brings gossip also carries it. Second, in a curious sort of justice, those who are gossips tend to be those who attract gossip about themselves.

Avoid gossiping. There are better things to talk about.

Become people of the truth

So much for the negatives about lying. But it is not enough to reject the bad – we need to take hold of the good. Being known as a man or woman of the truth means more than avoiding lies or gossip; it means affirming truth.

Facing up to the truth means being responsible for our guilt and our fallibility. It means admitting the things we do wrong and the way we sometimes don't seem to be able to help ourselves. It means that we have to avoid putting the defence of ourselves above everything, including the truth. Telling the truth is costly and uncomfortable, and it goes against our deepest nature.

Yet a moment's thought will show us that this is far from easy. Does this mean that we should never have any secrets? Does this mean that if we go to someone's new house and they ask us if we like it – and we don't – we have to tell them? What about telling 'white' lies? Should we tell our children about Father Christmas or the tooth fairy? Is it ever right to lie about our age?

What I want to do now is suggest some principles so we can deal with such questions in a way that pleases God.

Be open

Clearly, most of us would accept that God doesn't want us to be barefaced liars. Nevertheless, I suggest that most of us could go much further than we do in being open.

As we have seen, our inbuilt human tendency is to lean away from honesty. We always want to cover up, to blame others, to sweep things under the carpet, to have secrets. Now, of course, there are different types of secrets. Some secrets are good and valid ones: a surprise birthday party, the home telephone number of the Queen, my PIN number, your medical data. There is no reason why details of such things should be circulated. Yet there are also 'bad' secrets. These are things that are unhealthy or dangerous, or things that control and obsess us. Many people have things that happened in their past that continue to haunt and cripple them today. These need to be dealt with. If you feel affected by such bad secrets, whether about yourself or another person, then I advise you to go to someone you trust (a church minister, a teacher, an accredited counsellor or, where a possible crime has occurred, the police) and arrange to talk to them about these things in confidence. At the end of this book, there are some phone numbers of organizations such as the Samaritans that have been set up to give anonymous help and a sympathetic ear. It may be time to unburden yourself of something you have been carrying for years. There might be things in your past that you need to face up to, or be honest about.

But openness can help well before serious problems occur. One useful safeguard is making sure that we have what is called 'accountability'. The idea here is that you find someone you get on with, preferably someone older and wiser (and the same sex), and give them permission to ask you difficult questions about your private life. You, in turn, make a pledge not to lie to them and to be open and honest with them about your weaknesses, temptations and struggles. By being accountable, we can be forced to face up to problems well before they get serious. If we have been honest with another person, then it becomes harder to lie to ourselves.

Be an encourager

We should speak the truth, but it is important that we always do so in love. There is a famous story concerning the sharp tongue of Winston Churchill. At a dinner party one evening there was a heated exchange between Churchill and a female MP. At the end of the exchange the woman scornfully remarked, 'Mr Churchill, you are drunk.' 'And you, madam,' replied Churchill, 'are ugly. But I shall be sober tomorrow.' It was a clever reply, but it was hurtful and I suspect it earned him an enemy for life.

I knew a minister whose church was going through a tough time. There were many divisions, and things were being said behind people's backs and even to their faces. Finally, at one meeting, the minister said, 'We are going to start an MEF, a Mutual Encouragement Fellowship. We are going to encourage each other rather than discourage each other. How many want to join?'

Everyone present raised their hand.

'Well then, there's only one qualification for this – you need to *think* before you speak.'

He then went on to explain what he meant, by giving them an acrostic for the word 'THINK' based on five questions:

T – is it *true*?
H – will it *help*?
I – is it *inspiring*?
N – is it *necessary*?
K – is it *kind*?

As we make a commitment to telling the truth, we need to make a similar commitment to THINK before we speak.

One thing to be wary of as we set out to encourage each other is to avoid slipping into flattery. Flattery is insincere praise; we compliment someone – often to try and get something out of them – but we don't really mean what we say.

Flattery is an artificial sweetener and of no nutritional value. Flattery is, in its way, just as dishonest as lying, and results in the same sort of devaluation of our language. The Bible is very negative about flattery. 'A flattering mouth works ruin,' says Proverbs (26:28, NIV). You'll find that although flatterers may be popular in the short term, they are not trusted in the long term, as they cannot be relied on to tell the truth. They make unhelpful friends too, for sometimes we need to be told the truth.

Try to honestly encourage and praise what is good. The apostle Paul provided helpful advice to the church in Philippi that we would do well to heed: 'And now, dear brothers and sisters, let me say one more thing as I close this letter. Fix your thoughts on what is true and honourable and right. Think about things that are pure and lovely and admirable. Think about things that are excellent and worthy of praise' (Philippians 4:8–9, NLT).

Be true to your word

Finally, we need to be determined to be people of our word. Psalm 15 starts off with the question: 'Who may worship in your sanctuary, LORD?' In the four verses following, it lists the eleven characteristics of the righteous who can enter God's presence and it is interesting that four of them centre on the right use of words. The final characteristic, though, is challenging. It is that they are those who 'keep their promises even when it hurts' (Psalm 15:4, NLT).

As people of the truth we are to be people of our word. Jesus encouraged his followers to be people who keep their word whatever the cost. He said we should let our 'yes' be 'yes' and our 'no' be 'no' (Matthew 5:37). Broken promises break relationships, cause hurt and pain, spread mistrust and generate an unhealthy questioning of everything else that has ever been pledged. To be true to our word means to think carefully about what is involved before we make a promise, not after. It may mean that we need to be prepared to say no now rather than break our word later.

If we have been sceptical about the tenth commandment with its prohibition of unhealthy desires, then this ninth commandment with its reference to abuses of the tongue may seem only slightly less removed from what we think of as 'real sin'. Yet as we journey inwards through the commandments we can see that both raise very serious issues. The ninth commandment reminds us that speaking is a serious matter. In our modern society, we treat words far too lightly. Honesty in what we say is vital for the health of our society, for our relationships and even for us as individuals. We need to bring before God what we say, so that we may be known as trustworthy men and women whose words are both honest and fair.

COMMANDMENT **8**

You shall not steal.
(Exodus 20:15, NIV)

So what's the problem?

In our journey into the Commandments we started at the tenth commandment with our thoughts and desires and then, with the ninth commandment, moved into the world of words. Now, with the eighth commandment, we are firmly in the world of actions.

Unlike coveting or lying, the act of stealing is a physical action and because of this there is very solid evidence that a major national problem exists in this area. In early 1999 a national newspaper ran a lead story with the headline 'Britain; a nation of cheats and thieves', based on the evidence from a report on theft in the workplace. This had found that three-quarters of all Britons steal from their employers; a quarter of us will make opportunities to steal whenever we can and a half will steal if the chance arises. Apparently, only a quarter of us refuse to steal.

There are different types of stealing. Some theft, like burglary and shoplifting, is blatant and obvious. Much of this, especially where it targets *our* cars, houses, wallets or handbags, seems to be against us as individuals. However, some blatant theft is impersonal, directed perhaps against a council, a company or an organization. In many parts of Britain, this sort of stealing is such a major problem that almost anything that cannot be concreted into the ground is in danger of being stolen. So many road signs have been stolen to be melted down for scrap that most new ones are now made of valueless fibreglass and have a prominent notice on them pointing out that it is a waste of time stealing them. Even hospitals are forced to spend vast sums on screwing down or padlocking anything that might be remotely valuable. In a surreal twist, many police surveillance cameras are now surrounded by barbed wire to prevent them from being stolen.

Many people view those who carry out such types of direct, unashamed physical theft with a savage contempt. It is easy to sympathize with their demands for stiff sentences for the brutish yobs or thugs who ransack our houses or schools.

Yet there are many other ways to steal, and some of them are almost respectable. Some theft involves deception rather than physical effort. Consumer affairs programmes like *Watchdog* are full of stories of mail order firms that never delivered, investments that were spurious, workers who never worked, special offers that weren't special, price reductions that weren't reductions and dream holidays that were nightmares. The list could go on.

Much theft, though, is quiet and unspectacular. Far more stealing than we would like to think is carried out by apparently respectable and civilized men and women. VAT is fiddled, tax is evaded, mortgage applications are manipulated, grant applications are faked and phoney business loans are claimed on spurious cash-flow figures. The Serious Fraud Office estimates that financial crime costs British companies £29 billion annually, a figure that, they say, is probably just the tip of the iceberg. Tax evasion is an enormous issue today. One analysis of income tax fraud commented, 'Precise figures are impossible to obtain since no one knows the amount of income that escapes taxation through evasion, unrecorded financial transactions and other similar activities. Inland Revenue officials estimate that the amount is between 7 and 15 billion pounds a year.'

Another common but low-key way of stealing is in dishonest trading, where things are sold for more than they are worth. Here the line between shrewd marketing and fraudulent misrepresentation is a thin one. There are always people who will adjust the mileages of used cars, pretend that computer components are faster and better than they are, pass off copied clothing as the real article and pretend that cheap car parts are the manufacturer's own. These things are illegal and many of us would despise those who do them. Yet when we have to sell a business deal, a pension, a product or our house, are *we* totally honest about both its good and bad points?

Other acts of theft get ignored because we imagine that they fall below some invisible and unwritten level of what constitutes 'theft'. To take paper from our firm, a dozen sheets a day, is somehow acceptable, but we would never dream of walking out, once a year, with a full carton of paper. That would be stealing! We make our own phone calls from the office and acquire paper clips, laser printer cartridges and floppy discs. In a thousand little ways, we steal from our employers. Time may be money in business, but we ignore that when it suits us. We have phoney days off work, extended coffee breaks and make those little detours for shopping on our business trips. 'They'll never notice,' we say. 'They can afford it. They owe it me. It's not really theft.'

There are ironies with the current epidemic of theft that should cause us to think. On the one hand we are, as a nation, more prosperous now than we have ever been. That we have never had it so good is not political hype; it's true. Our houses are full of electronics, our wardrobes are full of clothes, our roads are full of cars and our shops are full of consumer goods. Many of us live a lifestyle (two or more cars, regular meals out, foreign holidays) that 20 years ago would have belonged to only the very rich. In the Western world we earn more and own more than any other people at any other time and place in history. Yet we still want more.

At the start of the twenty-first century, we are a mass of contradictions. There is, on the one hand, a naïve idealism. John Lennon's song 'Imagine', with its 'Imagine no possessions – it's easy if you try', was voted the nation's favourite lyric in 1999. On the other hand there is not the slightest sign that anyone (least of all rock stars) wants such a creed to be made the basis of serious economic policy. On the contrary, in a recent survey of young people, over half said that they would feel failures if, by the age of 30, they did not have a long-term partner, money in the bank, a senior career position and a good car and home.

We want more than ever. The problem is that in order to get what we want, many of us have no problems in helping ourselves.

The heart of the matter

I want now to try to look at what lies behind this extraordinary plague of stealing that we have come to live with.

Things, theft and idolatry

I believe that one factor is that we have made idols of money and things. We have already seen how the Commandments are interlocked. The tenth, ninth and eighth commandments, with their prohibitions of coveting, lying and theft, are all linked. It is impossible to seriously want to steal something without breaking the tenth commandment, and it is practically impossible to carry out a theft without breaking the ninth commandment. As we have seen already – and will see again – the Commandments hang together and reinforce each other. In this area of stealing, I want to suggest that yet another commandment is closely involved. This is the second commandment, which prohibits idolatry. I will talk about this in detail later, but I want to introduce the theme here now. Idolatry for most of us isn't about some carved wooden statues surrounded by joss sticks in the corner of a room, or gold images in a temple. It is far subtler than that. Idolatry is when things, often good in themselves, are worshipped as if they were God.

We might not see ourselves as an idolatrous nation. Yet imagine if some intelligent aliens were to arrive in the middle of one of our cities. As they surveyed the evidence of our civilization about them, what might they conclude was the centre of our lives? The answer is simple. They would conclude that we lived for possessions. All too often, when we are not consumed with earning money, we are consumed with spending it. Consumerism has become a primitive passion, as in the catchphrase 'shop until you drop' or the classic one-line meditation on mortality: 'Whoever dies with the most tags, wins'. The biggest, grandest and newest buildings are shops and malls; the most eye-catching posters are about sales and special offers; the greatest crowds are in the stores; the largest car parks are around superstores; the chief ceremony of the year is the January sales. The conclusion that British religion centres on material possessions – and especially buying them – would be inescapable.

Idolatry distorts values. It elevates to ultimate importance something that is not ultimately important. It can corrupt us and lead us astray and fill us with false hopes and aspirations. This of course is not exclusively a contemporary British problem. The worship of material things has always been a temptation for human beings. Jesus talked bluntly about the worship of possessions. He said, 'No servant can serve two masters. Either they will hate one and love the other, or they will be devoted to the one and despise the other. You cannot serve both God and money' (Luke 16:13). In the original Greek of the Gospels, the word Jesus used for money was 'Mammon', a word which has passed into English almost as the personal name of the god of wealth and possessions. In fact there is something valid in this use of Mammon as a god, because possessions are more than some abstract economic concept. They are god-like and they make god-like demands. As we have seen before – and will see again – such false gods are a deception, failing to deliver anything of what they promise. The point here, though, is that by making Mammon our god, we open the door to stealing. The reason is simple. Gods impose their own rules on their believers and Mammon's requirement of his followers is that they acquire more. *How* you acquire more simply doesn't matter. Just get it.

The epidemic of stealing that afflicts us is a result of having turned to possessions and wealth for fulfilment rather than the living God.

Whose things are they anyway?

Another factor that has affected our attitude to stealing is our flawed understanding of possessions.

For many people, the world and everything in it is a product of chance. Any rules to do with stealing – as with any other rules for living – arise simply because we as human beings need some sort of code to live together. They are not absolute rules; in a God-less world there can be no absolute rules. Others believe that this world has come about through the divine activity of some cosmic Creator God, but that the involvement of the Creator stopped a long time ago. He doesn't watch purses or wallets in the twenty-first century. Help yourself.

The Christian view is, of course, different. The God who made the world and who gave us the Commandments is still very much alive and active in the world today. This still is his world.

In the Old Testament we see that as David is about to reach the pinnacle of his achievements as king, he proclaims that everything he has is not his anyway – it is God's:

> Yours, O LORD, is the greatness and the power
> and the glory and the majesty and the splendour,
> for everything in heaven and earth is yours.
> Yours, O LORD, is the kingdom; you are exalted as head over all.
> Wealth and honour come from you;
> you are the ruler of all things.
>
> (1 Chronicles 29:11–12, NIV)

We need to think about this, for it goes against many views in our modern culture. What the Bible says here – and in many other places – is stunningly simple. Ultimately everything belongs to God and nothing belongs to us. We have no rights over property or wealth. It is not ours; it is God's. A few verses after the passage I just quoted, David says, 'Everything comes from you, and we have given you only what comes from your hand' (1 Chronicles 29:14, NIV).

This does not mean it is wrong to own things; after all, David himself as king was a rich man. In the Gospels, we see that Jesus himself assumed that people would have private property. He was supported by wealthy people (Luke 8:3), enjoyed their food and hospitality and appreciated their gifts (Mark 14:3–9). Some of his disciples appear to have had houses and to have owned or had shares in boats. There is no indication that this caused Jesus any problems. In the early church rich and poor coexisted. No, it is clear in the Bible that God allows people, and indeed gives them, wealth and possessions. These gifts are always a blessing and sometimes, especially in the Old Testament, there are passages that suggest they are a divine reward to those who honour God. The reverse, however, is never true: nowhere does the Bible say that if you don't have wealth and material possessions then you must have done something terrible. In fact it is quite clear from virtually every book in the Bible that the holiest people have the roughest time. There are far more stories in the Bible of people who suffer for being God's servants than there are of those who are blessed by material prosperity. Nearly 2,000 years of church history has reinforced this message.

The point is that everything we have comes from God. I no more own my house, my car and my bank balance than I own my library books. They have all, in different ways, been issued to me. They remain the possession of someone else, and one day will be returned to them. The difference is that while the librarian may then merely smile and say 'thank you', God will want to know what I did with all that he lent me.

The implications of this as regards theft are major in two areas. First, stealing is about increasing our possessions. Yet, in the Bible's view, 'our possessions' is precisely what they are not. We never *possess* them. We have them simply on temporary loan and we need to be reminded that they may be recalled to their rightful owner at any time without warning. When we think longingly about our neighbour's car or TV we need to remind ourselves that these things are not, in reality, their property. They are God's.

Second, this issue of God's ownership of everything affects stealing. When we steal, we do not wrongfully appropriate something from a company or another human being; we steal from God. That ought to make us pause.

Stealing insults God's generosity

Another factor we need to think about in connection with stealing is that when we steal we are denying God's care and love towards us.

God has graciously given us many gifts in creation, not because we deserve them but because God delights to bless us. We deserve nothing, yet God has given us great riches. The God who has given us life has also given us everything we need on this earth and now also sustains us. God has given so much to us that if we were to count his blessings, we would be unable to finish. If the Old Testament rejoices in God's love to us shown in the physical blessings we can touch, see and feel, the New Testament talks a lot about God's abundant, overwhelming, extravagant, measureless kindness to us in Jesus. So Paul writes, 'You know the grace of our Lord Jesus Christ, that though he was rich, yet for your sakes he became poor, so that you through his poverty might become rich' (2 Corinthians 8:9, NIV).

When we steal, we are denying God's goodness to us. By our actions, we are effectively saying, 'God, what you have given me is not enough.' We are demanding more, and in stealing we are accusing God of being an inadequate heavenly Father and showing our lack of faith and trust in him. Furthermore, when we steal we are saying to God that we know better than he does. We need something that he has not seen fit to give us; we have helped ourselves. Actually, God is not hard and skimping at all. He is generous beyond our wildest dreams and he has trusted us with the world he lovingly made.

So how can we live responsibly, recognizing what God has done, without breaking the eighth commandment? How can we keep our consciences clear in this area? How can we take a stand against stealing?

Standing up to stealing

In offering advice on how you can keep the commandment not to steal, I want to adopt a similar pattern to that I have used in the previous two commandments. First of all, I want to show how we can avoid theft. Then I want to show how, positively, we can adopt lifestyles and attitudes that are the opposite to the theft that the eighth commandment condemns.

Be honest about theft

The first thing I want to say to you is that we need to be brutally honest about what we are doing in this area. In almost no sphere of human life is there greater deception about what we do than in the area of stealing. Very few people are prepared to look at themselves in the mirror and say, 'I am a thief. I have stolen.' The result is a sea of words that obscure the reality of theft. Rather than admit they stole something we hear people say that they 'borrowed' it, 'acquired' it or 'helped themselves'. Things mysteriously 'fall off the back of a lorry', objects are 'surplus to requirements', software 'accidentally gets loaded' onto my computer and equipment gets 'creatively recycled'. People are 'less than totally transparent' about their accounts for the VAT inspector or engage in 'creative accounting' for the Inland Revenue. We need to stand firm here and point out that however soothing the alternative words sound, all stealing is stealing.

Sometimes something subtler occurs. Theft may be justified as a form of political or social protest. Shoplifting or the misuse of computers at work can be portrayed as a noble Robin Hood-like battle between *them* (who have unlimited wealth that they don't deserve) and *us* (who do deserve wealth). Of course, this is nonsense. In a democracy like ours, there are many legitimate ways of making a protest. Theft is not one of them. We need to be plain to ourselves and, if necessary, to others that theft is never noble and it is never right.

We need, though, to be scrupulous about ourselves. Some theft is so subtle that it may be both legal and perfectly acceptable to those about us. Yet it is still wrong. We may delay paying bills in order to maximize the interest to us; we may promise to meet deadlines and budgets when we know we can't; we may pretend that the house, car or insurance policy we are selling is better than it is. Financial advisers and brokers may give advice that is in their own best interests rather than those of the client. All too often, we are perfectly happy to pay someone less than they deserve and as we do it we can even manage to pride ourselves on our ability to 'control costs'.

We also need to be ruthlessly honest about what are considered more 'respectable' types of theft. We feel angry revulsion at the villain who steals a television from a children's ward of a hospital. Shouldn't we feel the same revulsion at the tax evader who deprives the Health Service of hundreds of pounds of income?

Remember the cost of theft

We need to remember the cost of theft. All breaches of God's Commandments have a cost and this one is no different. Of course, all this has to be paid for somewhere, whether in higher prices, elevated taxes or reduced social services. There is a direct financial cost of theft to us, whether it is having to buy burglar alarms or paying higher taxes to fund more police officers.

There are other costs to society. Many people will not take their cars into town centres at night, while other people become reluctant to leave their houses at all and are disinclined to open their doors after dark.

There are especial costs to the victims. I expect many of you reading this have been burgled (as we were last year). You can probably still remember how, as you entered your house, there was a different kind of feeling about it all; how the atmosphere seemed to have changed. Then, as you realized that your fears were true, there were the feelings of panic, of helplessness and of being violated and defiled as you thought of an unwanted stranger going through your most private things. Such theft produces a far greater reaction than would be warranted simply by the things that have been stolen. Our safety and security, our control over our own private space, have been shattered. The scars from theft can take a long time to heal.

There are the costs, too, to those who steal. Traditional wisdom has it that things that are illegally gained provide little lasting satisfaction or pleasure to those who get them. It is probably true. By its very nature, theft cannot satisfy. The thief will always want more.

By committing a theft, a person demonstrates that they are a slave of Mammon. And you cannot belong to God and Mammon. Let me leave this topic by giving you some solemn words of warning – and hope – from the Bible. Paul, writing to a church of new Christians at Corinth, says the following:

> Don't you know that those who do wrong will have no share in the Kingdom of God? Don't fool yourselves. Those who indulge in sexual sin, who are idol worshipers, adulterers, male prostitutes, homosexuals, thieves, greedy people, drunkards, abusers, and swindlers – none of these will have a share in the Kingdom of God. There was a time when some of you were just like that, but now your sins have been washed away, and you have been set apart for God. You have been made right with God because of what the Lord Jesus Christ and the Spirit of our God have done for you. (1 Corinthians 6:9–11, NLT)

Notice that Paul includes thieves and swindlers in those who will never be in the kingdom of God. That is the bad news. The good news is that, as in first-century Corinth, the work of Jesus and the Holy Spirit is able to transform the worst of thieves.

Making amends

I want to talk now about how we can adopt attitudes and lifestyles of integrity that can express the very opposite of what this commandment condemns. But before I do this I want to deal with a difficult but vital topic. As we have seen, there are many ways for us to break the eighth commandment. What I want to say here is that if you now realize you have stolen something, then I believe it is vital that you do what you can to make amends. The eighth commandment is one of the few commandments where we can make restitution for things we have done wrong.

One of the most extraordinary encounters Jesus had was with a man called Zacchaeus, who was the chief tax collector for the occupying Romans in Jericho (see Luke 19:1–9). Small, wealthy, probably corrupt and certainly loathed, Zacchaeus was shown love and acceptance by Jesus when he invited himself to Zacchaeus' house for a meal. There, Zacchaeus stood up and announced that he was going to give half his possessions to the poor and that he would give back to all whom he had cheated four times the amount they had lost. In doing this Zacchaeus was showing to everyone that he had wholehearted and genuine repentance, and that he was truly and utterly sorry for what he had done. He now wanted to do all he could to put things right.

The Inland Revenue once received an anonymous letter: 'I am having trouble sleeping because of my conscience. Please find enclosed £100. If this doesn't cure my insomnia I will send you the rest.' The motive there certainly wasn't wholehearted repentance. It was merely an attempt to buy off a troublesome conscience at the lowest price. The generous and unstinting action of Zacchaeus shows us the pattern of true repentance.

Time and time again when I speak on the subject of stealing, I encourage people to return stolen goods. If they can't return them to where they came from, I suggest they hand them over to a charity or a neutral party. When I ask people to do this I know that it may be hard. When I became a Christian, I realized that I should do something about some books I had stolen from a bookshop in London. I put the books into bags and, with a great deal of fear, took them back. It was difficult and embarrassing. The first assistant I talked to nearly fainted and I quickly found myself taken to the manager's office where I explained that, as a result of becoming a Christian, I now felt I had to return the stolen books. The dumbfounded manager explained that he could either call the police or bill me for the books. However, he concluded, as he had never encountered anything like this, all he could do was thank me and send me on my way. My relief as I left his office can be imagined!

Where we can, we must make amends for thefts we have committed in the past.

Seek integrity

I want now to move on to how we can live a life of integrity. Integrity is the state of being innocent, trustworthy, morally upright and free from dishonesty. It includes positive virtues rather than simply avoiding particular sins. The Bible makes it plain that there is more to being a follower of Jesus than simply avoiding sinful actions; rather, we are repeatedly told, we are to become more like God. We are to seek to reflect his character of openness, honesty and justice in all that we are as individuals. Integrity is a shorthand word for those aspects of our character.

A key element of integrity is the desire to seek justice. Justice is one of the biggest themes of the Bible – it is something that God demands of his people because he himself is just. The nature of God's character is shown in many places in Scripture.

To give one example, Jesus is called the good shepherd (John 10:11) who watches over the sheep flock, protecting, nurturing and leading them. This is the perfect image both of what God is like and of what we should aim to be ourselves. Satan, in comparison, is described as the thief, who comes only to steal and destroy the flock (John 10:10). Stealing and robbery belong to the characteristics of the evil one. It is a sobering thought that every act of theft makes us more and more like Satan and less and less like God. What would it be like to have a character of total integrity? The answer is that we would be like Jesus.

Seek integrity in personal relations

In the light of this we need to review all that we do as we seek to become people of integrity. Let me give just two examples of practical areas where we may need to take action.

We need to determine to be honest in the way we treat other people's money. Take, for example, where we have been made a loan. Have you ever borrowed money without having any intention of paying it back? Or have you conveniently had a memory lapse over some old debt? The Bible reminds us that it is the wicked who borrow and do not repay (Psalm 37:21). If you have done either, the advice I would give you here is simple: make amends. Practically nothing sours friendships as much as unpaid debts and unreturned loans.

This integrity does not just concern money but also applies to things. The fact that I used to own every Simon and Garfunkel album was a point of pride with me. I say 'used to' because I so wanted friends to share my pleasure in them that I would lend them out. The result was that they have never been seen since! The French novelist Anatole France quipped,

'Never lend books, for no one ever returns them. The only books I have in my library are books other people lent me.' Can I suggest that it may be worth looking round your attic, shed, garage, CD racks or bookshelves for things that you have borrowed and failed to return? Such 'extended loans' are simply theft by another name. And when you find them, act! If they are in the condition they were when you were given them, give them back. If they have been damaged, worn or have otherwise suffered, then offer to replace them. As a good general guideline in such matters, adopt the so-called Golden Rule, the one-line guide that Jesus said summed up all the Commandments: 'In everything, do to others as you would have them do to you . . .' (Matthew 7:12, NIV).

Seek integrity in work

If we need to pursue integrity in personal relationships, we also need to pursue it at work. First, I want us to be clear that God intends humans to work. That is not necessarily the same as having a job. I've always been of the opinion that the most hardworking people in this country don't get a wage, but the work women and men do in bringing up children is the most demanding and crucial of all. Any mother could perform the jobs of several air-traffic controllers with ease! What we must be wary of is laziness. I'm reminded of the manager who said to someone seeking a job, 'I'm sorry I can't hire you. There isn't enough work to keep you busy,' to receive the response, 'You'd be surprised how little it takes.' Not only is laziness wrong in itself, it also leads to all sorts of problems. As the old proverb wisely says, the devil finds work for idle hands.

Work is good and necessary, and is meant to be fulfilling and beneficial. Even when it isn't the job we would like, we should still do our very best. Within the sphere of the work we do, this command speaks to us of the need to act responsibly and honestly. The Bible makes it plain that we are to do our work as if we were doing it for God himself (Ephesians 6:7). Paul is here talking to slaves. How much more does it apply to salaried employees?

Integrity applies in every area of our work. So, for example, the Bible tells us that 'honest scales and balances are from the LORD' (Proverbs 16:11, NIV). There is to be honesty with the tools and measures we use; there are to be no attempts to short-change people, or to give them less than they require. If you are in a business in which you give quotations, make them realistic and fair. Don't rip people off. We should conduct our business transactions fairly and honestly.

This is true for how we advertise. Imagine if the advertising world was honest! It makes me smile just to think about it. Those who do work in that field must be morally scrupulous. Advertising, for instance, that 'sells' the idea that smoking is glamorous does a disservice to young people who are blinded by imagined status. Not putting 'a stumbling-block before the blind' (Leviticus 19:14) means not deluding those whom our popular culture has dazzled into believing they want and need certain things.

In the area of expense accounts and travel allowances, we must ask whether we handle these with integrity and complete accountability. Or, in the light of this commandment, are these things you are embarrassed about? Consider this true example of a man who was a civil servant. In the light of the Bible's teaching, he decided that he needed to take a very firm line on stealing at work. He knew it was widespread; one man's house was entirely decked out with fittings from work.

He determined to set an example. He decided that, instead of doing his own private photocopying on the office machine, he would walk to the nearby shop and do it during his lunch hour. Instead of using the phone on his desk for long private phone calls, he would either use the pay phone in the staff canteen or wait until he got home. His expenses were always genuine and much less than the full amount that he could have claimed. His actions were inevitably noticed and brought him a bit of leg-pulling and some snide remarks. Slowly, though, everyone else around him started to act in a similar way, and within a short time the department became far more efficient and motivated. Being completely above board might not automatically make us friends, but it will win us respect. It will certainly speak volumes about the different priorities we base our lives on.

But, as we have been reminded earlier, theft involves more than things or money; it also involves labour. We can also steal not only by what we take physically, but by what we refuse to give. The Bible says of labourers, 'Pay them their wages each day before sunset because they are poor and are counting on it. Otherwise they might cry out to the Lord against you, and it would be counted against you as sin' (Deuteronomy 24:15, NLT). So much for 'the cheque is in the mail'. People are made in God's image. Therefore, we can't let them barter their dignity by pleading for what is due them. And in the context of working with others, where one person doesn't pull their weight, everybody else is affected. We have stolen our labour from them.

This subtle form of stealing does not just occur in the workplace; it can be found in families, classrooms and even churches. Paul in the Bible talks about this again and again.

Everybody, he says, should contribute their gifts and talents with passion and presence.

What about you? Are you holding back in any area, whether at work, home or church? If you are, you need to be honest with yourself. It is theft, and you are stealing from those around you.

Seek corporate and national integrity

Our quest for integrity does not end in the workplace. We are part of a larger scene and we have an important part to play here. Stealing, unfortunately, is not confined to people. It can also be carried out by institutions, governments and even nations.

The Bible is clear that we are not simply responsible for what happens in front of our noses – our responsibility to have integrity extends to everything we are involved in. On this basis, we need seriously to consider how our actions and investments affect the wider world. It is all too easy for us simply to buy the cheapest product at the supermarket without thinking of why it is so cheap. It is equally all too easy to sit back and applaud the growth in our pension funds or investments without thinking about the possible costs to others. We buy trainers with little thought to the fact that barely a few pence of the price we pay may have gone to the person who made them. The same may be true of our clothes, coffee, chocolate or a host of other things we buy. Two hundred years ago Bible-believing Christians led the way, against considerable economic pressure, to abolish slavery in the West. It is perhaps time for us, as their descendants, to push for the modern equivalent of slavery to be abolished worldwide. After all, what greater theft can there be than making someone work for an entire lifetime for a completely inadequate wage?

The very least we can do is make an effort to find out where our money is invested and how our products are produced. Thankfully, today's companies are very sensitive to allegations of unethical practices. A few awkward questions and requests for clarification of positions can work wonders. Ignorance and comfort aren't good enough excuses where the exploitation and stealing of other countries' labour and resources are concerned.

Sadly, it is not just companies that are offenders here. The record of the developed nations in their dealings with the Third World is far from blameless. In the Western world, where less than one-third of the global population lives, we use over two-thirds of the world's resources. Furthermore, we have managed to load a crippling burden of debt onto many developing countries. Over the last few decades thousands of millions of pounds have been lent to poor countries by richer countries to help them fund various necessary development programmes. Not only are many of these debts still there, but they have continued to grow as they amass interest. The scale of this is enormous. In 1997 Comic Relief raised £26 million; yet African nations pay back as much in debt repayment *every single day*. This is just an impossible situation for them to be in, and plainly represents the breaking of the eighth commandment on an international scale. Significantly, Christians have been heavily involved in bringing this injustice to the attention of the Western world. The Jubilee 2000 campaign has called for the cancelling of all Third World debt as the most profound and appropriate Christian gesture to mark the new millennium, and some progress has been achieved towards this. I for one want to do all I can to support this campaign, as it seeks to make amends for the way many of these poor developing countries have been treated by the rich West.

Finally, there is another form of international theft that we must look at. This is the area of the environment. We saw earlier that we are only stewards, rather than owners, of our own personal wealth and possessions. They are merely lent us. The same principle holds true for this world, but on a much greater scale. Although we may see ourselves as lords of creation and free to do what we want with the earth, the reality is that we are responsible to God and one day we will be asked to account for what we allowed to happen to it. The devastation of the rain forests caused by reckless logging, the torn ozone layer produced by our CFCs, the imminent global warming caused by our senseless burning of fossil fuels, can all be seen as acts of theft, and against God.

There is another aspect to the environmental issues that should give us cause to think. A widely used term now is 'sustainable', as in 'sustainable development', and the definition of a sustainable environmental process is simple: it is 'meeting the needs of the present without compromising the ability of future generations to meet their own needs'. An unsustainable process is one that takes from future generations what should be theirs, whether it be oil, jungles, species or fish stocks. Sustainable development is therefore simply applying this eighth commandment to the environment. We mustn't steal the future from our children. On this basis alone, Christians need to be in the forefront of the battle to reduce pollution, save resources and preserve species.

Get the right attitudes

As we come to the end of our look at this searching and wide-ranging commandment, we should ask ourselves what other measures we can take to avoid sliding into theft. Let me remind you of three helpful attitudes to try and acquire. The first two are guidelines that we have already touched on in our dealings with the tenth commandment – hardly surprising when we see theft as the practical outworking of covetousness. The third, however, is new.

Hate greed

Greed leads to theft. We want so much that we don't mind how we get it. One problem is that we always seem to assume that when Jesus warns about the dangers of possessions he is speaking to other people, not to us. Amazingly, however wealthy we become we always manage to consider that 'the rich' (especially the rich Jesus wants to warn) are just above our level of wealth. *We* are merely 'comfortably off'. Yet by global standards – and the standards of Jesus' day – we are all rich, and his words surely apply to us.

A bishop in South America, Dom Helder Camara, once said, 'I used to think, when I was a child, that Christ might have been exaggerating when he warned about the dangers of wealth. Today I know better. I know how very hard it is to be rich and still keep the milk of human kindness. Money has a dangerous way of putting scales on one's eyes, a dangerous way of freezing people's hands, eyes, lips and hearts.'

In the light of what we have seen, it might be worth taking time to examine whether wealth is pulling our lives off course. Ask yourself what you are investing your time and energy in. What are you longing for? What would warm your heart more in tomorrow's post: a loving letter from a relative, or a dividend cheque from the bank? Where is your treasure? For where our treasure is, Jesus said, there our heart will be.

We need to have a sensitive nose for the first hint of the odour of greed about our lives, and learn to deal with it instantly. We should be those who are only loosely attached to our possessions.

Love giving

Every act of giving is an act of rebellion against a life dominated by possessions or wealth, and if we have made a practice of regular giving, then it is hard to be tempted to steal. If you have not acquired the habit of giving, I urge you to start. In fact it is well worthwhile getting into this habit as young as possible. My wife Killy and I encouraged our children to learn to give early, and they have three tins for their pocket money labelled 'Save', 'Spend' and 'Give'. Such a threefold division of our wealth is no bad thing for adults either.

Let me encourage you to really think about your giving. To give away a tenth of your income is one simple principle that many people use to work out what they should give. Of course our giving doesn't have to be only money; it can also be of time, hospitality and material things. I believe that we have to give of ourselves as well. Let me suggest that you search your hearts for the area (whether of money, possessions, time or something else) in which you are most tempted to steal, and make a point, *in that specific area*, of giving away to the extent that it hurts. I believe that giving is the best antidote for becoming a slave to possessions.

We must remember that however much we give away, God has always given far more. If we are to be like him, then we too should be generous. That is one of the reasons why giving is so important. When we give away we are, in a little way, imitating God.

Trust God

Finally, we need to turn back to and rely again on the God who gives us all we need. There is a wonderful prayer recorded in the Old Testament book of Proverbs: 'Two things I ask of you, O LORD . . . Keep falsehood and lies far from me; give me neither poverty nor riches, but give me only my daily bread. Otherwise, I may have too much and disown you and say, "Who is the LORD?" Or I may become poor and steal, and so dishonour the name of my God' (Proverbs 30:8–9, NIV).

We need to learn to live by relying on God rather than on possessions, investments and bank balances. We need to give God the space to be the provider and giver that he wants to be for us. I believe that we can rely on God for everything we need, and many times in my life I have known wonderful answers to prayer. If we do throw ourselves onto God, then our praying takes on a new dimension. Again and again Jesus encourages us to bring all our needs to our Father God. He knows what we need and is ready and waiting to give.

Stealing is an enormous area. Whether open or subtle, personal or impersonal, private or corporate, it is all around us and increasingly part and parcel of the way this world operates. Trying to live the way God wants us to in the area of possessions is going to make us stand out as very strange to those we live and work with. It seems impossible. Earlier, I was unenthusiastic about John Lennon's naïve idealism in the area of possessions. Yet I believe there is scope for a more biblical 'Imagine'. What if we simply took to heart these commands to neither covet nor steal? Imagine if there was no stealing. Imagine how it would change our working relationships and environment, our friendships, our fears, our communities, our economic policy.

The point is that we are not called by Jesus to imagine a perfect world. One day that world will come. In the meantime, he simply asks us to use whatever responsibilities and gifts we have been entrusted with to make a difference.

So what are we waiting for?

COMMANDMENT 7

You shall not commit adultery.
(Exodus 20:14, NIV)

So what's the problem?

Sex is inescapable. Today, if you've watched any TV, seen any advertisements, listened to the radio, flicked through a magazine or read any newspaper, it has been there. It may have been merely implied, so gentle that you barely noticed it, or it may have been so brash and blunt that you recognized it for what it was. We are a society almost submerged by sex; the media flood us with talk about sex, innuendo about sex, images of sex, advice about sex, questionnaires about sex, assertions about sex and problems with sex. Sex is used to grab our attention for anything. Advertisers use sex to sell cars, ice-cream, toothpaste, deodorant, holidays, classical music and even dog food.

The result is a stream of paradoxes and broken promises. The constant barrage of sex attracts and stimulates us, yet at the same time we find ourselves repelled and even jaded by it. The sexual revolution was supposed to bring us liberty and fulfilment, yet society seems to have more hang-ups than ever. We have – it is claimed – better sex education than ever (it is certainly more explicit), yet we have more single teenage mums and more abortions than we ever had. We are told that sex is recreational and purely for pleasure, yet we are also told that it gives our lives meaning and purpose. Can it really be both? The new openness about sex was supposed to be good for all, and yet we have more sexual crimes than ever and women seem to feel less safe on our streets than ever before. The freedom about sex was meant to get rid of those grubby backstreet shops that sold 'adult magazines'; instead we find a high-tech pornography business that, on a worldwide basis, makes more money than the entire car industry. With our inhibitions out in the open, we were told prostitution was to be a thing of the past, yet in red light areas it now operates on a bigger scale than ever. We know more about the mechanics of the orgasm than ever before, yet we seem to know less than our parents about how to make a relationship last beyond a few months. Is it possible that what we took to be the gateway to freedom was, in fact, the door to slavery?

Yet, as if to drown out the serious questions, the media hype about sex goes on. Take, for example, the 1998 film *Pleasantville*. Two teenagers from the 90s are transported back in time to a small American town during the 50s where everything is literally black and white. Into this stuffy, inexpressive, prim and proper town the modern teenagers bring liberation, signified by the characters coming into colour. The chief agent of liberation is, of course, sex and by the end of the film, boring, straight, black and white America has been brought into the multicoloured vibrant world of the new millennium. The message is clear: sex is liberation. The film reviewers loved it; especially those from the teenage magazines.

The problem in our sex-saturated society is not that we think too much about sex, but that we think about it so poorly. If sex is still sold as the key to personal liberation then marriage as an institution is badly under attack. Today there is a lack of public confidence in marriage and the figures are stark. From 1971 to 1990 the number of marriages taking place has more than halved. In the ten years from 1986 to 1996 alone, the number of people marrying for the first time dropped by 27 per cent. In a report in *The Guardian* in 1999 it was asserted that more than 70 per cent of couples in their first serious relationship choose to live together rather than marry. In contrast, divorce is up, with almost 60 per cent of marriages now ending in the courts and one in ten marriages breaking down within two years. Marriage in Britain is under threat.

There are complex reasons behind these statistics, but Dr Elaine Storkey's comments in her book *The Search for Intimacy* ring true: 'Marriage . . . seems to have failed to provide the intimacy it promises, because it has not been strong enough to withstand the pressures of stress, boredom and financial difficulties. The argument has been that marriage, far from meeting the deepest needs of people, has often been responsible for some of their deepest problems.' Certainly there is a lot of cynicism about marriage. There now seems almost a widespread expectation among marrying couples that sooner or later their own marriage will fall to bits. For many, marriage is now no longer for ever.

Against this constant background noise of the selling of sex and the diluting of marriage, there was never a greater need for clear thinking about sexual matters. The seventh commandment addresses exactly this subject. Its five words – 'You shall not commit adultery' – may seem so simple that we feel we can move quickly on past it. Yet such is the confusion we now have as a society that we need to think long and hard about this. You see, to understand what adultery is, and why it is a sin, we need to understand what marriage is. But to understand marriage we need to understand sex. And to understand sex we need to understand the body. It is time to do some hard work.

The heart of the matter

Let me build up to the issue of marriage and adultery slowly.

The beauty of the body

The first thing to say is that God is not opposed to either sex or bodies. Actually, he cares about both more than we do. He made our physical bodies, and in Jesus – to coin a phrase – he wore one himself.

This is important. There seems to be a widely believed lie that says that God is only concerned with 'spiritual' things: sacred thoughts, words and actions that are mysterious, untouchable and angelic and a million miles away from the whole very physical (and sometimes rather messy) business of making love. This of course is a clever lie because it suggests that God is not interested. Unfortunately, fairly early on in the history of Christianity the church became influenced by ancient Greek ideas and decided that bodies were bad and bodies having sex were even worse. The result was that if you wanted to be a serious Christian and become a priest, monk or nun, you gave up the whole idea of marriage. Presumably the rest of the population, while at least able to have marriage and sex, must have thought they were spiritually second class. It was only really 500 years ago, with the rediscovery of the Bible during the Reformation period, that the equation 'sex always equals sin' was broken. Yet such ideas still persist in popular culture. The same ideas occur in much religious music (those sexless pure angelic voices) and much church imagery (those unearthly stained-glass saints). They hardly encourage the idea that you can be holy and married. I mean, how do you make love when both of you wear halos?

The Bible, however, is refreshingly blunt about bodies. To take just one example, when Jesus talks about heaven and the future he frequently uses pictures of feasting and parties. It is all very down-to-earth and physical. This is important. We can't cordon God off, away from daily life; we can't ban him from the disorderliness of how we live and we shouldn't restrict him to some mysterious part of our inner life called 'spirituality'. He wants to be involved in every area of our lives.

The nature of sex

God's concern about bodies extends to sex. I want to plant the flag firmly in the ground of sexuality from the start and claim it for God. He made our sex organs and gave us hormones, and far from being embarrassed by them he decided which bits should go where, and how. We read in the first chapter of Genesis how, before sin had entered the world, God made people, male and female, in his image and how it was good. In the second chapter of Genesis, it is revealed that woman and man were designed to be mutual companions and helpers, and to relate to each other. Humans are unique as a species in that relationship, not reproduction, lies at the heart of the sexual act. It is presumably no accident that our species, alone of the higher animals, has intercourse face to face.

We are then, by God's design, sexual. Our sexuality, although twisted by our rebellion against God, is good and is one of his gifts. Rather than being, as it has sometimes been implied, a necessary evil for the perpetuation of the human race, marriage (and therefore sex) is good. Jesus' first miracle was at a marriage feast (John 2:1–11) and wedding imagery is repeatedly used about heaven and the Second Coming in the Bible. In fact there is even a whole book in the Old Testament (the Song of Songs) which, contrary to awesome efforts of generations of preachers to make it 'spiritual', is first and foremost a celebration of human love. God, the author of the Ten Commandments, is the foremost proponent of healthy sex. He is 'pro-sex'.

Because of the confusing times we live in, I feel, reluctantly, that I need here to make three clear points:

- To say that God is 'pro-sex' is not the same as saying that he is in favour of all sexual activity. As we will see, there is only one approved context for sex, and that is inside the secure framework of a married male–female partnership. While sex between a couple who are not married is not adultery in the strict sense of the word, it is still wrong. The thrust of this commandment – and the whole of the Bible – is that sex is for use within marriage only. Just because I concentrate on marriage here does not mean I am not concerned about unmarrieds. All research shows that couples who cohabit before marriage have a higher rate of divorce than those who do not. To put it bluntly, it seems that those who sleep around before marriage are likely to do it afterwards.
- The Bible is absolutely clear that men and women *alone* were made as counterparts to each other in physical, sexual and psychological ways. I am aware of the struggles of many in this area, and I genuinely sympathize, but I want you to understand that sexual relations between members of the

same sex are plainly against God's pattern for humanity. Where homosexual or lesbian practices are mentioned in the Bible they are always condemned, often in very strong language. I am fully aware that some people hold very strong views and are pro-homosexuality. It must be stated that these views are not rooted in the Bible. Equally, when I affirm marriage, it is exclusively the biblical pattern of marriage between one man and one woman that the Bible endorses. There is no way that the biblical definition of marriage can be stretched to cover a same-sex relationship, however stable or long term. The principle that men and women alone are each other's counterparts also rules out sexual relations with children and animals. Peering apprehensively into the future, I would also argue that it rules out sex with computer-synthesized systems, however life-like or alluring they might be. And if you haven't thought about that yet, *don't*!

- While sex in marriage is good and God-given, I also want to point out that the Bible affirms singleness too as being good. This is such an important point that I want to deal with it later.

Finally, while sex is good, it is also incredibly powerful, both for good and bad. Because the sexual relationship is at such a deep personal level, an enormous energy is linked with it. As such, sex can be destructive if misused. The illustration of sex as being like fire has much to commend it. In the right place and handled in the right way sex, like fire, can be good; misused sex – again like fire – can destroy us utterly. Another parallel with sex is creativity. This too is basically good and is also a gift from God. But our creativity has not just given us language and art and science, it has also given us nuclear weapons and pornography. Sexuality similarly has the power for enormous destruction.

In the last chapter we introduced the subject of idolatry – the serving and worship of things that are not God. The most dangerous idols are the best things of life and the better a thing is, the greater the danger that it will be mistaken for God. It is precisely because it is basically good and powerful that sex has the potential to be mistaken for God himself. And that is a fatal mistake, both for our relationship with God and our sex lives.

The meaning of marriage

Some of the most profound truths of the Bible are contained in the first few chapters of Genesis. There we see the blueprint of what it is to be fully human. In Genesis 2 we are given the basis of marriage: 'For this reason a man will leave his father and mother and be united to his wife and they will become one flesh' (Genesis 2:24, NIV). From this we see that marriage corresponds to three things:

- *Leaving.* When a man and a woman leave the familiar world of their own families and marry, they start something new that is independent of their parents' lives. Marriage marks the irrevocable start of a new legal and social unit in the community.
- *Uniting.* A marriage is a merging of the couple in every area of life. Marriage shows a wholesale commitment between a man and a woman that brings together every aspect of what they are, whether it be personal, emotional or social. There is to be no area where married people are to hold back from surrendering to each other.

- *Becoming one flesh.* A marriage involves creating a personal unity at a very deep level. In the sexual act, there is something far more than just physical contact happening. There is the generation of a total togetherness, of a union, to the extent that the two people concerned are in a real sense no longer individuals.

Anything less than this total relationship falls short of the definition of marriage. To underline this all-embracing and permanent bond, the Bible talks about a marriage relationship being a 'covenant'. The word 'covenant' means agreement or promise and comes with the implication of a lifelong commitment between two parties with mutual obligations. The model on which all such covenants are based is that of the divine covenant that God enters into with men and women. These are binding agreements with mutual responsibilities that are freely entered into by both parties and which are based on the promises of each side to be faithful and true to each other. Marriage is similar and equally requires each party to make promises to be faithful and true. In fact, in many places, God daringly uses the imagery of marriage as an illustration of his covenant love for his people. Adultery is also used as an image, but as an illustration of what it means to turn away from God and reject his love.

If we think of marriage in covenant terms, this helps us to see the place of sex within it. On the one hand, sex can be seen as the seal of the marriage relationship; the biological and spiritual equivalent of signing the wedding certificate. On the other hand, marriage provides the only safe place for sex. Only within the secure confines of a covenant relationship, where we are protected by security, love and commitment, can the power of sex be unleashed. It should come as no surprise in the light of this that sex outside marriage is always seen in the Bible as a dangerous and wrong abnormality.

In our society, where freedom has been elevated to be the rule of life, it is no wonder that such a binding covenant basis to marriage is disliked. As Elaine Storkey says, 'It would not be an exaggeration to suggest that in spite of even the most lavish and detailed wedding preparations, every marriage in Britain and America today potentially gets off to a bad start. That is because the very meaning of what those two people are doing is fundamentally out of step with the ethos of contemporary society.'

I would want to argue that actually it is only by binding ourselves to each other with unbreakable commitments that we find freedom. We can only be secure enough to open up to be the people we really are, when we know that we can utterly trust the person we are with. Far from marriage restricting freedom, it actually brings freedom. We have the freedom to love another, without holding anything back. Only within the thick, secure and private walls of a permanent marriage can we become psychologically and spiritually naked. To be loved unconditionally without strings attached, and to love in return, is true freedom.

Let me point out something about what I have just written that you may have overlooked. In the last few paragraphs I have said almost nothing at all about feelings or emotions and *nothing whatsoever* about 'being in love'. The fact is that the key elements of marriage (leaving, uniting, becoming one flesh) do not require the emotional state that the modern media insist is the only basis for marriage. In fact in an arranged marriage 'being in love' was either the icing on the cake or something that came later. The emphasis in marriage lay elsewhere. This may seem strange and even heartless to us, but it had its merits. The point is this: 'feeling in love' with someone is in fact what it says – a feeling. And a feeling, even a strong one, on its own may fade. To hold a marriage together over many years, a better glue than emotions is needed. God knows this. That's why he wants marriage to be broadly based and bound by promises. Ironically, within the secure framework of marriage where other things are doing the cementing, the emotion of love may thrive and persist.

This wide-ranging giving and sharing under the guarantee of a sworn solemn covenant is the pattern of marriage given to us by God. But before we move on I want to say that what I have described as the biblical pattern is not some abstract dream, like some scheme for eliminating all human poverty, or devising a London public transport system that works. Although its implications were probably rarely spelled out, it has formed the basis for marriage in Britain for the last 500 years. Indeed, I could have illustrated much of what I have said by quoting from the Marriage Service found in the 1662 *Book of Common Prayer* under whose words many, if not most, of our ancestors were wed. And, as our sobering contemporary statistics on divorce illustrate, we have nothing to teach our forebears on the subject of making marriages work.

Avoiding sexual immorality and adultery

If you have read the previous chapters, you will be able to guess my strategy in the pages ahead. What I want to do is first address the sin of sexual immorality in general and, more specifically, adultery, and show why it is so serious. Then I want to discuss how we can affirm and strengthen the institution of marriage. But before I can do either, I want to remind you that we need to think and talk straight about sexual matters.

Be honest about sex

There are lies about every area of our lives. But there is no part of our existence where the lies are bigger, more widespread or more seductive than in the area of sex. We need to be honest and to think hard in order to challenge today's sexual myths.

First of all, let me warn you to beware of sex. Don't treat it lightly. Never ever say, as you see some scandal in the paper, 'It can't happen to me.' Our sexuality is such a powerful force that it is capable of tripping up presidents, politicians, princes and even preachers. Whether it wrecks more careers than greed or lying I don't know, but what I do know is that there is nothing the press likes more than to see a man or woman who aspires to morality, caught in the act of sexual immorality. Sex has an astonishing ability to make victims. Men in particular can labour for years with families and jobs, earning love, security and respect from many. Then, in order to possess a few moments of sexual gratification, they can throw it all away. A moment of pleasure, and a lifetime of guilt. It is extraordinary what wreckage sex can produce. Take the actor Michael Douglas, who when charged with adultery in his divorce proceedings pleaded 'diminished responsibility'. 'Sex', he claimed, 'is a wave which sweeps over me, the impulse that is, and when the urge comes I am helpless, every time.' And this, we remind ourselves, is not some adolescent struggling with his glands on overdrive but a man who is over 50!

Second, see through the lies. Don't be persuaded by the soft words. It may be termed by the media, or even your friends, as 'a fling', 'a bit of a romp', 'a harmless bit of fun', or even 'a romance'. You should call it what it really is: immorality or adultery.

Third, remember that, as with other idols, sex promises what it cannot deliver. If you are a teenager, sex can offer maturity and fulfilment. If you are lonely, sex can offer closeness and companionship. If you are bored, sex offers excitement. If you are hurt, sex offers comfort. If you want to be intimate with someone, sex offers you intimacy. Yet outside the context of marriage, it actually delivers none of these things but instead gives only guilt, emptiness and yet deeper hurts and regrets often experienced years later.

Fourth, sexual temptation is not irresistible. To many people today, including Michael Douglas quoted above, the sexual urge is something unstoppable. The urge for sex is something like a flu or cold virus. It's just in the air and if you catch it, then hard luck. All you can do is give in to immorality. No, you need to tell yourself that wrong desires can be fought and can be defeated. Sometimes the battle is not easy and sometimes the victory is gained at a high cost. But the biggest lie is that there is no point in resisting.

Fifth, we need to be aware that there is more to adultery than the physical act of sex. In the pattern of marriage that I outlined earlier, of leaving, uniting and becoming one flesh, a marriage is based on more than physical relations. Technically, it might not be adultery to have merely a deep, non-physical, tender relationship with someone other than your spouse. But it is still an action that strikes at the heart of a marriage. The popular expression 'cheating on your wife' (or husband) catches this sort of thing very well. We need to shun it, and work to make sure that it does not happen.

Remember the cost of adultery

If marriage is, as I have described it, an all-embracing covenant arrangement where both parties commit themselves to each other for life and give each other everything they are, sexually, psychologically and socially, then the horror of adultery becomes plain. We need constantly to remind ourselves of how serious an act of adultery is.

Marriage is a whole web of links of intimate giving and sharing between a man and a woman, and with the act of adultery all these bonds are severed. Adultery smashes the deepest and most intimate levels of trust, shatters the covenant promises and breaks down the walls of privacy and exclusivity that protect the heart of marriage. It is, in short, an abomination.

Of course, it is not portrayed as this in the media. There, adultery is rarely if ever portrayed as what it really is, a shabby betrayal of the deepest and most intimate trust. At the lowest level, what is generally referred to as 'an affair' (*adultery* has rather negative overtones) is portrayed as something exciting and stimulating. Driven by the unstoppable and glorious emotion of falling in love, the hero or heroine slips into what is essentially a harmless and life-enhancing bit of sweaty, physical fun that brightens up their humdrum existence. At a more sophisticated level, adultery is portrayed as something that allows us personal fulfilment. Through it, we can somehow 'move on' beyond our marriage and in moving on we become more 'what we ought to be' or we 'achieve our own potential'. Adultery here is far more than lust. It is part of 'our deep quest for self-realization'. However it is portrayed, you can be sure of one thing: nine times out of ten, the media – and Hollywood in particular – will sweep under the carpet all the shame, the anger and the pain that all adultery brings. Adultery hurts. It shatters trust and severs friendship. Please look out for the truth, not the illusion.

There are other costs. My friend Dr Chris Bignell, who specializes in sexually transmitted infections, recently summarized the situation for me. 'People risk their physical (and psychological) health for adultery and immorality. Sexually transmitted infections are common and have a disproportionate effect on the health of women. They are a major cause of infertility, ectopic pregnancy, chronic pelvic pain and cervical cancer. In 1998, the number of sexually related infections treated in GU (Genito-Urinary) medicine clinics in England exceeded half a million for the first time. Despite widespread awareness of AIDS the number of people infected with HIV continues to rise, particularly among heterosexuals.' The best way to ensure you never catch a sexual disease is either not to have sex, or only to have it with someone who has only ever had sex with you. From the health point of view alone, it would be impossible to invent a better system than a lifelong exclusive marriage. God (surprise, surprise) knew what he was doing.

Adultery and immorality also affect others. Sexual sin is a social sin and the effects are staggering. The social cost of family breakdown in the UK is put at around £5 billion a year. If trends continue, one in four children will experience family breakdown before they are 16. Sexual crime too is rising every year. Four times more rapes have been reported to the police in the last decade, while the number of rapists convicted has gone down from 24 per cent to 9 per cent. A recent Home Office report stated that more than 70,000 children a year are believed to be the victims of sexual abuse. There has been a massive increase in date rape, and in 1996 half of all sexual assaults were from people in 'intimate relationships'.

Behind these cold figures lies a sea of individual human misery. We have as a society paid a very high price for turning our backs on the seventh commandment and on emphasizing the sexual act at the expense of relationships.

Adultery denies love, degrades people, destroys families, defiles marriage and defies God.

Clean up your act

When I talked about theft in the last chapter, I asked you to make amends where you could. I want to be similarly practical here.

If you are involved in an adulterous relationship, end it now. Not tomorrow, not next week, *now*. Pick up the phone and do it. There is no easy way out, and, yes, someone is always going to get hurt, but the only way to end it, is to *end* it. When Jesus talked about adultery, he said some strong things:

> If your right eye causes you to sin, gouge it out and throw it away. It is better for you to lose one part of your body than for your whole body to be thrown into hell. And if your right hand causes you to sin, cut it off and throw it away. It is better for you to lose one part of your body than for the whole of your body to be thrown into hell. (Matthew 5:29–30, NIV)

What Jesus is saying here, beneath the imagery, is simple: we need to take drastic action and do some radical spiritual surgery.

Where there has been adultery, you and your marriage partner will probably need to see someone who is able to work through the issues of broken trust and violation that will be there. It is very delicate and painful, and needs to be done with God's help in the context of repentance and forgiveness. But healing of a marriage can happen. Obviously, very few couples talk openly about how their marriage survived adultery, but I know of many cases where God has enabled restoration to occur.

In this context, I want to warn you against the peril of despair. The lie is that you cannot get out, or that you can't be forgiven and made clean: 'It is too late now. You are in too deep to ever get out.' I believe that with a loving, caring God the door for repentance stays open. But if we stay in a wrong relationship, then the chances are that habit will make it harder and harder to deal with. However painful it may be, *now* is the time to act.

As an encouragement to you, look at one of the most powerful stories in the Gospels, where Jesus was directly confronted with adultery. In John 8:1–11 we read how the religious leaders dragged before him a woman 'caught in the act of adultery'. In fact the text makes it plain that their real interest was to trap Jesus. Would he endorse the religious death penalty for adultery and in so doing break the Roman rule that only they could pass a death sentence? Or would he let her off and thus go against the Jewish law? So waiting for him to condemn himself, they asked Jesus whether she should be stoned. 'What do you say?' they asked. In answer Jesus simply bent down and began writing with his finger in the dust. Incidentally, we do not know what he wrote, but it is quite possible that it was the list of the Ten Commandments. They kept badgering him for an answer until he straightened up and said, 'The sinless one among you, you throw the first stone.' Then as he bent down again to write some more in the dirt, they slipped away one by one, beginning with the oldest, leaving the woman alone. Jesus stood up and spoke to her. 'Woman, where are they? Does no one condemn you?'

'No one, Sir.'

'Neither do I,' said Jesus. 'Go on your way. From now on, don't sin.'

In this I see three things. First, there is a condemnation of those who were willing to use the sexual sins of others for their own purposes. Then, as now, sexual sin brings out the worst in bystanders. We need to be very careful about our own motives when we criticize in this area. Second, I see how Jesus showed mercy to the woman. He, as the one without sin, could have thrown the first stone, but he chose not to. He offers her, in effect, a new start. But third, I also see how he balances it with a requirement that she turn from her sin. I believe that he holds out the same offer of mercy matched with a call for repentance and a changed life to all who are in sexual sin today.

One of the most notorious adulterers in the Bible is King David and I recounted earlier one how his covetousness of Bathsheba led him into sin. The writer of many of the psalms, David was a wise and godly man, but in this area of his life he was weak. The Bible recounts (in 2 Samuel 12:1–14) how, under the challenging rebuke of a holy man of God, David confessed and repented of his sin. Psalm 51 was written by David at this time and is a moving model for repentance in the circumstances of sexual sin. If you have committed adultery, you would do well to spend a long time looking at and reflecting on this psalm.

I do urge you that if you are caught in this net of sin, let Jesus Christ free you. Admit to sin, confess it, repent of it and promise to do all you can never to repeat it. Ask his power to help you overcome it.

Affirm marriage

Having spent some time talking about adultery and sexual sin, let me turn to how you can positively affirm marriage.

Work at being married

Often when I speak on this commandment I give the talk the title 'How to "Affair-Proof" your Relationships'. Adultery happens because no marriage is perfect and all of us have something in our lives, for example a need of love, acceptance or intimacy, that can sometimes make adultery seem attractive. I believe that God wants our marriages to be satisfying, so let me suggest what I call 'The Five Rs' of a successful marriage.

Respect. Love is built on the foundation of mutual respect. Paul tells us, 'Each man must love his wife as he loves himself, and the wife must respect her husband' (Ephesians 5:33, NLT). One of the most unpleasant things to witness is people being rude to their partners in public – interrupting them, ignoring them, contradicting them or putting them down. As they say, you can bury a marriage with a lot of little digs. Husbands, don't criticize your wife's judgement – look at who she married!

A public lecture was once advertised under the title 'How to Make Your Wife Treat You Like a King'. The lecture hall was absolutely packed out, with men from all sections of society waiting to hear where they were going wrong. Finally, the speaker stood up to address the packed and expectant gathering. 'Gentlemen,' he said to them, 'the answer to the question being posed is very simple. If you want your wife to treat you like a king there is one thing you must do: treat her like a queen.'

Respect is vital. The alternative is contempt, and frankly where there is contempt it is almost inevitable that eventually you will be in one of those dangerous conversations where you find yourself looking longingly into someone else's eyes and saying, 'You know, I don't get this sort of respect at home.'

If you are not yet married, let me give you some advice. Never consider marrying anyone you do not thoroughly respect as a person, however good-looking or charming.

Responsibility. One of the ways you can help keep your marriage going is to take responsibility. This means fixing the problem, not fixing the blame. You can often see in relationships that couples spend much more time and energy attacking each other than attacking the problems. Marriage is, as I have said, a covenant and is about commitment and 'stickability' rather than feelings. To make a marriage work takes an act of the will so that both the heart and the mind act together. One of the things God encourages us to do is to be honest about our weaknesses and failings, to own up and take responsibility when something is our fault. The trouble with the world is that so many people who stand up for their rights fall down miserably on their responsibilities.

Not only are we to take responsibility for our own actions, but we should try to take responsibility for our partner. It is often better to pick up the blame rather than win an argument. The apostle Paul wrote to one church, 'Each of you should look not only to your own interests but also to the interests of others. Your attitude should be the same as that of Christ Jesus' (Philippians 2:4–5, NIV). The same rule applies to marriages.

Relate. The figures on how little time couples spend together today are alarming. One Gallup poll found the average husband and wife spend less than ten minutes a day in conversation with each other. Now I know in these days we talk about quality time not quantity time, but it seems to me that nothing beats quantity quality time. In a marriage we need to give time to nourish and cherish the relationship. We need to learn to talk and listen to each other.

Romance. I think that if there was more courting in marriage there would be fewer marriages in court! I don't know whether you were surprised by what I said earlier on in this chapter about God being pro-sex, but I am convinced not only that it is true, but that marriage is the place to demonstrate it. God, the author of the Ten Commandments, is the foremost proponent of healthy sex. Intimacy in marriage should be unashamedly erotic. As Elaine Storkey says, 'A couple in marriage is called to worship God as much by their truthful, erotic sex as by their prayers for each other.'

Resolve. Decide to make it work! For a successful marriage you need to make a resolve to be committed to your wife or husband not only in the one-off wedding ceremony, but on each day of your married life. Both partners have to make a firm commitment to faithfulness, fidelity and honesty at all times. Tell yourself that you are going to make it work or die trying.

Now please do not get me wrong. I'm not suggesting that marriages will never run into problems or have to endure storms. But I believe that the kind of commitment God is talking about means that when we hit a difficulty in our marriage, we make a decision to face it and carry on together. Trying times are not the times to stop trying. It might be that you are aware of problems in your marriage. If so, you need to be honest about those with your partner and also seek professional help. In all this, we need to treat the gift of our marriage with the highest respect and value.

Support singles

Wait a minute, you say, *singles*! I thought this was about marriage and adultery? It is, but I believe that the roots of many disastrous marriages go back to the mishandling of the whole issue of singleness. One reason, I believe, why there are so many disastrous marriages is that people have been so misled by our culture that they feel that they *have* to be married, and they are so scared of singleness that they flee from it at the earliest opportunity.

One of the biggest lies around is that sex is the same as sexuality, so if you are not sexually active you are not sexual. Freud said something similar: 'Those who are not sexually active are socially retarded, unbalanced and disturbed . . .' This, of course, is nonsense. A person may not be sexually active, but this certainly doesn't mean that they are not sexual. Linked with this lie is another. This says that if you live a single, celibate life you are missing out and are unfulfilled. My response to this patronizing attitude is to point to Jesus. Here was a single man who was not sexually active, but would anyone dare to suggest that his life was unfulfilled, or sad and boring? No, on the contrary. No one has ever lived as fulfilled a life as he had. In his many friendships, his love of fellowship, his daring friendliness that cut across the rigid contemporary barriers of gender, race and even religion, he is the model for what a human life should be. We need to let Jesus be our pattern, not the magazines and TV programmes that scream out at us that we must be having sex in order to live a fully satisfying life.

It is clear from the Bible that God calls some people to be single. I believe the single state is not for the majority, but I also believe that God equips those whom he calls that way. Singleness is not in any way an inferior or less godly way of life. In fact it might be the opposite. It may be that because God can't trust some of us to be on our own, he gives us spouses. However, we are all social people and it needs to be said that a single person will have relational needs that the married person would have met by their spouse. We need to find ways of integrating single people into families and communities better than we do and affirming their value as both single and sexual people. We need to build deep, strong and encouraging relationships with them, so that they do not feel lonely. In particular, we need to remember that to be called to singleness is to be called to celibacy and as St Augustine said, 'Celibacy without community is impossible.'

While God may have called some of us to be single, he has called none of us to survive on our own. We are all made as relational beings who need each other. It is selfish to ignore those who are single, and we need to do all we can to integrate singles into our lives. From my experience of singles, I have no doubt that we will benefit as much from this as they will.

Get the right attitudes

Finally, I want to suggest that we arm ourselves with the right attitudes.

Guard your minds

Whether single or married you might be thinking, 'Well, I've never actually committed adultery, so how does this relate to me?' Listen to what Jesus does with this commandment in the teaching on how to live that we call the Sermon on the Mount. There he says, 'You have heard that it was said, "Do not commit adultery." But I tell you that anyone who looks at a woman lustfully has already committed adultery with her in his heart' (Matthew 5:28, NIV).

What Jesus is doing is shifting the emphasis from the action back a stage further, to the desire. Clean hands are not enough; we need clean hearts. The look of lust or desire is, Jesus says, also adultery. He does not say that the look is equally as bad as the physical act, but he says that it does count as adultery. As we think about this, we realize that if our desires are to be judged, then none of us can escape condemnation. We have all sinned. This is typical of Jesus, getting at the core of the issue and reaching to examine our thoughts, our desires and our hearts. There is a chain of things in our lives that can be summarized as follows: thoughts become words, words become actions, actions become habits and habits become character. We need to start at the root with thoughts.

As I close, it is worth being utterly frank about our thought life. I remember hearing of a man who had just committed adultery. 'I don't know how it happened,' the man protested in bewilderment to his minister. The minister turned to him and said, 'I do. Had you ever committed the act in your mind with this woman?' Of course he had, and his actions had finally just followed his thoughts.

We are all prone to temptation, and living in the world that we do, we are bombarded time after time by images and ideas that try to divert us from God's way. Temptation isn't wrong in itself. The question is what we do with it. The Bible encourages us to 'remember that the temptations that come into your life are no different from what others experience. And God is faithful. He will keep the temptation from becoming so strong that you can't stand up against it. When you are tempted, he will show you a way out so that you will not give in to it' (1 Corinthians 10:13, NLT). We can't stop being bombarded by sexual images, but we can stop them getting a foothold in us. It is better to shun the bait than to struggle on the hook.

Here, though, we need to drag our wills and action into line. We need to choose purity. The stimulus of the erotic pictures, films and words we inevitably meet in this sex-obsessed world can play havoc with our internal desires. They can act as fuel to a fire that is often already in danger of burning out of control. Many people who have everything else in their lives under control feel completely overwhelmed in this area. They feel enslaved and taken captive by thoughts they are ashamed of. If that describes you, then make a decision to choose God's way in this area. You don't need to live as a slave, under the domination of things that aren't pleasing to God. Allow Jesus to deliver you.

For some of you reading this, I need to issue a stronger warning. While others may have blundered into images that have aroused them, you, in contrast, have deliberately sought them out to feed your sexual appetites. By watching particular films, reading certain magazines, letting your eyes roam over whatever they choose, you have relinquished control over your own life and are heading into slavery of the most pitiable sort. A mind that persistently dreams and schemes is a mind that needs cleansing. If we don't confess and turn away from mental adultery and immorality, it will eventually dominate our thought life. And if we encourage it with sexually stimulating films, books, magazines or social settings, our fantasy dreams will one day turn into nightmare realities.

The only solution is to deal uncompromisingly with the problem using the radical spiritual surgery that Jesus calls for. Rather than plucking out your eye, cancel the sex channel on cable television. Rather than cutting your hand off, erase those pornographic images on the computer. If you need help, then find someone wise whom you can trust to be accountable to about your internal thought life. If struggles and pain can be shared with another, they often lose their power and hold. This is nowhere more true than in this whole area of our sexuality.

If you choose God's way of living, I promise you that, far from missing out, you will become truly human.

Guard your behaviour

It is also important that our public behaviour is appropriate. In social situations, if you see someone who attracts you, for whatever reason (and we know that whether we are single or married, it happens), then don't take a second look. That does not give you permission to take a long first look! In the Bible, one man of God says, 'I made a covenant with my eyes not to look lustfully at a girl' (Job 31:1, NIV).

We need to be aware of how our actions come over to members of the opposite sex. God wants us to have right relationships. Do you know that most affairs happen with friends? If you are married, never flirt. If you are single, never flirt unless you have a serious intent and the object of your attentions is both unattached and suitable. Keep your boundaries with members of the opposite sex clear and firm, and never give any ground for misunderstanding or ambiguity.

Choose purity today; choose God's way. I cannot encourage you enough to make up your mind to be sexually pure. Whatever you have done in the past, from this day forward you can choose purity.

A final word

I believe that for all of us as individuals – and for our society as a whole – our sexuality is the most damaged and broken part of our humanity. Yet with God there is wholeness through healing and right relationships, through his help and his example.

In the *Guinness Book of Records* 'Marriage' is under the category of 'Human Achievement'. But frankly, if we are honest here, we need more than human achievement. We need God's help. The wonderful thing though is that God does wish to help us. He, after all, is the great lover, the faithful partner, the one who is utterly committed to his covenant people. He doesn't show his love by sending us a romantic poem or dropping a bunch of red roses onto our doorstep. 'But God showed his great love for us by sending Christ to die for us while we were still sinners' (Romans 5:8, NLT).

He shows he cares, not by a poem, but through cries of agony and excruciating pain. It's not champagne he drinks, but bitter wine. He doesn't bear roses in his arms, but a crown of thorns wedged on his head. He doesn't bathe us in fine-smelling perfume, but saves us through sweat and blood. God's proposal was nailed to a cross. And he did it for us. That's true love.

The only way to resist temptation to infidelity is to root our single life or our marriage in the rich soil of God's confirming love. Let go of your regrets about the past, and experience God's forgiveness and healing for previous poor choices. It is when we allow ourselves to be loved by Jesus that we are free to love like Jesus – faithfully, unconditionally, purely and selflessly. Not for what's in it for ourselves, but for what the other person is worth.

A national newspaper was able to run a story a couple of years ago with the title 'Christians make the best lovers'.

No wonder.

COMMANDMENT **6**

You shall not murder.
(Exodus 20:13, NIV)

So what's the problem?

The sixth commandment prohibits unlawful killing or, more precisely, the intentional killing of an innocent human being. As such, it seems a straightforward rule (who is in favour of legalizing murder?), but as we look at it, we will find ourselves forced to think about some unfamiliar matters. Most of all, and perhaps to our discomfort, we will have to look at anger, a subject that we may be all too familiar with.

For a start, though, we need to think about death. There are fashions in attitudes as well as clothes. In the Victorian age, everyone talked about death, and the taboo subject was sex. In our generation, dying and death is taboo while we are preoccupied with sex. The whole business of dying is hidden behind a screen of words: 'passing away', 'the departed', 'chapels of rest' and so on. The change is fascinating, because we face the same risk of death as our Victorian ancestors did: 100 per cent of us will die too. Yet unless we work in hospitals or funeral parlours, most of us will only rarely see dead people during our lives.

Bizarrely, though, we are more familiar with death and

killing than any previous generation. On our television and cinema screens, we have seen fictional death in a thousand ways. Violence is being pumped into our culture by the megaton. We have spawned a new generation of movie heroes – Rambos, Terminators, lethal weapons who Die Hard – who are not exactly walking models of 'anger management'. Over our popcorn, we have watched men and women shot, drowned, burned alive, crushed by cars, eaten by sharks, swallowed by snakes, consumed by aliens and even (but more rarely) die quietly in bed. Nightly, our children stalk around their computer worlds armed to the teeth, generating body counts worthy of a respectable war. In the game *Carmageddon*, drivers get points for running over pedestrians.

In reality – or as near as it gets on television – we gawp at the bloodied dead of wars, shudder at the earthquake-crushed bodies and wince at terminally malnourished infants. Then we switch channels. Occasionally, worryingly, as we stare at the screen, the worlds of reality and illusion merge. Was that film of a NATO air strike or was it a clip from a computer game? Are those really burned bodies or are they Hollywood dummies?

There are strange parallels between our modern views of sex and death. We know more about the mechanics of both sex and death than ever before, yet we seem to know less than ever about the reality and significance of either.

Our confusion is unfortunate because there is a lot of death about. The final toll for the twentieth century has not yet been released, but it is probable that war and war-related deaths totalled well over 500 million people. In a recent radio phone-in people were asked to pick one word that summarized the last hundred years. The most common words suggested were 'holocaust', and 'ethnic cleansing'. The past hundred years have seen truly horrific acts of evil against humanity: Hitler's extermination of 6 million Jews, the tens of millions who perished under Stalin, the millions killed in Cambodia, Uganda and Rwanda. Famine and disease have killed hundreds of millions more. And there is no sign that the new century will be much better.

The sixth commandment raises other issues. In thinking about killing and murder, matters that are literally problems of life and death emerge. How unique and valuable is a human life? How should we regard each other? How do we relate to each other? How do we cope with difference and disagreement?

The principles behind these four words, 'You shall not murder', are far-reaching and go way beyond simply putting a law on the statute book.

The heart of the matter

The value of life

Life is from God. The first chapters of the Bible declare that God made heaven and earth and created men and women. Speaking of Adam, the first human, we read, 'The LORD God formed the man from the dust of the ground and breathed into his nostrils the breath of life, and the man became a living being' (Genesis 2:7, NIV). Behind the pictorial language lies the plain fact that life comes from God.

Recently there have been all sorts of scientific advances in the area of genetic manipulation and research, and there is much talk about 'making life in the laboratory'. Even if this is done, it will not be us creating life. It will simply be us copying God.

God created life first and he remains the origin of all life, whether formed in the test tube or the womb.

This is important. Life is not something that we automatically have or some sort of natural right. It is a gift from God. And because God has given life to each of us, he alone is the one who gives life and he alone is the one who takes it away. The pivotal point around which the sixth commandment hangs is once again *God*. He is the God who freely, generously, wonderfully and mysteriously gives life to each one of us. To murder is to take away someone's life. That, simply, is beyond our authority.

What is more, human life is special. *Homo sapiens* is not simply the top of the evolutionary tree or the dominant ecological species. Instead, we have a unique honour and dignity, as we alone are the ones God made in his image. We read on the first page of the Bible, 'So God created people in his own image; God patterned them after himself; male and female he created them' (Genesis 1:26, NLT). That doesn't mean, of course, that God looks like us and has two eyes, a nose and a mouth! Rather it means that God gave us the potential, denied to all other animals, of relating to him on a personal level. It also means that we bear his image or likeness and are to show it to each other and to the world about us. We are – or were supposed to be – his representatives and little imitations of him. We were made to be like him, to act like him, to love like him and to relate as he does. Jesus in fact confirms our status. By God becoming man in Christ, we see a new way in which people are in God's image.

People are special. That whole idea underlies the issues raised by this commandment about taking life. A few chapters after the story of the creation of the world we read one of God's first warnings to people: '. . . for to kill a person is to kill a living being made in God's image' (Genesis 9:6, NLT).

Another way, I believe, in which human beings are made in the image of God is that we are social beings who interrelate with each other. The Bible reveals that God, though one being, is Father, Son and Spirit. Between these three persons of the Trinity there is a deep relationship. As God's image-bearers we show that image most when we are with other people, whether it be in a marriage, a family or at work. God gives us each other; it is the plan of God for us to be interdependent, living in a society where each person is valued and able to make their unique contribution to our life together. The poet and preacher, John Donne, well expressed the significance of death in such an interlocked society this way: 'No man is an island, entire of itself; every man is a piece of the continent, a part of the main. . . . Any man's death diminishes me, because I am involved in Mankind; And therefore never send to know for whom the bell tolls; It tolls for thee.'

So at this point, we see there are three reasons why human life is sacred. First, God alone has the power to give life and therefore is the only one authorized to take life away.

Second, as we are made in the image of God, to take the life of another human is to destroy someone patterned after God and close to God's own heart.

Third, God made us to live together, each contributing what we have and are to others. Murder is the most brutal breach possible of that interlocked social life together.

Think of the most valuable object you can. Perhaps it is a painting, some wonderful sculpture, a stunning piece of jewellery or even a great building. Such is its value that it is beyond price and it cannot be insured. Now think of a human being, any human being, perhaps a relative, your neighbour, a colleague. Now ask yourself this: which is more valuable? The answer is plain. It is the human life. To say otherwise, even to hesitate, is to insult the very God in whose image we are all made.

The value of human life, *all* human life, is something we need to learn today. We live in a disposable society with disposable razors, disposable contact lenses, disposable pens and disposable nappies. We need to protest loudly that the one thing that is not disposable is human life. To regard human beings as expendable, as if they were merely pawns in a chess game, is very wrong. To treat the death of other human beings as if it were of little consequence ignores the intrinsic value of the human being. It is actually a crime against the God whose image we bear.

In the light of this, I want to look, very briefly, at some important issues of life and death that this commandment addresses. Then I want to look at how Jesus extends the scope of this commandment so that it affects all of us.

Issues of life and death

Two groups of issues emerge here. These are whether killing in the name of the law or the state is ever right, and how we are to respond to the issues of abortion and euthanasia. Neither of them is easy, but neither of them can be ducked.

Killing under authority

I can imagine that the question has already been raised as to whether, in light of the value of the human life, it is ever right for the state to take a life. What about war or capital punishment? After all, in the time of Moses the Israelites had both. Let me briefly touch on both issues.

Killing in war. Let me deal with the complex issue of war first. Apart from some appalling aberrations, of which the Crusades are the most notorious, almost all Christians have agreed that war is only to be undertaken as the very last, desperate resort. Every other option to resolve a situation must be tried first. There are no Christian holy wars. Some Christians have gone as far as to say that all fighting is always wrong and have taken the pacifist position. Others have said that limited and restrained wars may, at times, be justified as the lesser of a number of evils. The classic example is the defeat of Nazi Germany, which presumably spared yet more millions from the gas chambers. The issues over justified war are complex and need more space than I have here. All Christians today would, I think, agree that because of the value of human life even a war that is justified should be restricted in its scope, and care should be taken to avoid civilian casualties. But, as the bombing of Dresden, Hiroshima and Nagasaki shows, even justified wars have a way of getting out of control.

If you are directly involved in these issues, perhaps as a soldier or politician, I can only urge you to do some hard, serious, prayerful thinking. A good lead into the issues is the relevant chapter in John Stott's *New Issues Facing Christians Today*. The rest of us, however, cannot escape by shrugging our shoulders and hiding behind our newspapers or Bibles. Let me give you some brief guidelines.

- Beware of any simplistic glamorization or glorification of war, whether it is by the cinema, software-makers or the military industry. Even where (and if) war is justified, it is always no more than an appalling necessity.

- Beware of military euphemisms. We need to remember the human cost behind such phrases as ‘mopping up’, ‘taking out’ and ‘the degrading of enemy capabilities’.
- Beware of hate, the language of revenge or retaliation or the lowering of the enemy to the subhuman level (‘rats’, ‘animals’, ‘scum’). Wars kill men and women, mothers and children; all are made in the image of God.
- Beware of military operations expanding beyond a limited focus. When you hear terms such as ‘broadening the campaign’, ‘the inflicting of unavoidable collateral damage’ and ‘punitive air strikes’, things are probably going beyond any sort of justified action.
- There must be serious questions asked about the very large-scale sales of weapons we make as a nation, particularly to poorer countries. For example, with the cost of military jets now starting at around £5 million is it right to sell them to countries that can’t afford to feed or educate their citizens?
- The goal for us as individuals is always clear: to pursue love, peace and righteousness across all barriers of race, language and culture. That – not warfare – is what will bring in God’s kingdom.

Killing in punishment. Largely speaking, capital punishment is not a major issue in Britain, where you have to be over 50 to remember the last hanging. However, after every brutal mass murder or act of terrorism, someone suggests the return of the gallows. In other countries, though, debate continues more actively. As with attitudes to war, there are differences between Christians, as well as considerable agreement. All Christians today would, I imagine, accept that capital punishment, if it is to be employed at all, is to be reserved exclusively for those who murder. There would also be, or should be, agreement that if a death sentence is carried out, it ought to be done with great sorrow and all possible dignity.

Christians who support capital punishment for murder would argue that it is *precisely* the value of human life that justifies the death penalty. Nothing less, they say, will show our high assessment of the victim's life. Those opposed to the death penalty would say that capital punishment is barbaric, that it dehumanizes any society that imposes it and that, as legal systems make mistakes, we should not impose a sentence that is so irreversible. A compromise position is to propose that while the death sentence for murder should be passed (to show society's high view of life), it should always be converted to life imprisonment (to avoid the problems of enacting capital punishment). The debate will, I imagine, continue.

Killing at the beginning and end of life

Abortion. Christianity teaches that life is valuable from the moment of conception and that the child in the womb expresses consciousness, pain and humanness. Since the legalization of abortion in the UK in 1967, well over 4 million pregnancies have been terminated. In 1998, more than 170,000 pregnancies in England and Wales alone ended in abortion. If capital punishment is a remote issue for our society, then, sadly, abortion is not.

At the outset of discussing what is a difficult and emotive topic I want to say two things. The first is that, as a man, I feel very awkward about writing this. The responsibility for an unwanted pregnancy must be shared by a man and a woman alike, yet all too often the cost in guilt and pain is borne only by the woman. Second, I wish to try and be as sensitive as I can. I am well aware that there will be women who read this who have had abortions, often because they were pressured into them. Abortion can cause crippling guilt and regret, and I believe that God doesn't want to increase those feelings but to take them away. If you have had a pregnancy terminated, I would urge you not only to seek God's healing, but also to talk to a wise listener who can work through some of the issues that will probably remain in this area of your life. It would probably be good if this person had professional counselling qualifications, and at the back of this book there are the names of organizations that are able to help anyone in any position of pain. You need to know and experience the living, forgiving God who lives to heal you.

I should also say that I am not someone who believes this issue is settled by making blanket statements and slogans. I do however believe passionately that the current rate of abortion in Britain is horrific and scandalous. The justification for abortion given in nearly 98 per cent of cases is the 'risk of injury to the physical or mental health of the mother or her existing children'. In most cases, this is simply because contraception either failed or was not used and the pregnancy is inconvenient or simply unwanted. Rape, or even alleged rape, is cited in less than 1 per cent of all abortions. Barely 1 per cent of abortions occur because there is a likelihood of foetal handicap and only a tiny fraction of 1 per cent of abortions occur because the mother's life is at risk. In short, most abortions appear to be for convenience or as 'retroactive contraception'. I think it must break God's heart to see how this disposable society will even dispose of its own unborn children. I cannot understand how a mother's 'right to choose' can be exercised without any regard for an unborn child's 'right to life'.

Even in the case of potential abnormality, I have my doubts about abortion. I believe every single human is made in the image of God and that God makes no value judgement on our physical or mental capability. Those who argue that an 'abnormal' child should be aborted seem to suggest that we should only value that which is physically and mentally perfect.

In the face of such figures I believe that we must stand up for the voiceless and question the values of a society that allows such actions on such a scale. Having said that, I believe it is important that we offer care, practical and financial aid, and a welcoming attitude, to those who have chosen not to terminate their pregnancy. We cannot just proclaim our opinion and retreat. If we are serious about protecting the life of the unborn, we must put our money and time where our mouths are.

Some medical students were attending a seminar on abortion where the lecturer presented them with a case study. 'The father of the family has syphilis, and the mother, tuberculosis. They have had four children already. The first is blind, the second died, the third is deaf and dumb and the fourth has tuberculosis. The mother is now pregnant with her fifth child, and is willing to have an abortion if that is what you suggest. What would your advice be?' The students overwhelmingly voted to terminate the pregnancy. 'Congratulations,' the lecturer responded. 'You have just murdered Beethoven.'

Euthanasia. The literal meaning of euthanasia is 'dying well', but the term has come to mean the intentional medical termination of a person's life. It is important to distinguish euthanasia from two other practices. The first is that of allowing a patient suffering from a fatal disease to die in peace without being subjected to painful treatments that cannot ever restore them to health. The second is the use of pain-killing drugs to control severe pain, even at the risk of shortening life. The intention in both practices is to allow patients to end their days in as peaceful, dignified and pain-free a way as possible. Such methods, although not without medical issues, are widely practised and raise no significant moral problems.

In theory, euthanasia sounds harmless. The terminally ill decide voluntarily that 'enough is enough' and, at the time of their choosing, are given such drugs as will cause a speedy and painless death. Supporters of euthanasia are careful to avoid any phrases that might suggest that the doctors 'kill' the patient and, as with abortion, the language of 'choice' and 'rights' and 'freedom' is widely used.

There are, however, many problems with euthanasia, particularly in providing safeguards. Proposed candidates for euthanasia are generally elderly and are almost always those who need a lot of looking after. The pressure to allow or encourage euthanasia, especially in a time of limited medical resources, can become very strong. Not even relatives can be relied on to provide a guarantee that the 'right to die' will not be abused. After all, they are probably going to benefit from the will.

Euthanasia also sets worrying precedents. A psychiatrist who worked with the Nuremberg Tribunal described the process that led in Hitler's Germany to the horrors of Auschwitz, Belsen and Treblinka:

> The beginnings at first were merely a subtle shift in emphasis in the basic attitude of the physicians. It started with the attitude, basic in

> the euthanasia movement, that there is such a thing as a life not worthy to be lived. This attitude in its early stages concerned itself merely with the severely and chronically sick. Gradually the sphere of those to be included in this category was enlarged to encompass the socially unproductive, the ideologically unwanted, the racially unwanted and finally all non-Germans.

Both of these medical issues raise similar questions about what life is. Abortion and euthanasia allow us to become judges of what is a valid life and what isn't. The view that *all* human life is valuable is not popular today, and those who object to it are plain that it is the belief in God that is the problem. We must be grateful to Peter Singer, the controversial Princeton professor, for bluntly expressing this fact: 'Once the religious mumbo-jumbo surrounding the term "human" has been stripped away . . . we will not regard as sacrosanct the life of every member of our species, no matter how limited its capacity for intelligent or even conscious life may be.' In Singer's view (and he is not alone) you have to reach some biological or mental level before you are to be allowed to live. The mentally handicapped, the brain-injured, the unborn and even newborns have no right to life; indeed killing them may, in such views, be morally acceptable. What those standards are, who sets them, and whether you and I – and our children – will always reach them, are alarming and disturbing questions.

The value of all of us

Clearly the command not to murder plays a vital role in providing healthy limits to a society. Yet this commandment isn't just about the negative concept that God is against murder. It is also about affirming a wonderful positive truth. That truth is that we all have value. We are to see each other as being made in the image of God.

Now this truth relates not just to such difficult areas as war and euthanasia, but also to everyday life. It applies not just on the battlefield and in the operating theatre, but also whenever we meet and deal with other people. It also applies every time we look in the mirror. We need to assert, and reassert, that all human beings are special. This is important, because the media give the impression that only the beautiful people we see on television and at the cinema, with their perfect teeth, hair and figures, really count. Let me say again that we are *all* made in the image of God. That applies whether we are world-class athletes or wheelchair-bound paraplegics; whether we are models or scarred burn victims; whether we are academic geniuses or struggling to pass a GCSE.

When we look at any other human being, whether they are a tramp or a superstar, we need to remind ourselves that in them we see reflected something of God. Because he made us in his image, we all have a priceless dignity and value.

I want also to remind you that we can break this commandment by simply doing nothing. There have been disturbing accounts of people being attacked in public while onlookers did nothing, and of people abducted at knifepoint with crowds watching passively. Of course we are aware of the dangers of interfering in this brutal society, but by not intervening we are allowing the wrong to happen. Sometimes it is required of us that we act in defence of others. Such actions are not just required on the streets of our towns; they may be required at an international level. For instance, I do not believe that we as a nation should stand passively by while genocide is committed, whether it be in Europe, Africa or anywhere. I believe that we are in danger of committing sin by doing nothing when we ignore people in rags whom we could clothe or people who are hungry whom we could feed. If the poor freeze to death, won't we be to blame? If the hungry starve, won't we have their blood on our hands?

The roots of murder

What I have dealt with here, however briefly, are the practical issues that arise whenever we discuss murder and killing. The Bible, however, goes further and suggests that breaking the sixth commandment is not as far from each of us as we might like to think. The classic example, the prototype of this, is to be found as early in the Bible as the fourth chapter of Genesis. Here the first story of family life soon becomes the story of the first murder as Cain kills his brother Abel.

Anger and murder: Episode one

I believe that the Bible tells us about Cain and Abel, not to illustrate how bad some people can get, but rather to emphasize that every one of us could end up like Cain. Cain and Abel were the sons of Adam and Eve, a family line that we all belong to. The story starts with the two brothers, who could have been both equal and unique, but who grow up differently. This may reflect a different treatment by their parents. Cain, the first-born and heir, is given a significant name, and becomes a land-owning farmer. With Abel, we are not even told what his name means (in fact, it is rather belittling, meaning 'breath' or 'temporary') and he becomes only a shepherd. The two brothers come to bring their offerings to God. Wealthy Cain brings some of the fruit of the ground, but Abel brings the best portions of his best animals. We are told that God looked with favour on Abel's offering and not on Cain's. What matters, it seems, is not so much the offering, but the attitude of the heart that lay behind the offering. Only Abel's motivation and attitude were acceptable to God. This annoyed Cain and his pride was hurt. The Bible tells us what happened next: 'So Cain was very angry, and his face was downcast. Then the LORD said to Cain, "Why are you so angry? Why is your face downcast? If you do what is right, will you not be accepted? But if you do not do what is right, sin is crouching at your door; it desires to have you, but you must master it"' (Genesis 4:5–7, NIV).

Notice that God here both offered Cain the possibility of change and warned him of the peril that his anger was leading him into. Yet instead of Cain looking to God in repentance, he ignored the caution, took his brother into a field and there killed him. God then asked Cain where his brother was. Cain pretended ignorance and denied any responsibility for his brother. God revealed that he knew of the murder and pronounced judgement on Cain.

Despite its antiquity, there are many ingredients in this story that we recognize. Envy, anger, deceit, lack of responsibility, lies, refusing to heed a warning and, ultimately, murder can be found in many real-life tragedies today.

Anger and murder: Jesus makes the link

When Jesus taught on the sixth commandment he broadened the scope of it:

> You have heard that it was said to the people long ago, 'Do not murder, and anyone who murders will be subject to judgment.' But I tell you that anyone who is angry with his brother will be

> subject to judgment. Again, anyone who says to his brother, 'Raca,' is answerable to the Sanhedrin. But anyone who says, 'You fool!' will be in danger of the fire of hell. (Matthew 5:21– 22, NIV)

Now I am aware that 'Raca' isn't one of the top insults we hear today. It is actually an Aramaic insult, a strong term that literally means 'empty-head' or 'fool', but in a harsh, contemptuous way that implies that the person doesn't actually deserve to be alive. The nearest modern equivalent is probably something along the lines of 'I wish you'd never been born!' or 'Do me a favour and drop dead!'.

What Jesus is teaching us here is that murder is simply the ultimate and most destructive form of anger. It is where anger, if unchecked, will ultimately end up. God wants not only to stop the action of murder, he wants to go further and stop those things in our thought life that act as the seeds of murder. In the previous chapter you will remember that Jesus did exactly the same thing with the seventh commandment. There he pointed out that adultery was not simply the outward physical action; it was also the inward action of the heart in lust. Here he makes it plain that the crime of murder is not simply the shedding of blood. It is about the hatred that leads up to it.

Certainly we see the linkage in the story of Cain, where uncontrolled anger led to a murderous rage. Jesus, focusing on the seriousness of anger, should make us think. There is no shortage of rage in today's society. One of the new words to be recently added to the Oxford Dictionary is 'road rage'. I doubt if any of us haven't been a victim of abusive or aggressive driving from others, and some of us have at times, I'm sure, returned the compliment!

There is a lot of anger about today, not just on roads but also in offices, shops and, worst of all, homes. While domestic violence isn't a modern phenomenon, what does seem new today are the levels of violence against women and children. I am going to deal more with the whole issue of anger and how we handle conflict later. However, before I start, I want to mark out domestic violence as something so big and serious that it can't just be treated glibly under phrases like 'come to terms with anger'. If you are in a situation where you have been subjected to domestic violence, or if you fear it, then I can only advise you to try to calm things down and then try to get out of the situation as soon as possible. Take whatever steps you need to take for your own safety, and seek professional help from either the organizations listed at the end of this book or from the local social services. If you yourself are the abuser in this situation, then I urge you as strongly as possible to get professional help before you do more damage. Abusive violence is never an appropriate way to show anger, and the home is the last place it should occur.

How to handle anger

I now want to spend some time talking about how we can handle anger.

Right anger

At the start, I need to say that not all anger is wrong. Anger is an emotion that often shows we care. Imagine if we didn't get angry about things; it would betray a 'couldn't care less' attitude, a sort of moral apathy. Saint Augustine said, 'Hope has two beautiful daughters: anger and courage.' Anger at the way the present situation is, and courage to believe it doesn't have to stay that way. Given some of the injustices in the world today, *not* to feel anger would be sinful.

Interestingly, the word 'anger' appears 455 times in the Bible and in 375 cases it refers to God. God gets angry. Let's face it, if he didn't get angry, what kind of God would he be? God becomes angry at injustice, hypocrisy and lies, and at people who inflict pain on each other. Jesus himself became furious in the temple at the way the changers of money and sellers of sacrifices had got in the way of people meeting with God.

However, there is God's righteous anger and then there is our anger. Sadly, there are differences. God is perfect and all-knowing and is always justified, both in the reason why he is angry and the way he expresses it. With us, things are both worse and more complex.

Types of human anger

When it comes to dealing with anger, at least four types of reaction can be identified. The following types can be characterized:

- The ***maniac***. The maniac is a pressure cooker just waiting to explode. These people have a short fuse and can blow up at any time and in any place. Their anger spills out and is obvious. When they are angry, you – and everybody else around – know about it. These people can get angry at the slightest thing. If this is you, remember your temper is the one thing you don't get rid of by losing it!
- The ***mute***. Mutes don't blow up, they clam up. They are people who cannot, or will not, show their anger in public

or in a relationship. Instead, they just bottle it up. The problem is, when we don't express our anger, our bodies keep the score. Anger eats us up, sometimes literally, and it does us no good. Many of those who mute their anger end up with ulcers, depression and other symptoms as a direct result of their bottled-up anger. Sometimes people think that this kind of attitude is Christian, but personally I cannot see how. It is more like the Roman Stoics who tried never to show any emotion. Be assured that if you try and bottle up anger it will still find other ways to come out.

- The ***martyr***. Martyrs never get angry because everything is always their fault. They act like guilt magnets, always blaming themselves for what has happened. These are the people who throw a pity party and invite only themselves.
- The ***manipulator***. Manipulators are those who express their anger by getting even. The situation that has annoyed them may never be mentioned again, but they make sure by their actions that they inflict revenge on the person who angered them. Some people can do this by always being late, or deliberately forgetting things.

Now if you are anything like me, you have probably seen yourself in all four of those categories. Apart from the manipulator, there are healthy things about the other three responses to anger. The positive side of the maniac is that at least they let their anger out, and you know where you are with them. The negative side is that as you really don't want to be around them when they blow up, it can be quite tense either living or working with them. The positive side of the mute is the high level of self-control. Negatively, they ignore the fact that God wants us to be honest and genuine about our feelings of anger.

If problems are not brought into the open, it is hard to see how they can be sorted out. Martyrs don't ever consider themselves to be in the right and therefore have a humble attitude, but to always consider yourself at fault doesn't seem to be honest. It may even result in agreeing to something that is wrong. Allowing yourself to always be treated like a doormat is neither wise nor honest. Even though Jesus allowed himself to be sent to the cross, the accounts of his trial show that he challenged those who tried him.

The ancient philosopher Aristotle said, 'Anyone can be angry – that is easy. But to be angry with the right person, to the right degree, at the right time, for the right purpose and in the right way – that is not easy.' Let's face it, most of us do not do very well in managing our anger.

Count to ten first!

So how should we handle our anger? The book of Proverbs isolates at least three causes of anger: injustice, humiliation and frustration. We can see here some of the things that led Cain to be angry. Causes, of course, are not excuses and do not justify anger. With Cain's anger, it seems that he felt grieved because he had expected that his offering would be accepted. It was certainly the case that he wasn't humble enough to learn a lesson and admit he had been wrong. Whenever we get angry, it is good advice to try and analyse the reasons for our anger and to be honest about them. Unfortunately, being angry is quite the wrong frame of mind in which to try and analyse anything! Attitude is the mind's paintbrush – it can colour any situation.

President Lincoln's secretary of war, Edwin Stanton, had some trouble with a major general, who accused him, in very abusive terms, of favouritism. Stanton complained to the president, who suggested that he write the officer a sharp letter. Stanton did so and showed the strongly worded note to the president who applauded its powerful language. 'What are you going to do with it now?' he asked. Surprised at the question, Stanton said, 'Send it off, of course.' Lincoln shook his head. 'You don't want to send that letter. Put it on the fire. That's what I do when I have written a letter while I am angry. It is a good letter and you had a good time writing it and feel better. Now burn it and write another one.'

Speak when you are angry and you will make the best speech you will ever regret. As we saw with lying, the Bible warns us of the danger of the tongue: 'Everyone should be quick to listen, slow to speak and slow to become angry' (James 1:19, NIV). Words have power. Can there be any more untrue playground rhyme than 'Sticks and stones may break my bones but words will never harm me'? Many of us can still remember unkind words that were said to us in anger and we may still bear the wounds of them. To understand our anger, we need to take time, and that will mean, in certain situations at least, keeping a hold of our tongue until we are sure we know what we should say, rather than what we want to say.

But taking time to understand our anger, and being careful of how we express it, doesn't mean not expressing it at all. Marriage counsellors have said that it is often not the relationships where there are cross and angry words spoken that are in trouble, but the ones where there are never any cross words said. One of the healthiest statements in a relationship is 'I'm angry at you'.

Have self-respect and *humility*

We saw that one of the things that made Cain's anger burn, was that he couldn't handle the fact that his younger brother was preferred over him. His previously superior position as the first-born was overturned and he could not cope with the reversal. His self-worth seems to have been based simply on his status.

A proper self-respect is the key to managing our anger properly. Self-respect means that we are secure enough in ourselves to know when we are in the wrong and humble enough to admit it. The problem with some people is that they think so little of themselves that they think they are always in the wrong. The problem with others is that they are so proud that they get angry because they think they are always right. We need a correct view of ourselves. On the one hand, because God made us in his image and loves us, we are of very great worth. On the other, as weak, fallible and sinful human beings, our assessment of ourselves may be flawed. We need to have both humility and self-respect.

Deal with the anger you feel

The Bible teaches that when we feel there is a problem between us and another person we should go to them and sort it out. In Matthew 5:23–24 Jesus taught that it was such a priority to deal with disagreements that if someone was worshipping and there was something between them and someone else, they should go and sort it out immediately. The Bible also says that we shouldn't go to sleep angry, but should sort it out first. There is a great value in this because if we go to bed angry we will lie down with the anger unresolved and it will start eating into us. We may have to stay up pretty late to deal with it, but the right thing to do is to sort out our anger in order to clear the air.

This, of course, doesn't give us the excuse to vent our spleen on anyone who crosses our path. Neither does it give us the right to give people a good talking to, just because they have made us unhappy. There are always two sides to each issue. We need to do everything in humility, love and respect, and we need to be prepared to listen to the other person's point of view. Often situations that could escalate into big rows can be prevented by our attitude. It is always very helpful to listen and try to refrain from making value judgements about someone else's actions or words.

Forgive – don't bear grudges

'Do not take revenge but leave room for God's wrath. For it is written, "Revenge is mine to avenge, says the Lord; I will repay"' (Romans 12:19). In all our disputes, the Bible works on the principle that God is a just judge and he is in charge of handing out punishment in due time. Our job is to forgive, and not to be eaten up by our desire for revenge. It takes more inner strength to forgive than it does to inflict revenge. There are times when the most disarming thing to do in a situation of conflict is to offer appropriate apologies and forgiveness.

Forgiving others doesn't just happen because we feel like it. It happens because we make a decision of our will. Clara Barton, the founder of the American Red Cross, never bore grudges. She was reminded by a friend of a wrong done to her some years earlier. 'Don't you remember?' asked her friend. 'No,' replied Clara firmly. 'I distinctly remember forgetting that.'

Anger grows and festers in an atmosphere of unforgiveness

and revenge. But where there is forgiveness and the decision to move on, anger can be constructive and actually good for a relationship or situation. This is how God deals with us. In the Psalms we read:

> The LORD is merciful and gracious;
> he is slow to get angry and full of unfailing love.
> He will not constantly accuse us,
> nor remain angry for ever.
> He has not punished us for all our sins,
> nor does he deal with us as we deserve.
>
> (Psalm 103:8–10, NLT)

At the start of this chapter we talked about the dignity that each one of us has because we are made in the image of God. It is in how we deal with other people that we can most reveal the fact that we bear his likeness. Are we like God in the way we deal with others? In the Bible Paul encourages Christians to show the fruit of God's presence in their lives: love, joy, peace, patience, kindness, goodness, faithfulness, gentleness and self-control (Galatians 5:22–23).

When you squeeze a tube of toothpaste, what comes out is what's in there. So it is with us. When we are squeezed, what comes out is what's inside. If we are full of God, there will be evidence of that when we are squeezed. As with the other commands we have looked at, what we need to be able to live God's way isn't a self-help manual, but to be changed from inside out. Jesus does that by transforming us. We all need this transformation because, on Jesus' own interpretation, we have all broken the sixth commandment by our angry words and attitudes.

Find the way of love

Finally, the good news is that it is exactly with people like us that God works. Think about some of the main figures of the Bible: Moses, David, Paul. What do they all have in common? Yes, they were all followers of God, they are all credited with writing large sections of the Bible, but, astonishingly enough, they were all people who had committed murder. Yet we do not remember them for this. We remember them for what God did in and through them. And if he can do it in them, he can do it in us.

A little under 2,000 years ago God gave his Son to be murdered, so that we could be given life. That death allows us to be transformed from those who hate and whose desire is to take life, to those who are loving peacemakers and who want to give life. We are to be witnesses to a different way of living.

Never in the last 2,000 years has that witness been more needed.

COMMANDMENT 5

Honour your father and your mother, so that you may live long in the land the LORD your God is giving you.
(Exodus 20:12, NIV)

So what's the problem?

The endangered state of the traditional family was brought home to me recently, not by some new statistic, but by the ending of a series of television advertisements for – of all things – gravy. For 18 years, Britain had followed the Oxo family through various meal-centred stages of their life together. Finally, as the new century dawned, Oxo announced that the advert series had run its course, because the image of Mum and Dad and three children sitting round a dining table 'no longer reflected the average family'. There was the need, we were told, to move with the times and portray home life in a far more varied way.

Certainly modern family life is very different from what it was 50 years ago. Then you knew who everybody in the family was and exactly how they related to each other. The family was a tightly defined unit. It was also stable; its fixed order was only modified by births, deaths and marriages, events so major as to be marked by official ceremonies and certificates. Nowadays, a family is an altogether vaguer, more fluid structure. Partners change with the seasons, people come and go, there are fewer certificates and ceremonies, and without DNA testing it's very difficult working out who is the father of the baby. Today's family has a very different look and feel to its predecessor.

Now it is easy to be nostalgic about the 'good old days' of the nuclear family with Mum, Dad and 2.4 children. But I believe that to call for such days to be brought back is a temptation we have to resist. For one thing, we can't go back. The family then was part of a whole society that has vanished. Another reason for being negative about such 'forward to the past' solutions is simply that we are called to live in the present, not the past. Besides, memory can easily be over-romantic and selective, and behind the golden glow, painted by nostalgia, there were problems. In fact there are some current social patterns that have much to commend them: parents taking joint responsibility in the raising of children, the possibility of victims being able to get out of abusive family situations and the empowerment and dignity that have been given to women. It is interesting that the most intense nostalgia for the good old days seems to come from men.

But if we don't want to return to the past, neither can we be complacent about the pain and brokenness that accompany so many people's family life experiences today. Consider these figures: by the time children reach the age of 16, around one in four of them will have experienced the divorce of their parents; last year 150,000 divorces were granted; four out of ten children are now born outside marriage; and people living on their own now represent more than a quarter of all households, whereas 20 years ago the figure was 18 per cent. These figures, of course, represent only the families that have failed enough to count as statistics; they do not show the far greater number of families that are under strain. Another sign of the problems is that we have absorbed a whole new vocabulary; of 'maintenance agreements', 'access arrangements', 'current partners' and 'pre-nuptial agreements'. And behind all these statistics and words lie real people and real lives. In fact the truth is that we don't need figures to prove any of this to us – the statistics only confirm what we have seen happen to friends, neighbours, relations and even ourselves.

Why are families failing? In detail the answers are complex but, put simply, families are breaking up under pressure. Today's pressures on the family have probably never been greater and come from many areas.

In the area of *work*, we see that changing labour patterns have wreaked havoc among family life. The days when it was the full-time (if unwaged and unpraised) job of the mother to mind the family have largely gone. In the absence of a full-time family minder, things tend to be done by the frequently unsatisfactory methods of consensus ('I thought we'd all agreed . . .') or delegation ('But it was *your* turn to do it. . .'). Equally, having more than a sole breadwinner means negotiating complex timetables just so that, occasionally, we all manage to eat together. The fact that few jobs now are for life has also combined to put strain on families. Do you move for Mum's job or for Dad's?

In the area of *lifestyle*, there are new pressures. Families might live under the same roof, but it can sometimes seem that that's about all they have in common. Whether because of different timetables, microwave meals, or the tyranny of TV, the average household only sits down to eat together around a table once every week. Technology has contributed here. We no longer even have to watch the same programmes on the television; we can always watch it on the video later. In fact we are told that the average teenager watches 28 hours of TV a week, much of it in the privacy of their own room. Video and computers, personal stereos and now the Internet, all encourage us to spend time on our own rather than together. Houses are smaller today and everybody has more things, so there is no room for grandparents to live in anyway.

With respect to *personal development*, there have been major changes. Children mature faster and face life-determining decisions at an ever earlier age. There are many pressures on them to be adults sooner. Most teenagers have to deal with sexual issues that only adults faced in previous generations. Cynically, children are now targeted as consumers and customers by fashion firms, music companies and even banks. Some social commentators talk about the 'erosion of childhood as we know it'.

Perhaps, most worryingly, is the fact that failure in families is an infectious social disease. Let me explain. No one is born a naturally good parent. Parenting skills have to be learned. A child growing up in a failing family is likely to pick up bad habits rather than good ones. So, sadly, the chances of their own marriages failing in turn are heightened. Unless there is a dramatic change, one dysfunctional family is likely to breed others.

How can the family be saved? With the pressures on the family being so great, no amount of governmental intervention, however worthy, with 'Initiatives for the Family', is likely to do much good. Something more drastic is needed.

It is against this background that we come to the fifth commandment – to 'honour your father and your mother'. What, we ask, does it mean for us to 'honour' our parents in families that are so fragmented? What can this commandment, based on a culture so different from ours, have to say to us in a world where the dysfunctional family seems to be normal?

The first thing to say is that it is easy to overestimate the differences in this area between twenty-first-century AD Britain and the fifteenth-century BC Near East. Moses' day was hardly the golden age of the family either. In those days families didn't consist of Mum, Dad and 2.4 kids but were huge, extended and intermingled groups of everybody related by blood or marriage: uncles, aunts, grandparents and hordes of children. There were also problems. Frequent wars, famines or epidemics gave rise to many vulnerable widows and orphans, a fact widely recognized in the Old Testament. And where some men practised polygamy and had several wives or concubines (essentially wives with fewer legal rights) there was the obvious potential for conflict. The Bible, in its honest and unflattering way, gives us tales of families that are as spectacularly dysfunctional as any we see on our television screens. Actually, the fact that they lived in such close proximity to each other (if not under the same roof, at least in the next tent along) must have encouraged friction. These people knew about complex and difficult families. They were just complex and difficult in a different way to ours.

The second thing to say is that in these extended families it was the links between parents and children that held everything together. It was the way in which parents brought up, disciplined and taught their children and the way the adults looked after their own aging parents that tied these extended families together. In Hebrew society then, as in many similar cultures today, the key links were always up and down across the generations. That is why the Bible so often has genealogies listing how 'X was the son of Y'. Your bonds with your own parents, and with your children, were the cement that held families – and indeed the whole structure of society – together. The rebellious child, particularly the son, who failed to look after his parents was an outrage. In explaining why the disaster of the exile had come upon the people of Israel, the prophet Ezekiel says that, among other abuses, 'Father and mothers are contemptuously ignored' (Ezekiel 22:7, NLT).

Before moving on, though, I need to spell out what it means to 'honour' parents. Basically, it means giving them value and respect. It means esteeming them of worth, even if we disagree with them. It rules out entirely any attitude where we reject our parents as worthless. It does not mean automatically obeying them. If it did, we would have the awkward case of Jesus, who as we will see went against his mother's wishes, breaking a commandment. But I want us to avoid seeing this commandment as being exclusively to do with the relations of parents and children. It *is* to do with that, but it is to do with much more. Ultimately, the fifth commandment addresses the whole concept of the family.

The heart of the matter

The family is a gift of God

The good news is that the Bible is positive about families. The family was God's idea. If we return, as we have done before, to the earliest chapters of the Christian and Jewish Scriptures, we are struck by the fact that the family is an integral part of being human. We are meant to relate to others. God has made us and shaped us for relationships – with each other and with him. Families are the God-designed structures where we can grow and learn to understand ourselves and to relate to others. It is plain that God intended children to be raised by their natural parents and for a monogamous, lifelong male–female relationship to provide the intimate, secure and supportive environment for a child's nurture until maturity. When, in adulthood, the child leaves his or her father and mother to start, by marriage, a new family unit, the old family links are not severed but are transformed. The new family acquires a distinct individuality of its own, but the parents are not neglected.

God affirms families. There are biblical standards for family living; norms for parental care and nurturing of children, for unconditional love, respect and honouring of parents by offspring and a commitment to the welfare of the whole family. We may find these standards hard to keep – we may fall short of them – but they exist.

The family is always under threat

If the Bible is positive about families and sets forward the family as God's ideal, it is under no illusions that making a good family is easy. That is the bad news. The fact that there are so many rules and guidelines about families in the Bible suggests that there were always problems to be addressed. Proof that making a family work is hard, comes from the pages of the Bible. There we see, in many of the families it records, examples of failures in this area. Some of these failures happen with even the best of men and women. For example, neither Jacob, David nor Solomon can be held up as a model of a good father. In fact, as we saw in our discussion of murder, in the first family history recorded for us (that of Adam and Eve), relations broke down to the extent that one of their children killed another.

For me, the honest portrayal of these calamitous families in the Bible demonstrates the truth of a simple but wise saying that states, 'The abuse of the best is the worst.' God intended families to be something powerful for good; to be places of belonging and trust, of learning and loving. Yet when they go wrong, their very power can make them sites of long-lasting bitterness and hurt.

But that isn't God's fault; it's ours.

God wants to help the family

Faced with these threats to the family, the encouraging news is that God does more than simply lay down a commandment and then frown at us when we mess up. Time and time again we are told in the Bible that God isn't distant and remote and that he is not some unfeeling ogre. He cherishes us and grieves over us. We are told that he knows the number of hairs on our heads – a task that with some of us gets easier every day!

One thing God does is set us an example of how to behave in a family. He does this first of all by being the model father who cares for and nurtures us. God endorses parenting by being happy to be considered a parent himself. This idea is there in the Old Testament and it is there, most of all, in the language of Jesus. Jesus talked of God as his Father and encouraged his disciples to use similar language. In fact the word he used, 'Abba', is respectfully intimate, and corresponds to our word 'Dad'.

Now I am aware that to introduce the idea that God is a father is problematic for some people. Some object to the concept of 'Father God' as 'sexist language' reflecting an offensive patriarchal culture. I can only briefly touch on some of the issues here. There are, for a start, problems with describing God as male, female or neuter. Second, there is also a gentle but progressive thrust throughout biblical history that is subversive of the patriarchal culture and seems to quietly undermine it. Interestingly enough, we see it in this commandment, which encourages the honouring of not just the father, but both mother and father. The high point of this trend is seen most plainly in the ministry of Jesus, who risked scandal for treating women as intellectual equals. He also – again risking scandal – used the image of himself (and by extension God) as a mother hen (Luke 13:34).

Others have problems with the idea of a Father God because they have had difficult relations with their own fathers. The idea that God is like such a father, only larger and in heaven, is enough to send them running. After all, why on earth would we want, trust or feel safe with a God like *that*? I can sympathize. It is, however, worth getting to the root of what the Bible (and Jesus) is really saying by using 'father' language of God. He is *not* saying, 'You know your dad? Well, God's like that.' What he *is* saying is that God is everything a father should be. He is the perfect Father, the true ideal. God is like no father anyone has ever known. He is perfectly good, faithful, true and trustworthy. He is the heavenly Father who can always be relied upon. He is the ultimate parent, like the closest, most caring guardian or the most gentle mother, and he particularly cares for those who are broken by their upbringing. He is a 'father to the fatherless' (Psalm 68:5). If you find that the image of a good father is hard for you to hold on to because of your own experience, let me offer a rather banal illustration that may help. Imagine, say, that the first time you are given a 50 pound note, it turns out to be counterfeit. 'Never again!' you promise and refuse to accept them ever after. Of course, that would be foolish because genuine 50 pound notes do exist. The same goes for fathers. If you have been hurt by a 'counterfeit' earthly father, don't let that put you off a relationship with the real, heavenly one.

I have spent some time on this idea of God as the loving and perfect Father because it helps us to understand how we are to behave in a family context. We are to model our heavenly Father. The way he loves us is the way we should love each other, both within our families and outside them.

God does more than provide an example. He provides the power for healing in families through the Holy Spirit, whom he gives to all who have come to him through Jesus. This is extraordinarily helpful. For instance, you may feel that the idea of God as our role model for family relationships is impossible and that all I am doing is setting you up for a guilt trip. Yet the wonderful truth is that not only does God command us to be like him, through the power of the Holy Spirit he also enables us to be more like him. Over and over again this comes out in the New Testament. For instance, some of the deepest teaching on families is to be found in Ephesians 5:21–6:4, where Paul talks about the duties and responsibilities of wives and husbands, children and parents. But he prefaces his remarks by commanding the Ephesian Christians to let the Holy Spirit fill and control them (Ephesians 5:18). The Holy Spirit is God's power for the healing of our lives with others. Only with his power can we hope to live out God's pattern for families.

Creating families that work

Let me now make some practical suggestions as to how we can work at making better relationships within families. I want to talk about some general principles for families, based on a biblical example, then I want to apply these to how we relate to our parents and how we relate to our children. Finally, I want to end on a note of encouragement.

Learning from failure: a biblical case study

There are good and bad ways of being family, and some patterns of living bring greater blessing than others. The best thing we can do to be part of healthy families is get into healthy patterns of behaviour; not just to deal with the fall-out, but to stop the hurtful behaviour at the root. To illustrate some principles on which to build family life we're going to do a case study – learning from a family that lived over 3,000 years ago.

At the end of the book of Genesis is the story of Joseph, the one of Technicolor Dream Coat fame. This saga is a classic example of how families can get into bad patterns. Joseph was the son of Jacob, a man with a complex family. In the Bible the unhappy situation with Jacob's children is rapidly and skilfully painted.

> When Joseph was seventeen years old, he often tended his father's flocks with his half brothers, the sons of his father's wives Bilhah and Zilpah. But Joseph reported to his father some of the bad things his brothers were doing. Now Jacob loved Joseph more than any of his other children because Joseph had been born to him in his old age. So one day he gave Joseph a special gift – a beautiful robe. But his brothers hated Joseph because of their father's partiality. They couldn't say a kind word to him. (Genesis 37:2–4, NLT)

Incidentally, the one thing everyone knows about Joseph – that he had a multicoloured coat – may be incorrect. We really don't know the exact meaning of the word that the older versions translated as 'multicoloured'; it may be 'long-sleeved', but then that wouldn't make such a good title for a musical. What we do know is that it was an ostentatious and rather posh coat that clearly indicated to everyone that (a) Joseph was special and (b) he wasn't going to do any hard work. Joseph was given this coat, we are told, because 'Jacob loved Joseph more than any of his other children'.

As a result of his father's favouritism, Joseph was hated and despised by his brothers. This is so frequently true in family life that it is hardly surprising. Often when one child is preferred over another it causes great consternation, jealousy and huge feelings of inferiority and of being overlooked. The fact that Jacob had twelve sons by four different mothers (some wives, some concubines) would hardly have produced a stable and secure family setting and must have, instead, bred insecurity and competitiveness.

This family background clearly had an effect on Joseph, who comes over, at least at this point in his life, as an arrogant and unpleasant young man. Whether his telling tales on his brothers was a result of his brothers' hatred or a contributory factor to it, we do not know. Either is psychologically credible. However, matters got much worse when Joseph had some dreams, whose obvious interpretation was that his brothers and his father would one day bow down to him. Of course, Joseph revealed these to his brothers, doubtless as a way of scoring points.

Irritated beyond their limits, the brothers decided that enough was enough and planned to murder Joseph and blame it on an attack by a wild animal. However, Reuben, the eldest of the twelve brothers, intervened and persuaded them not to kill him. Finally, a compromise was agreed and Joseph was merely thrown into a pit. Reuben left, intending to come back later, recover his brother and take him home. But when he returned it was too late; Joseph had been sold into slavery.

I find it interesting that Reuben, despite being the eldest brother, lacked the authority to simply stop the whole business. In fact, as we have learned in an earlier chapter, Reuben had slept with one of his father's wives. This act of immorality (and flagrant breach of the parent–child relationship that the fifth commandment was later to address) probably undermined any authority he had. There is no evidence that his father had disciplined him over the matter and it requires no great stretch of the imagination to see that the children probably despised Jacob as a father. Certainly their intention to lie to their father suggests that they held him in low esteem.

Now although it would be fascinating to trace further the story of Joseph and see how, after many twists, God worked it all out for good, we cannot do it here. Yet even in this brief introduction we see a classic dysfunctional family, with its fractures developing between parents and children and between the children themselves. I think we can draw a number of general lessons from this situation about principles for family life.

Lesson 1: Learn to learn

'Learn to learn' may sound strange advice, but it is crucial. In some ways, the most important thing we ever do is be part of a family. Yet most of us drift through, muddling along, and only really consider how we are doing when we hit a family crisis. I want to challenge you to think about how you are working in a family situation and to seek to learn how to do it better.

Jacob was a man who needed to learn. He himself had been at the rough end of some poor parenting (Genesis 26:28) involving favouritism, sibling rivalry and a split between his parents. Yet he seems to have learned nothing from it. As we have seen, the really bad news about bad parenting is that it gets passed on down to the next generation. Indeed, I wonder if the Bible is giving us a nudge that way when we read at the start of the Joseph story the strange words, 'This is the story of Jacob' (Genesis 37:2, NIV). Hold on, we say. Jacob is hardly the main figure in the story. Surely it ought to be 'This is the story of *Joseph*'? But as we watch what happens in the story, we see that the events are an almost inevitable outworking of Jacob's bad family management.

Jacob's parenting was bad and he seems to have simply, dully and automatically passed on his bad habits to his children. This pattern has been repeated ever since. For example, it is said that king George V was a remote and distant man, always abrupt and cold with his children. Once, when a member of the royal court mildly suggested to the king that he might be a little more relaxed with them, he chillingly replied, 'My father was frightened of his father, I was frightened of my father, and I'm damned well going to see to it that my children are frightened of me.' This expresses with painful clarity the way that failure in families can, if unchecked, echo on for generations. Yet it doesn't have to be that way. Can I urge you, particularly if you are from a family that did not function well, to 'learn to learn'? Try and get a chance to observe families that work, and model your behaviour on them, not on your own past. Over everything you do, say to yourself, 'Is this good?' or, 'Can I do it better?' Don't let the past ruin the future.

Lesson 2: Learn to be fair

Clearly, a major problem in the family of Jacob was his clumsy and blatant favouritism towards Joseph. While we may not flag it quite so openly as he did, a thousand generations later favouritism is alive and well in twenty-first-century Britain.

We need to avoid favouritism and being unfair in our treatment of others in the family. Now of course we cannot make everyone the same, nor should we try. Some members of our family are more like us and we relate to them more easily. An introverted, musical mother will probably have closer relations with a shy, artistic daughter than with her extrovert rugby-playing son. That is not favouritism. Favouritism is when she treats the daughter with more affection than she does the son and gives her preferential treatment. The problem of favouritism is that it hurts the child who is not favoured and fuels the fires of sibling rivalry.

It is easy to slip into being unfair. When, say, a son gets mediocre results compared to his brilliant sister, it is tempting to make hurtful comparisons. We need to learn to stand back, take a deep breath, put aside our natural emotions and learn to be absolutely and completely fair.

Incidentally, favouritism is not confined to parents with children. It is also possible for children to takes sides with one parent against another. The same principles hold true: we must be absolutely fair there too.

Lesson 3: Learn to communicate

Another problem in Jacob's family seems to be that they did not communicate with each other. When I read the story, I get the feeling that here are people from the same family who do not know each other. I have no doubt that they *talked* to each other – we know that – but whether they *communicated* is another matter. There seems little evidence that the brothers ever really talked things through, either with Joseph or their father. Their hatred seems to have simmered quietly until it exploded in nearly lethal anger.

The problem has not gone away. A lot of talking in families today is simply making words, not making communication. We have all been part of a dialogue like this. A 16-year-old daughter went into the front room and asked the assembled family members, 'Has anyone seen my new jumper?'

Her dad replied, 'You mean the one that cost £50?'

Her gran replied, 'You mean the one with the low neckline?'

Her mother replied, 'You mean the one that has to be washed by hand in cold water?'

Her brother replied, 'The stupid one that makes you look fat?'

Her sister replied, 'You mean the one that you won't let me borrow?'

Everyone was talking about the same jumper, but no one answered her question. There were many words said, but no communication took place.

Let me say that good communication has to have both quantity and quality. First, good communication requires quantities of time. We all too often hear ourselves saying that we haven't got time. The most shocking statistic I heard last year was that on average a father spends 38 seconds a day talking face to face with his children. Our work and lifestyles demand more and more time, and the result is that we are made frantic keeping all the plates spinning in the air. At least two sad things happen as a result. One is that the gap develops and gets bigger until the gap has become a chasm. Shared times become increasingly marked by stilted conversation, criticism or silence. Another thing is that it sends out the message to a child that he or she is less important than work, conferences or even anyone else who might ask for Mummy or Daddy's time. I heard recently of a wife who, when driving her husband to work, was horrified to hear her four-year-old son say to their visitor, 'And this is where Daddy lives.' Many young people do feel very let down by their parents simply not having the time for them. We need to make time to communicate.

Second, good communication requires quality talk. It is not enough to set aside time to talk. We need to use it wisely. Ironically, it is often good to use time to talk about life, music, films, sport. That allows us to develop natural links. It is a dreadful state of affairs that whenever a child hears a parent say, 'I want to talk with you,' they know that it is about something serious, something they have done wrong. Equally, though, we need to be able to be honest and express irritation, hurts and even anger.

Where there is intense love, there is also the possibility of intense anger. If we keep brushing things under the carpet, we will only trip over them later. The family ought to be the best forum to discuss problems, because it should be the place of security and acceptance, where people can be honest about their feelings, their expectations and their hurts, and face them head on. How this works out in practice is something every family must work out for themselves, but I cannot stress how healthy it is to talk things through. Even if things may get quite heated at times, it saves them growing and mushrooming into bitterness and resentment.

I want to make a particular plea here for fathers to become

involved more in talking to their children, especially their sons. A recent national report on young men talked about the 'Dad deficit', where some fathers had little or no involvement with their sons. We need to beware of this. Bringing up boys cannot be 'left to Mum'. If fathers take an interest in their sons, it helps to encourage self-confidence. Susan Faludi, a social commentator who spent six years working on a book about masculinity published at the start of the twenty-first century, said, 'From the start, I intended to talk to the young men about such matters as work, sport, marriage, religion, war and entertainment, but what they really wanted to talk about was their fathers . . . "My father never taught me how to be a man" was the single line I heard again and again.'

We need to learn to communicate with each other now, or we will shout at each other later.

Lesson 4: Learn to forgive

Perhaps the most basic attitude we need is to be givers (and receivers) of grace, kindness and forgiveness. If we are not, then not only will we carry hurts and wounds around with us, but we will pass them on to others.

Even in the best families, we will often need large doses of forgiveness. With several people making up a family there are inevitably going to be different temperaments and personality characteristics. These give the potential for tensions and deep divisions, and sooner or later result in disagreements and clashes. The problem with dealing with disagreements within families is that unlike, say, work, the people concerned are not simply going to go away. While you can choose your friends and, to a lesser extent, your enemies, you have to live with your family.

The key ingredient to resolving disagreements and clashes within a family is our willingness to forgive and to be forgiven. Now of course forgiveness is never easy and this is especially so when the other party is not sorry. Nevertheless, I believe that – for our own good if nothing else – we must sometimes forgive unconditionally. Only that way can we release the pain we feel in being let down and hurt by members of our family, and move on. One very respected doctor wrote in *Making Peace With Your Parents*: 'The psychological truth is that holding on to our past resentments towards parents robs us of our current peace of mind and our ability to experience satisfaction in the here-and-now relationships.'

Now I know that asking anyone to forgive unconditionally is difficult. If you have been significantly hurt by your family, it can often be of great benefit to receive professional help. If you do feel that you carry huge burdens and resentment because of some family problem, I urge you not to hide or ignore these burdens, but to begin to deal with them.

To help you here I want to attack two commonly heard statements that I believe are very harmful. The first is '*To forgive is to forget*'. I think that this is rather patronizing and belittles the horrendous experiences that some children and spouses have undergone. Many people hold back from forgiving because they incorrectly assume that if they forgive they will have to minimize (or even forget) painful things that happened to them. I can forgive my parents without minimizing the pain they caused me. Forgiveness allows us to build something positive in the present while still making sure that we don't repeat what happened in the past. While forgetting is not automatically linked with forgiving, the act of forgiveness means a start to healing, and from that forgetting *may* come in time.

The second cliché is *'Time is a great healer'*. It may be, but without forgiveness it is all too possible that the hurt is simply driven underground into the subconscious where it festers away. Frankly, it is important to deal with a grievance as soon as we can. Again, God helps us here. He is a God who is forgiving and gracious, and he knows all about unconditional forgiveness and what it can cost. What do you think the cross was all about?

I believe that God wants us to be enabled to forgive those who have hurt us and that he promises to give us all we need in order to do it. Even with the power of the Holy Spirit working in your life, I cannot, in all honesty, guarantee you a quick fix or tear-less solution. But I am certain that God has all the resources you need to enable you, if you are truly willing, to forgive the one who has hurt you and to leave that resentment behind.

Relating to our parents: giving honour

We've looked at qualities we are encouraged to have in our families, things that provide an environment for our children to be able to obey this command, but what does it mean to really honour our fathers and mothers?

Accept them

The first thing we need to do is to accept our parents. The Bible gives us some helpful advice about what that means in practice: 'Listen to your father, who gave you life, and do not despise your mother when she is old' (Proverbs 23:22, NIV). We are to respect our parents and not despise them.

Now, God isn't asking us to pretend that they are perfect

when they are not, or that they are always right. We are instructed to honour our parents despite their faults and failings. In court, for example, we address the judge as 'Your Honour'. That has nothing to do with our attitude to his or her personality; it simply shows our respect of a judge's position and authority. Likewise, 'honouring' is simply an act of duty that applies to our parents.

For good or ill, we must remind ourselves that they are *our* parents. Nothing we do can change that fact. We must learn to accept them.

Appreciate them

Even if we find our parents difficult, we can appreciate them for their effort in bringing us up. Parenting is a very difficult, time-consuming and demanding job. I've said before that any mother could perform the jobs of several air-traffic controllers with ease! It is easy to criticize parents, but interestingly enough the criticisms tend to wane when the children become responsible for parenting themselves. In fact we have probably learned far more than we think from our parents. Many of the skills, abilities, attitudes and interests that we pride ourselves on are in fact things that have been passed on to us by our parents.

One of the greatest things our parents pass on to us is their wisdom – a fact repeatedly recognized by the Bible: 'My son, obey your father's commands and don't neglect your mother's teaching' (Proverbs 6:20, NLT). Often children think they know best and there is nothing their parents could possibly say to them about the situations they find themselves in. Actually, one real way in which parents can be honoured is by their children asking, listening, and even heeding their advice and wisdom.

It does not hurt to find practical ways to express our appreciation. A card on Mother's Day, a regular phone call, a diversion off some trip to pass by and see Mum and Dad are all ways of appreciating them. Simple appreciation and gratitude can make all the difference in family relationships.

Affirm them

We honour our parents by affirming them. To affirm someone means to strengthen and support them. One way we can affirm our parents is by voicing our praise to them. We all thrive on praise. Praise, of course, is not the same as flattery. We all know flatterers whose smooth tongues will say anything to get on someone's right side. Praise is different; it is affirming something about someone that we know and have experienced to be true. Have you ever told your parents how grateful you are for all they gave you, for all they shaped in you, for all they taught you? If not, why not do it now? A letter is perhaps the best way. Even to hear simple words of thanks means a great deal to all parents – I can vouch for it.

Another way to affirm our parents is by involving them in our lives. This is especially true if we have left home. It doesn't hurt to discuss work and home issues with them. At the end of the day, we may not take their advice, for whatever reason. Yet for them, to feel that they have been consulted is a good way of honouring them.

Still another way we can affirm our parents is in the way we speak to them. Respect and regard often seem to be in very short supply when you hear the younger generation talking of those older than them. We need perhaps to be more respectful in the way we talk to the 'older generation'. After all, one day we will be part of it.

Avoid abandoning them

Practically, as parents get older the way we honour them is by not abandoning them. The question of how to deal with the needs of ageing parents, without compromising our responsibilities to our own immediate families, is a complex issue and one that is not easily solved by simple maxims.

The New Testament does lay down the general principle that there is a duty to care for the elderly and vulnerable within our families: 'If a widow has children or grandchildren, these should learn first of all to put their religion into practice by caring for their own family and so repaying their parents and grandparents, for this is pleasing to God' (1 Timothy 5:4, NIV). Each family will need to weigh up the particular situations their parents face as they get older. There is no doubt that at times we may feel put out, inconvenienced and frustrated. However, honouring our parents is a duty that should continue whether it is easy or hard.

Act now

There are two distinctive features about the fifth commandment: it is the only one with a promise attached and it is the only command that doesn't last a lifetime. This last point is one worth pondering. A day will come when, at a hospital bedside or in the funeral parlour, we will realize that death has removed the opportunity for us to carry out this commandment. This, then, is an urgent command. When our parents die, it is too late and our chance has gone. A friend of mine is a vicar who takes many funeral services. He finds that when he visits the families, he only hears praise for the dead parent. He says it seems that they only bury saints! Underneath the words, he often knows that the families didn't get on, that there was a huge amount of pain, remorse and anger around, and there was so much that was left unsaid and unforgiven at death. No amount of expense on a fine funeral or wonderful wreaths is equal to a thank you, a visit, a letter, a phone call, while we still have the opportunity.

We must not wait for a crisis, in which death threatens either us or them, to make peace with our mother and father. There are compelling reasons to start right now.

To honour our parents means to obey them in our younger years, to support them in their older years, and to respect them through all the years.

Let me here add a personal and hard-earned footnote to this advice on honouring parents. This is a hard commandment. I have struggled with what it means for me to honour my father and mother. To say that my relations with my parents have been strained is an understatement. They both refused to come to my wedding, and even tried – a week before the ceremony – to bribe me into marrying another woman. It is hard to honour your parents when what they do seems to be so dishonouring to you. Yet my wife, Killy, and I have endeavoured to fulfil our side of this commandment. It has not been easy.

Relating to our children: earning honour

This commandment works both ways. Yes, it says that children have a duty to honour their parents. But I believe that it also implies that parents need to earn the right to be honoured. Let me briefly give some suggestions as to how this might be done.

Work at parenting

As we have seen earlier, parenting ability is not an automatic skill, and unfortunately no manual comes attached to the baby. In fact it seems to me an extraordinary inconsistency that to be allowed to adopt a child in Britain, you have to pass any number of stringent tests and meet all sorts of criteria. But anyone can have a child the good old-fashioned way without having to pass any test at all.

Earlier, I challenged you to 'learn to learn' about parenting. I repeat it now. I would, however, counsel caution about using rigid and doctrinaire methods. Parenting involves the careful use of a series of flexible skills, not the rigid, unyielding application of an exact science. Parents do not deal with uniform and predictable silicon chips – they have to work with living and developing creatures with very individual (and often wayward) temperaments and wills. Flexibility is a great virtue; what may work with one child may not work with another. I sometimes think that by the time we get the hang of parenting, our children have left home. The Earl of Rochester said in the seventeenth century, 'Before I got married I had six theories about bringing up children; now I have six children and no theories.' Frankly, in the 300-odd years since, all that has happened is the number of theories has multiplied while the success rate has stayed the same.

In the sorry story of Joseph's upbringing we read how he was singled out for preferential treatment. Partly it was because he was born to Jacob in his old age, but it was also because he was born to Rachel, the wife whom Jacob loved above the others (Genesis 29:30). Now I know we do not live in those times and few Western families rival Jacob's for complexity, but one thing that is pivotal in family life is the stability of the parental relationship. Part of the problem with Jacob's children undoubtedly came from the unstable relationships between him and the four women who bore him children. The nature and quality of the parents' relationship has life-long consequences for the children. As we have seen elsewhere, one commandment reinforces another; keeping the 'no adultery' rule is a good basis for this fifth commandment to be kept. A stable marriage is the best possible foundation for a solid family and the greatest gift any parent can give a child is to love the other parent.

Over 20 per cent of all British families are single-parent families and at this point I feel it is important to say something to those who are in such a situation, whether it results from divorce, separation or death. You belong to a group of people I especially want to affirm and in everything I write here I want to build you up, not pull you down. Remember that God knows you; he knows your situation and he knows all the circumstances you face. I can only guess at how tough it is to bring up children on your own. My wife Killy and I have found it hard enough bringing up children together. That single parents manage at all (and some manage very well) fills me with awe and respect.

What I do know is that again and again there are stories in the Bible of God supporting a lone parent – comforting, healing, establishing, providing, taking away any shame and blessing them. I believe that one of the great things church provides is a family for us all. Jesus again and again invites people into his family. At one point, he talks about people becoming his brothers and sisters if they do the will of his Father (Mark 3:35). He gives us a wider family to be part of; one far greater than simply our blood relations. There will be different times, depending on different situations, where we all need to lean in different ways on this family. It may be in invisible things like support, advice and prayer; it may be in little practical things like baby-sitters or meals; it may even be in big practical things like shelter, finance and holidays. Please do not think that if you do have such wants or needs it is because you have failed. It is because God allows us to need each other. That's what families are all about.

I want also to put a question to those of you who are involved in leading churches. It is simply this: Is your church a place where the single parent – or even the single person – can find a home? You may need to think about it when you next meet. But can you read the paragraph above and say, 'Yes, thank God, that is true of our church. We are a family for those without family.' I'm sorry to ask such an impertinent question. But I just feel it may be easier if it comes from me now rather than Jesus later.

Enforce discipline

Let me say something briefly here about the unpopular subject of discipline within families. Discipline is badly needed these days. There are too many parents who tie up their dog at night and let their children run loose. Some families can trace their ancestry back 300 years, but can't tell you where their children were last night.

No parent enjoys discipline and I'm sure all of us wish for families in which it is never needed. Yet the principle of discipline is good, and indeed the Bible tells us that it is one of the characteristics of God that he 'disciplines those he loves' (Hebrews 12:6). God disciplines us because he cares, because he does not want to see us hurt. That pattern should be the model for our discipline. The purpose of discipline is never to inflict pain or shame. It is to help teach a child, so they will learn and not harm themselves in the future. A failure to discipline is a failure to love – a point made by the book of Proverbs: 'If you refuse to discipline your children, it proves you don't love them' (Proverbs 13:24, NLT). Jacob, it seems, refused to punish Reuben for his immorality. This caused them both harm, making the father seem ineffectual and stripping the son of respect. Had there been punishment, both Jacob and Reuben would have had their respect restored.

The actual practice of discipline is beyond the scope of this book. But discipline is vital. One way of imposing discipline may be the removal of privileges (TV or computer time is a good start), but however punishment is imposed, a number of rules must be obeyed.

- It should be strictly limited and there should be no risk of physical harm.
- It should not be psychologically hurtful. It is worth noting that some non-physical punishments such as humiliation can be very damaging.
- It should never be carried out in rage.
- It should be agreed between both parents.
- It should be appropriate to the offence.
- It should not be carried out unless there was a clear and wilful breach of some previously defined limit.
- It should be explained.
- It should not be cruel.
- It should be followed immediately by an affirmation of love.
- Once punishment is carried out, the matter should be closed as the price has been paid.

By whatever means discipline is carried out, we parents must be careful. The Bible says, 'Fathers do not embitter your children or they will become discouraged' (Ephesians 6:4). Centuries ago Martin Luther said, 'To spare the rod and spoil the child is true. But beside the rod keep an apple to give him when he has done well.'

And on that note let me move on to the positive counterpart to discipline: praise.

Praise them

An atmosphere of praise is the best environment for children and parents to grow in. Often parents can set an example and lead the way in this regard. One of the saddest things is to see a parent who, time and time again, just grinds down their children. Those children end up being crushed and without self-confidence. Yet if parents can learn to create an atmosphere of praise by being quick to compliment and credit and slow to criticize and condemn, their children will thrive and grow. Not only that, but they will be teaching them lessons on how to relate to others that will be of great blessing in the future.

Learn to let go

Parents can nurture an atmosphere of acceptance by giving space to their children. Tempting as a close control is, we can be too protective. One couple had just had a child, but following the birth there were complications and the baby girl had to be taken away from her mother to the intensive care ward. The new mother was distraught; her baby was just hours old and already she had been taken away from her. Later on that day, her own mother came to visit her. 'Daughter,' she said, 'today – the day you gave birth – you have had to learn the most difficult but the most important lesson of parenting: to let them go.'

Letting go doesn't mean letting children do anything they want, but it does mean freeing them to be themselves, letting them make their own mistakes and letting them learn the hard way. However much we might want to, we parents cannot live our children's lives for them. Accepting love frees, protects and ultimately releases.

Be encouraged

Let me end this chapter positively. Even if our experience of family has been a positive one, we would all agree that it is hard work. Both parenting and relating to parents is tough. Two mothers were talking. The first said, 'My daughter doesn't tell me anything. I'm a nervous wreck.' Puzzled, the second mother looked at her and replied, 'My daughter tells me everything and *I'm* a nervous wreck.'

If you are struggling with parenting

If you are struggling with parenting, then let me remind you that God is for you and what you are doing. He understands. Indeed, it may help you to realize that Jesus probably understands far more than you think about running a family. You see the last we hear of Mary's husband, Joseph, is when Jesus is twelve. Afterwards there is no mention of him and it seems probable that he died sometime before Jesus started his ministry. If this is so, then Jesus, as the eldest son, would have taken on the task of being head of a household that included a number of younger children. Yes, he does know what it is like.

Not only does God sympathize, but he longs to help. He has

provided us with resources in Jesus, the Holy Spirit and the church to enable us to parent faithfully.

If you are struggling with parents

Again we need to be reminded that God is involved in our families. In this area too Jesus understands. One of the most fascinating incidents in the Gospels comes when Jesus' mother, together with his brothers and sisters, came to take him away from the crowd (Mark 3:31–35). They had heard rumours of what he was doing and we are told that they were worried he was going out of his mind, so they thought they were doing it for his sake and for the sake of the family. Jesus was forced to defend his own ministry against the well-meaning attempts of his family to intervene. Often the cry of children caught up in family difficulties is, 'But no one understands.' Jesus does. His family misunderstood him. If you feel everyone else is against you, make sure you remember that God knows what you are going through. Yet at the same time, Jesus was actually the model son. Some of his last words on the cross were to arrange for the apostle John to look after his mother.

Again, we see that not only does God sympathize with us, but he desires to help. Whether we are parents – or we have to deal with parents – the resources of Jesus, the Holy Spirit and the church are available to us.

Have hope

Above all, I want you to remember that God can transform things. It is easy to be discouraged about the family. Families are an area where we all make mistakes. There are casualties of 'family' everywhere – not just those openly broken families, but the ones that appear secure but have tensions below the surface. Your experiences and regrets over your experience of family may have cast a mould that you feel powerless to be free from. Yet God can forgive and can change things, even the worst things.

The good news is that God wants to help us make families work. Jesus came, died and rose again so that the gap between people and God might be healed. He also came so that the gaps between individuals might be healed.

The best and most urgently needed place for that healing is in the family.

COMMANDMENT 4

Remember to observe the Sabbath day by keeping it holy. Six days a week are set apart for your daily duties and regular work, but the seventh day is a day of rest dedicated to the Lord *your God. On that day no one in your household may do any kind of work. This includes you, your sons and daughters, your male and female servants, your livestock, and any foreigners living among you. For in six days the* Lord *made the heavens, the earth, the sea, and everything in them; then he rested on the seventh day. That is why the* Lord *blessed the Sabbath day and set it apart as holy.*

(Exodus 20:8–11, NLT)

So what's the problem?

Time is relative. Albert Einstein remarked, 'There certainly seems less of it about than there used to be.' I wonder how often you have heard yourself say:

- 'I'm too busy.'
- 'It's been all go.'
- 'There never seems to be enough time.'
- 'I don't know where all the time goes.'
- 'The week's simply flown.'
- 'I haven't had a moment to spare.'

In fact, I could list many more similar sayings, but I don't have the time! Do you see the problem?

Technology has achieved wonders in almost every area. Bookshelves of encyclopedias have been shrunk into silver discs the size of beer mats, British sporting defeats can now be watched live from the other side of the world and you can now jog and be deafened by pop, rock or classical music at the same time. Yet no one has done anything about time. The best that technology has achieved is to allow us to measure ever more accurately how fast time flies. Our ancestors, listening to the ticking of clocks, were reminded that their time was slipping away. We stare at spinning digits on screens, a million times more accurate, but the feeling is the same. Time is fixed and unalterable, and whatever we do it slips away from us.

It is because time is so basic and unchangeable that it is the most precious commodity we have. We are masters of so much but, whatever our wealth, we still cannot create more time. Time passes at the same rate for the rich as it does for the poor. In fact, attempts to create more time are often counter-productive. Consider the following story:

A business executive, talking into a cellular phone, is walking across a beautiful sun-drenched beach. Over his phone conversation all he can hear is the sound of the waves and the gulls crying. Ahead of him, a man in simple clothes is dozing in the shade of a fishing boat that has been pulled up onto the beach. As he passes, the fisherman wakes up and the executive, now waiting for a call to be returned, decides to make conversation.

'The weather is great, there are plenty of fish; why are you lying around instead of going out and catching more?'

The fisherman replies gently, 'Because I caught enough this morning.'

'But just imagine,' the executive says, 'if you went out three or four times a day and brought home three or four times as many fish. You know what could happen?'

Puzzled, the fisherman shakes his head.

'Why,' says the executive, becoming enthusiastic, 'you could buy yourself a motorboat. Then after, say, two years you could buy a second one. Then after perhaps three years, you could have a cutter or two. And just think, one day you might be able to build a freezing plant – you might eventually even get your own helicopter for tracing shoals of fish and guiding your fleet of cutters. You could even acquire your own trucks to ship your fish to the capital, and then . . .'

'And then?' asks the fisherman.

'And then,' the executive concludes triumphantly, 'you could be calmly sitting at the beach side, dozing in the sun and looking at the beautiful ocean!'

The fisherman replies, 'What do you think I'm doing now?'

In our pursuit of time we sometimes lose more than we gain.

'Time is money,' we say, but we mislead ourselves. Time is more than money. Money can be replaced, time cannot. We would be better off saying that 'time is priceless'. If we did, we might treat our hours and days with more respect. Because time is unchanging and cannot be traded, how we use it is vital. In fact, as in so many other areas of life, when it comes to our use of time, we are in an utter mess.

Our modern lifestyles are ruthless. It is a well-known fact, proved both by statistics and experience, that while we now work harder and earn more, we have less time or energy to enjoy the money we've made. Certainly, as our working hours have increased, so too have our stress levels. Sixty per cent of successful professionals say that they are suffering chronic stress or depression, and 48 per cent of top American corporate executives report that their lives are 'empty and meaningless'. You can't stop, because to stop is to risk being surplus to requirements. Yet it is not just our bosses who drive us on, it is ourselves. It has been claimed that during any 24-hour period we receive an average of 3,000 messages seeking to persuade us that we need something we do not have. I can well believe it. Far too much of our time goes in working to pay for things that we couldn't afford and didn't need anyway.

On top of earning a living, there is so much else to do today. For most of us, if we were to list everything that we had to do it would run onto several sides of paper. There are friends to phone, family members to talk to, exercise to take, appointments to make, shopping lists to write up, books to read, videos to watch, e-mails to answer, web pages to browse, hobbies to pursue, bills to pay and even socks to sort out! We know that our time is finite, but the demands on our time seem infinite. The responsibilities and requirements we face day to day seem overwhelming. And to make it all worse, we are bombarded by ever more messages urging us to do what we are already doing better, and to do what we are not doing. 'Buy! Write! Visit! Phone! Read!' they scream. The chances are that if I asked you to tell me how you are, the word 'busy' would come up in the first few sentences. We end up having so many irons in the fire that we put the fire out.

Any moments of time we save in one area of our life seem to be snatched away from us. For example, there was a time when the moment we left the office our work ended. Not any more.

Technology promised us modern conveniences that would make our lives easier, but computers, faxes, mobile phones and e-mail have increased the pace of work rather than diminished it. Notebook computers allow us to work on the train and mobile phones mean that the boss can catch us wherever we are. From transport to communications, from production to entertainment, time saved is constantly eroded, whether by greater travelling distances, more appointments or 'enhanced productivity requirements'. In fact so bizarrely twisted is human nature that we can easily get ourselves into the position that if we are not rushed off our feet we begin to fret. 'What's wrong with me?' we say, as we look up from our novel and realize that everyone else on the train is working. In twenty-first-century Britain things are so messed up that some people seem to feel more guilty about relaxing than they do about adultery.

All this ceaseless rushing around inevitably has a physical effect on us. If your body could talk, what would it say to you at this moment? I expect it would be 'slow down', or 'take a break'. When we refuse to co-operate with God's laws for our body's proper maintenance we run an increasing risk of malfunction. Our modern lifestyle of hustle and bustle places us in the grip of what psychologist Paul Tournier calls 'universal fatigue'. We constantly complain about how tired we feel. Often the first reaction we have when we wake in the morning and look at the clock is disbelief: 'It can't be morning already – I'm still tired!'

How many times have you said, 'I wish I had just a few more hours in the day'? The assumption is that, given more hours, you would accomplish everything you need to with less stress. But there is just as much chance that, given this wish, it would only mean a few more hectic hours to live through in any given day. Perhaps we should actually be wishing for a shorter day, in which the crazy pace of our lives is limited to fewer hours. We have bought into the idea that the busier we are, the more important our life is.

In the middle of such overwhelming pressures, everyone agrees that one of the things that we need to do is to evaluate our priorities so that we can better order our lives. If we don't live by priorities, we will live by pressures.

This chapter is about the fourth commandment, where God speaks directly to us about how we order our time. One day in seven, we are told, we need to have a holy day in which we do not work. It is my strong belief, based on the Bible but supported by my own experience, that at the start of a new century we need to revive the historic practice of setting aside one day a week to rest. I believe that for the sake of our health, our sanity, our families, our relationships, our spirituality and our society, we all need to have a Sabbath.

I realize that to suggest this now is harder than it has ever been. Only 20 years ago, if you were to walk down a road on a Sunday, the only shop open would have been the newsagent; if you wanted to watch football, you'd have been limited to a scrappy amateur game in the local park, and your town centre would have been eerily silent. Now all that has changed. Sunday has become a major shopping day, town centres and shopping complexes echo to the sounds of people and traffic, and there is football everywhere. The fact is that many of us have grown used to shopping on Sundays and having things open. The idea of going back to solemn and silent Sabbaths is hardly going to be popular. Besides, people will protest that they don't have time to take a day off.

Now, let me say right at the start that we profoundly misunderstand this commandment if we think of it in any way as God making yet another burden for us. On the contrary, the Sabbath is God's gift to us. If human beings were not so distorted by sin, God could perhaps have dealt with this topic in the Bible simply as a 'Maker's Recommendation' along the lines of 'Your Creator advises you that you will function better if you take one day in seven off'. The fact is, because God knows that taking a day off is so much against our desires, he has made it a rule. In this commandment God is ordering us to take a break.

The heart of the matter

Taking this commandment seriously doesn't mean simply putting the clock back to the 1950s and trying to get everything shut down on Sundays. In fact, as you have probably found out by now, all the Commandments require serious thought as to how we apply them today. This one is no different. What we need to do first is to delve a bit deeper into why this commandment was given.

This is the longest of the Ten Commandments. That is not only because God wants to make it clear that it applies to everyone (sons, daughters, workers, visitors and animals!), but also because God sets out the reasons for it being given. It is linked with how God himself works. Now, as we have seen several times already, we are made in his image and we are patterned after him. On this basis, it is not a bad idea if we listen carefully.

The rhythm of life

God bases his ruling of a Sabbath rest on the way that he created the universe. Now I know that there are different theories on how the first couple of chapters of the Bible are to be interpreted. Personally, I think to have an argument about whether it took God six 24-hour time spans in order to make the universe sadly misses the point of what it is all about. The point of the account in Genesis is not to tell us scientifically how God created the universe; it is to tell us *who* made the world and *why*. Everything, it says, was brought into being from nothing, not by chance but by the will of the one supreme God who has revealed himself to us. The universe, far from being the result of squabbling or breeding gods and demons (as other ancient cultures have seen it) or the product of a random and impersonal nature (as modern atheists see it), is the deliberate creation of a personal, all-powerful, perfect and loving God.

Into this vast universe, God himself has imprinted an order and rhythm that can be seen at every level, from how subatomic particles hold together, to the way that living things interact. Whether in the cells of our body, the flow of our blood or in the vast carbon and oxygen cycles of the atmosphere, there are regular pulses and beats as energy and elements are interchanged. The most prominent and unmistakable examples of rhythm occur in the heavens: the earth rotates on its axis, giving night and day; its path around the sun gives seasons; the moon's orbit produces monthly cycles and tides. These rhythms come from God who ordered, 'Let there be lights in the expanse of the sky to separate the day from the night, and let them serve as signs to mark seasons and days and years'

(Genesis 1:14, NIV). As human beings, a response to these daily, monthly and yearly rhythms occurs at a very deep level. We sleep and wake, eat and drink, grow and develop in similar rhythmic patterns. Attempts to modify or ignore the frequency of these cycles can produce very negative results – just ask anyone with jet lag.

As if to emphasize that he is a God of rhythm, God tells us that he worked in creating the universe on a daily basis (whatever that means in terms of actual time) and that he himself rested at the end of his efforts. The principle of regular work followed by rest has therefore the highest endorsement possible: it comes from our Creator himself. Not only that, but as human beings are made in his image, this rhythm of labour followed by leisure is something that we have inherited from our heavenly Father. It's in our blood.

What is God's day of rest?

Before I deal with all the practical implications of what it means to keep this commandment I need to discuss briefly what God's day of rest is for us today.

A brief history of God's day of rest

The commandment, as it was originally given, refers to the seventh day of the week – our Saturday. Keeping the Sabbath by refraining from all work and holding religious services was one of the great distinguishing marks of the Jewish faith in the Bible – a tradition that modern Judaism has kept. In the Old Testament there are various other laws that were given about the Sabbath that strictly limited the extent to which, for example, you could travel or prepare food. In the Gospels, we see that Jesus and his disciples attended the synagogue services on the Sabbath, and presumably they kept the Sabbath rules given in the Old Testament. By Jesus' day, however, the God-given Old Testament laws on the Sabbath had been added to by a vast number of restrictive and often petty rules from the religious authorities. Jesus came into conflict with these, and had a number of disputes with the religious leaders over what the purpose of the Sabbath really was. This is something that I will talk about more later.

After the resurrection of Jesus something very remarkable happened. Although most of the first Christians were Jewish and kept the old Sabbath, very soon Christians started worshipping on the Sunday, the first day of the week. The fact that the resurrection had occurred on a Sunday must have been the key factor in making the switch. Sunday was the day Jesus was raised back to life and was an appropriate day to remember all the things that God had done for his people through Jesus' death. That the Holy Spirit had been given on a Sunday was probably also an important factor. There may also have been a practical element. If some of the Christians from a Jewish background were observing the Sabbath, the only time they would have been able to meet with other Christians for worship would have been either before the start of the working week on a Sunday morning, or in the evening (as in Acts 20:7). There is no evidence of early Christians applying the old Sabbath rules on work to a Sunday. In fact for several centuries, the first day of the week must have been a normal working day, marked only by fellowship meetings outside work hours.

As the church grew and spread, so did the importance of meeting together. The pattern that churches all around the Mediterranean got into was to meet on a Sunday. In AD 321, the first Christian Roman Emperor, Constantine, decreed that Sundays were to be an official public holiday, on which most work was forbidden. Since then Sunday has been the normal Christian day of rest and worship.

The Jewish Sabbath and Christian Sunday

If Christians have always worshipped together on a Sunday, there have been differing views on how Sunday relates to the old Jewish Sabbath. There are two extreme positions. Some Christians have felt that at least some Old Testament rules on the Sabbath should be transferred to Sunday. For them, Sundays are solemn days of rest and devotion; reading fiction or kicking a football would definitely be out. To support their position, they would point out that nowhere in the New Testament does it say that the Sabbath is abolished. Other Christians, however, consider that the new era that Christ brought in rendered this part of the Old Testament law as obsolete as it did the laws on diet. Sunday for them is very different from the Jewish Sabbath and they don't see a problem in reading a novel or having a bit of a kick-around in the park in the afternoon. Opponents of the first view say that with it you run the risk of legalism; of trying to please God by doing things, rather than just accepting his grace in Jesus. Opponents of the second view say that you run the risk of using grace as an excuse for moral sloppiness, and that soon Sunday will blur into any other working day.

In fact, there is something to be said for both sides. While I do not believe that all the Sabbath laws can be brought over to Sunday, I am concerned that under the relentless pressure of modern society we may end up throwing away a precious rule and one of the Ten Commandments that we badly need to keep. As I have suggested earlier, our need for a one-in-seven day of rest seems to be unalterably built into the human frame. At the same time, I am unhappy about adding rules and restrictions to what should be a joyful day of liberation from work. In a phrase, I would say that for Christians the Sabbath *rules* are dead but the Sabbath *principles* remain. So when I talk – as I do – about 'observing a Sabbath', it does not at all mean that I am suggesting keeping all the Old Testament laws. I mean keeping the Sabbath principle of enjoying God's day of rest.

When do we keep God's day of rest?

One other linked question needs tackling here. Does this mean that God's day of rest for us must always be on a Sunday? No, not necessarily. For one, many people cannot avoid working on a Sunday: for example those in medical professions, on the emergency services, in charge of the public utilities, and last – but not least – church staff! However, it is still the case that, because of traditional working patterns for most people in this country, Sundays make the best Sabbaths. Despite all the changes in working practices, it is usually the case that Sunday is the day that most people have free. It is because of this that I supported the 'Keep Sunday Special Campaign' in 1993, which attempted to stop the large-scale lifting of restrictions on Sunday shopping. I should say that this was not because I was under any illusion that if shops were closed people would go to church. Rather it was because I believed – and still do – there is a great value in keeping a common day of rest. After all, if everyone in a family has a different day off, much of the value of a Sabbath rest day for family and society will be lost.

Although Sundays generally make the best Sabbaths, sometimes it may be impossible to take a day of rest then. In most

Islamic countries Sunday is a normal working day and Christian believers there often have Friday as a day of rest instead. Even here in Britain, circumstances and shifts may be such as to make it impossible for some people to have a Sunday off. If this applies to you or your spouse and Sunday is a working day, then I believe it is vital that you make sure you get another day off during the week. If it can be the same day off every week and you can get into a regular routine, then fine. If, however, that is not possible, I encourage you to arrange for a full 24-hour stretch off: plan it out and guard it. I will make some practical suggestions later on how to do this.

The important thing is that we all need to inject into our lives a regular weekly break, whether on Sunday or on some other replacement day. But before I look at how we are to use that day, I feel it is important to look at the whole issue of work first. This commandment says something about that too.

The blessings of work and rest

I want to make two suggestions here with regard to work and rest. The first is that we thank God for work. The second is that we take God's designated day of rest seriously.

Thank God for work

A key feature of this commandment is that it upholds the goodness and privilege of work. Yes, we are told to take one day of rest a week, but the clear assumption is that we will spend the other six days in productive work. Not working on one day is tied to working on the other six. Doing nothing is the most tiresome job in the world, because you can't stop and rest.

There is a distinction between work and employment.

Employment implies a paid position, while work is something you can have and not be paid for it. Many people – most of them women – work very long and antisocial hours to care for children or families. Yet these jobs (surely the most valuable of all) are unpaid.

I believe that work is good. We read that Adam was given work to do in Eden (Genesis 2:15) before he and Eve broke God's commands and were punished. Work was part of God's good design for humanity. Only after the calamity of humanity's fall into sin do we find that work became burdensome (Genesis 3:17–19). The fact is that human beings were designed to work.

I believe that each of us has a part to play in maintaining and developing our society. Each of us has different skills and talents, and because God gives these to us, we glorify him by using them. A tragic but often overlooked element of being unemployed is that it results in our inbuilt God-given desire to work lying fallow and frustrated. That is one of the reasons we should support policies to enable the long-term unemployed to get back to work. There are of course those who are unavoidably unemployed, through disability or illness. For such people we need to implement what the Bible says about 'the strong supporting the weak' and make sure that financial provision is made for them. We should also try to find something for them to do that is rewarding and which fulfils their innate desire to work.

Despite the negative press that work has and continues to have, those of us who are in employment need to thank God for it. I know that in some work situations the idea of thanking God for our job can, at best, raise a grim smile. Let me say two things. First – and I am not being flippant – I urge you to count your blessings. There have been many times in British history when large-scale unemployment has been common and, in some places, it still is. Unemployment is a cruel and depressing situation. Second, can I encourage you to work at trying to thank God for your work? I believe that the general rule is that not only should we be working but our work should be a positive and good thing for us. Does that phrase 'a positive and good thing' describe your current attitude to your work? Would you say that you enjoy your work and that you are fulfilled in what you do?

One thing you may find helpful is to remember that whatever you are doing at work you are doing for God. Writing to the Colossian church, Paul gives the following instructions to – of all people – slaves: 'Work hard and cheerfully at whatever you do, as though you were working for the Lord rather than for people. Remember that the Lord will give you an inheritance as your reward, and the Master you are serving is Christ' (Colossians 3:23–24, NLT).

Taking such an attitude is actually possible. Brother Lawrence, a seventeenth-century cook in a French monastery, had it. He learned to bring a devotional attitude into virtually every action of his day. This enabled him to find not only meaning, but also purpose in all his work. He wrote:

> I turn my little omelette in the pan for the love of God. When it is finished, if I have nothing to do, I prostrate myself on the ground and worship my God, who gave me this grace to make it, after which I arise happier than a king. When I can do nothing else, it is enough to have picked up straw for the love of God. People look for ways of learning how to love God. They hope to attain it, I know not from how many different practices. They take much

> trouble to abide in his presence by varied means. Is it not a shorter and more direct way to do everything for the love of God, to make use of all the tasks one's lot in life demands to show him that love, and to maintain his presence within by the communion of our heart with his? There is nothing complicated about it. One has only to turn to it honestly and simply.[1]

We all need to have some of that attitude to our own work.

Now before moving on, let me make an important point. I have been anxious here to defend work in general. That does not mean I am saying that every job is fine and all you need to do is just thank God for it. There are some jobs that are wrong, perhaps because they involve dubious practices, or because they are producing things or services that the world doesn't need. Equally, there are some jobs that are right but which may be wrong for you. I can hardly tackle all the issues raised by that here. All I can say is this: give your job its best and pray for those you work with. Thank God for whatever you can about your job and seek guidance about a way forward.

I believe it is God's will that we all have jobs that are fulfilling. But I should warn you: his idea of what is a fulfilling job may not be quite what *we* had in mind.

Taking rest seriously

If this commandment shows us something of the value of work, it also allows us to see the value of rest. The problem is that we tend to consider work as being important and rest as being trivial. We can think of rest as merely 'not-working'. I want to point out that a day of rest is far more than that.

---

1 Brother Lawrence, *The Practice of the Presence of God* (Hodder, 1997).

At the most basic level, a day off every week is good for us physically and mentally. It gives us the opportunity to relax the pace at which our body's machinery is working. We can rest eyes strained by computer screens, ease backs stressed by office chairs or give a break to metabolisms kept going on caffeine. Although many people insist that their workload is such that they cannot take a day off, the fact is that keeping going without a break is often detrimental for overall productivity. A day off may help to re-energize us, to the point that we work at a higher level of efficiency on subsequent days. In contrast, continuously working may soon result in us working at a low level of efficiency and competence. A well-known vicious circle effect cuts in, where we refuse to take time off because we have so much to do. We then become so tired that we aren't able to do what we have to properly, so it takes more time to do our tasks. This then leaves us with even less time, and reduces still further the chances of taking time off. Taking a day off a week is not a luxury; it is the way we were made to exist.

A day of rest is also important because it enables us to assess what we are doing. The problem with continuously working is that there is no opportunity to stand back, get things into perspective and see the big picture. Deadline after deadline forces us to focus on immediate crises rather than the overall design of our lives. Many people today have a work style that is reminiscent of some racing cyclist, head down and pedalling furiously along the road. A day of rest allows us to stop pedalling, sit down, look around, pick up the map and work out where our efforts are taking us. I have often found that it is when I am recharging, away from the place of my restless 'doing', that I discover what exactly it is that has to be done.

William Wilberforce (1759–1833), who will be remembered

in British history as the MP who after decades of labour brought forward legislation to ban slavery, knew the truth of this. Wilberforce was a committed Christian and never felt it right to work on a Sunday. Within a few years as a politician, he had made a great impression, and was being tipped for a high position in the cabinet. The atmosphere around Westminster at the time was heady and Wilberforce felt flattered that his hard work was on the point of being rewarded. However, after resting during the following Sunday, his view of his possible promotion changed and he was able to write in his diary that 'these earthly things assume their true size'. His day of rest had given him a sense of perspective. Incidentally, Wilberforce was also well aware of the physical and mental value of a Sunday's rest. Later in life, he was to write sadly of his contemporaries who had broken under the pressure of politics, 'With peaceful Sundays, the strings would never have snapped as they did from over tension.'

Taking a day of rest also makes a statement about who we are and who runs our lives. It deliberately dethrones work from being central to our existence. In the passage in Genesis 1 that this commandment refers back to, we read how, as God made everything, he stopped and stood back and saw 'that it was good'. Even on the ultimate job of making the entire cosmos, God does not become work obsessed. We who are made in his image would do well to learn the same principle. In fact, if our lives are only about working, we need to do something to change that. We need to remember that who we are isn't defined by what we do. We are human *beings* not human *doings*. If all we do is *do*, then we will stop being. It is no accident that many people who have worked intensely in jobs find retirement or unemployment profoundly stressful. They have let their jobs take over their lives, and the ending of the job comes as a deep-felt savage blow to who they are.

In Leo Tolstoy's short story 'How much land does a man need?', a man travels to a tribe in the Russian hinterland. They offer to give him as much land as he can cover in one day. Anxious to cover as much ground as he can, the man makes a frantic journey. As the sun sets, he collapses with exhaustion and dies. Ultimately, the amount of land that he actually gets is the six-foot plot that is his final resting place.

In our grasping for the material benefits of our society, we are no different from Tolstoy's character. If we judge ourselves and others only by the goods and services that we produce, if we believe that to *do* more is to *be* more, then we are, in fact, slaves to what we do. Work becomes an end in itself. We eventually conclude that if we are only what we do, then to *be* more, we must *do* more.

Now this is no less than a demonic lie. Instead of liberating us, work enslaves us and owns us. As Diane Fassel wrote, 'Work is god for the compulsive worker, and nothing gets in the way of this god.'[2]

Work becomes an end in itself, a way to escape from family, from the inner life, from the world. Workaholism is literally fatal. Its toxic fruits are heart disease, hypertension, depression and more. In Japan, *karoshi* or 'death from overwork' is the second largest killer of working males and accounts for 10 per cent of Japan's death rate. Like other addictions, workaholism consumes the addict's time, energy and thoughts.

Forcing ourselves to take a break is also helpful because it reminds us of our limitations. We tend to think that we are

---

[2] Diane Fassel, *Working Ourselves to Death.*

indispensable in the great scheme of things. All too frequently this is an illusion. We love to be busy and to be needed, and there is no greater boost to our egos than to think that we personally hold everything together. However, making ourselves take a step away from the action can give us a healthy sense of proportion. Very often when we do stop, we find that not everything stops with us. As someone has written, 'To act as if the world (or worse still, God) cannot get along without our work for one day in seven is a startling display of pride that denies the sufficiency of our generous maker.'

Sometimes, though, we are indeed so genuinely important that it is difficult to say 'no' to people. Yet even here a forced break is good and it guards us from becoming slaves to other people's demands. Besides, if we get into a regular pattern of taking time off, then people come to respect that and learn to work around it. If it is known that we are always available, we not only create an unhealthy reliance on ourselves, but we can also end up becoming effectively the property of other people. Taking a day off is actually a really good test of our freedom. As Dorothy Bass has said in *Practising Our Faith*, 'Slaves cannot take a day off; free people can.' Which are you?

Yet despite all the virtues of a day of rest, for many people it is something that is just too risky. 'How would I survive?' they ask. That we can trust God to provide for us if we keep his commandments is one of the lessons that the people of God learned just before Moses was given the Ten Commandments. After the Israelites crossed the Red Sea, they journeyed through the desert of Sinai. Faced with insufficient food, they made their needs known to God. In response, he miraculously provided manna for them, a substance which appeared like dew in the morning and which was 'white like coriander seed, and it tasted like honey cakes' (Exodus 16:31, NLT). With the manna came strict instructions: for five days they were to collect only what they needed for that day and if they tried to collect more it would rot and be full of maggots by the next morning. On the sixth day – the day before the Sabbath – they were told to collect twice as much, because on the Sabbath itself none would be given. The manna of the sixth day stayed fresh and did not rot, and on the Sabbath they were able to eat what they had stored. The lesson they learned from this was that God would provide for his people in every way and that they were not going to suffer for keeping his day of rest. We need to learn a similar lesson.

Making God's day of rest special

In this section I want to give some guidelines on how we can get the most benefit from God's day of rest.

Guard your rest

Paradoxically, you may need to work hard to keep God's day of rest special. A day of rest does not just happen; the phone will not suddenly stop ringing just because you have decided to take a day off. You need to make a definite effort to make a day of rest and to take care to guard it. This is particularly a problem if your day of rest is not on a Sunday: everybody will assume that you are working. You will need to take positive and proactive action to make sure that your much-needed Sabbath rest is not shattered by interruptions.

It is interesting that Jesus, in the midst of a busy ministry, was proactive in taking rest. We often read in the accounts of his life how he went to a solitary place in order to escape the crowds. Sometimes he took his closest friends to be with him and at other times he went on his own. There are lessons there for us about making firm resolutions to ensure that we do have rest.

Some of the actions we can take to guard our days of rest are concrete, physical ones. For example, if you can, divert phone calls somewhere else and refuse to check your e-mail. Make the rules you have for your day of rest widely known to others, and if you have responsibilities try and get someone else to deputize for you. Getting out of the house also makes it harder for people to find you and removes the temptation to finish off that report or write that letter. Just leave the mobile phone at home, rest from the things you do during the week, and create a day of distinction.

There are other less obvious actions that we can take to enhance the benefit of our days of rest. If you are a news addict, then give the radio and TV a break. If doing personal administration leaves you anxious, then postpone paying bills or sorting out your diary. Don't try to tackle household tasks that will leave you drained. You may want to discipline yourself not to talk, or even think, about a nagging work situation or project.

Resolve to guard your rest. Unless you do, pressures will inevitably erode it. The time to relax is when you don't have time to relax!

Be refreshed in your rest

The Sabbath is to be a day of physical non-productivity, a day to rest and recharge our bodies. Resting is about recovering from the week that has been; recharging is about getting ready for the week to come. One doctor said, 'The periods of rest I prescribe for my patients are often Sabbaths in arrears.'

Make the most of your day of rest. Force yourself to do things that are not stressful. If you don't have young children you might want to sleep in a bit longer. Find out what makes you relax and do it. In our household we often relax with a film or food. Other people like to listen to music or read a book. Many people have found that they feel refreshed by the beauty of God's creation, and are especially aware of God by lakes or rivers and in woods or gardens. The Sabbath should be a time when we step back to admire nature, rather than figure out how to change it. I believe that God gives his creation to us as a gift, and through it he can refresh us and rebuild us. And if on the other six days of the week rushing is your norm, walk slowly and calmly on the Sabbath. In the most famous of the Psalms we read that God 'makes me lie down in green pastures, he leads me beside quiet waters, he restores my soul' (Psalm 23:2–3, NIV). While this might be symbolic language, many have found it to be literally true.

Not only do you need to guard your Sabbath day of rest, you also need to monitor it over a period of time to make sure you are getting the most from it. Do you feel better as a result? Are there ways that you could make it of greater benefit to yourself? Are there things that you do on your day of rest that are stressful? Some people who are very committed to working hard can bring the same dedication into their hobbies and sports. The result is a new area of stress. If this is you, ask yourself some hard questions. Does it really matter if you don't break your personal record for the marathon? Do you need to remodel *all* of the garden? Is it really relaxing to learn Chinese?

You need to be blessed by your rest: make sure that you are.

Have freedom in your rest

One of the extraordinary abilities of the human race is that of being able to totally mess things up. You would have thought that a simple divine ruling about having a day of rest would be hard to damage. However, with perverse ingenuity, generations of people from all sorts of cultures have managed to turn this command from being a liberating gift of God into a wearisome day-long obstacle course. As I have mentioned, this happened at the time of Jesus to an extraordinary extent. The religious leaders had worked out a whole list of things that must not be done on the Sabbath. You couldn't prepare a meal, sew on a button, light a fire, or walk more than 3,000 feet from your home. There were, in total, 1,521 of these rules, all of them inventions of the human mind, to try and prevent this commandment being broken. Ensuring that no work took place on the Sabbath had become very hard work!

What happened with Jesus and the Sabbath is fascinating. Time and time again his actions brought him into trouble and open conflict with the religious leaders. Jesus felt free to heal, to pick corn and to cast out demons on the Sabbath. These were all actions that, in the opinion of the religious leaders, broke their rules on what could be done on the Sabbath. The fact that there were so many controversies about Jesus breaking these Sabbath rules may suggest that they were a religious abuse that he felt very strongly about. At one point, when criticized about his lax attitude to such rules, he replied, 'The Sabbath was made to benefit people, and not people to benefit the Sabbath' (Mark 2:27, NLT). The religious leaders had taken a blessing and turned it into an unbearable burden.

Such attitudes can occur even today, and we need to beware

of them. This commandment was given to set us free, not to enslave us. That you rest is essential; *how* you rest is up to you.

Enjoy others in your rest

The most important things in life aren't things, but people. Sabbaths are given so that we spend time with those we are closest to. So God's day of rest should also be used to develop and extend our relationships with friends and family. Not just in brief moments, but with quality (and quantity) time. Jewish people have the practice of gathering the family as one of the focal points of their Sabbath, and central to that family time is a shared meal. One of the casualties of the last few decades has been the family meal. We have less time for meals than we once did and they are frequently snatched or abbreviated by the demands of the phone or television. Even if this is our pattern for living for six days of the week, on our Sabbath day of rest I believe that it is important to rediscover leisurely family meal times. For us, as a family, one thing that helps us is our rule that the telephone will be out of bounds during a mealtime. We just ignore it: whatever it is, it can wait. In all the years, I can hardly ever recall an occasion when being instantly accessible was a necessity. We need to learn to master the telephone rather than remain enslaved by it. This allows us to give our full attention to those nearest to us – those for whom we have primary responsibility.

Enjoy God in your rest

God's day of rest is a day to worship. It is not the *only* day to worship and not the *only* day to pray and praise, but it should be the day when we have time to focus on God and our life in him. It is a day to tune in again to God, to refocus and to reprioritize all that we do and are, in the light of the reality of God.

Normally, one part of our day of rest should involve worshipping with other members of God's family. If we can take our Sabbath rest on Sunday, then giving God the first part of the first day of every week serves to remind us that he is first in our lives. Christians have always set time aside to be together: to listen to God's word spoken into their lives, to remember Jesus' death for them in the breaking of bread, to pray together for the world, and to praise God for his goodness. To meet with God and his people is something that serves to nourish and feed us spiritually. Ceasing to meet together is bound to have a negative effect on our Christian lives. An old and useful image is that fellowship is like a burning coal fire; if you take a hot coal out of the fire and place it somewhere in isolation it will soon go cold. Experience over centuries has shown that this is what happens if individuals are isolated from a church fellowship. We need to make time for regular meeting together. Of course, in Britain, if your day of rest is not a Sunday, using it for both rest and worship is not easy and you may have to make other arrangements. But whenever we take our Sabbath rest we should spend time with God.

'Remember the Sabbath day by keeping it *holy.*' The Sabbath day was created holy, but God wants it to be holy to you. The Sabbath is not just about time off; it is about sacred time. Sunday does not belong to business, it does not belong to industry, it does not belong to the government. It belongs to God.

So many people now have no room for God in their thoughts, in their schedules, or in the fabric of their lives. Let me ask you this: Do you keep going along with the flow of the world and let it erode your relationship with God? Does God have a chance to look into your heart? Do you give him time to do so? If not on Sunday, then when?

Stand up for the right to rest

Rather quaintly to modern ears, this commandment also includes the instruction that God's people are to ensure that their sons, daughters, servants, animals and foreigners (visitors) also keep the Sabbath. The principle, though, is plain and very up to date: we are to do all we can to make sure that others have the right to rest too.

Now of course that is not easy in a society that is driven by 'market forces' (frequently a polite synonym for *greed*). The battle to 'Keep Sunday Special' is far from over and we need to support efforts to give anyone who wants to, the right to have a day of rest without being pressured into work. And pressures there are. I have a good friend, Gary Grant, who is the managing director and owner of 'The Entertainer' chain of toyshops. Gary knows the challenge of keeping God's day of rest. What he said to me about how he had responded to the pressure for Sunday trading is so helpful that I want to share it.

> We started our business in 1981 with one shop in Amersham, and for the first two years worked exceedingly long hours, seven days a week, to build the business. In 1991 I became a Christian and then had a new set of parameters. This changed many aspects of our business, from product selection, to the way we treated our staff, to the hours that we worked, and especially Sunday trading.
>
> In 1994 Sunday trading became lawful, and I was really concerned about how it fitted in with my Christian belief of having a day of rest. I prayed as to whether I should open my stores on a

> Sunday. I was annoyed that God hadn't answered my prayers, but one night God said to me, 'Gary, you've had the answer, but you've been praying for the answer "yes".' And to this day, I know that the bit in the Bible where God says that he will honour those who honour him is absolutely true. I can testify that God has prospered our business as we have gone from strength to strength. We have gone from three stores back in 1991 to twenty today.
>
> The last few years haven't been easy. Many of the sites that we would have liked to open in, we have been barred from, as the landlords are only interested in people who are doing seven day trading. However, we have found that our staff of 300 are pleased we are taking a stance over Sunday trading, as it gives them the opportunity to be at home with their family and their children. As the owner of 'The Entertainer' I am in a very privileged position to be able to make the decision not to trade my business on a Sunday. We only trade for six days and our business is financially viable.

God has honoured Gary's decision. If you have to make similar decisions then I am sure that God will honour them too.

The challenge of God's day of rest

While we like the idea and the appeal of the Sabbath, we resist the reality of actually observing it. We have become Sabbath-phobic. But ignoring the Sabbath carries a heavy physical, psychological, emotional and spiritual price tag, and one that increases along with the modern pace of life. Unless we start to change now, there will come a time when it will be too late to do so. Too late, because others will have already suffered too much as a result of our obsessive haste. Times will change for the better only when we change.

Let me end this discussion of God's day of rest by pointing

out to you that it represents a deep challenge. The issue that this commandment addresses is a fundamental one: who controls our time? By keeping God's day of rest we proclaim to ourselves – and to the world – that God runs our lives. If he is Lord, he is Lord of our time.

That is why there is a battle in this area. It is not simply a question of legislation on trading hours or about cultural practices; it is about the lordship of our lives and of our culture.

I believe that we all need to follow the pattern that God has established for us. Not in some dry and wearisome ritual, but in a way that liberates us and rejuvenates us. This is not selfishness. The effects of observing the Sabbath principle are wider than just our own lives; they ripple out into wider society. As one Jewish rabbi taught, 'It was not Israel that kept the Sabbath, so much as the Sabbath that kept Israel.' It is true today; a society without Sabbaths is a society that is heading for trouble.

For one day a week, the Sabbath is a reminder that we are dispensable to work and the world, but not to our families, community and God. We need to set an example, and by our use of our precious time, show that God is Lord.

COMMANDMENT **3**

You shall not misuse the name of the L*ORD your God, for the* L*ORD will not hold anyone guiltless who misuses his name.*
(Exodus 20:7, NIV)

So what's the problem?

The shifting popularity of children's names is a fascinating aspect of our changing society. As this new century began, the most popular names were Jack for boys and Chloë for girls. A hundred years earlier, William (followed by John and George) was the favourite name for boys, with Mary (followed by Florence and Edith) the most popular for girls. You will have to look long and hard for any Williams, Florences or Ediths in today's school playgrounds. Clearly there are fashions in names, just as there are in clothes and cars.

Yet names are important. We can all remember when someone who should have known our name forgot it, or when we were mistaken for someone else. We can probably remember the emotion we felt too – hurt. We feel hurt when our name is forgotten, and there is an uncomfortable sense of losing importance. We feel that we are insignificant. Equally, think what happens when we go somewhere and we see our name misspelled on a notice. What do we do? We correct it, of course. Not because it makes any difference to how it is pronounced, but because we feel it is important that people get our name right.

In fact, we go to great lengths to protect our names. An entire branch of the legal profession exists to govern the use and abuse of names. Almost any newspaper will have an account of some court case where a newspaper, TV company, publishing house or individual is being taken to court for libel or slander. 'I need to clear my name,' those involved protest. We are very protective about our names.

The reason why we are so protective is because a name stands for something. Just to mention a name will often call up a whole set of images. For example, take a name like Adolf. Even without a surname, it conjures up images of indescribable cruelty, concentration camps and persecution. But take a name like Teresa. Especially if it's coupled with 'Mother', we see good, we are full of respect and admiration. If we have a bad name, the images people will have will be negative; if a good name, then they will have a positive and praiseworthy image. And unfortunately, not only do first impressions count, but they are hard to change. We all want people to have a positive impression of us and can feel very offended if there are malicious stories or unfair criticism going round about us. As the book of Proverbs says, 'A good name is more desirable than great riches; to be esteemed is better than silver or gold' (Proverbs 22:1, NIV).

It is not just our own names that we are sensitive about. I remember how at school we were warned about our conduct on the bus on the way home: being in school uniform, any bad behaviour would bring the school's name into disrepute. We have all watched embarrassed football managers on television, trying to distance their clubs from some act of urban devastation wreaked by their drunken fans. Clearly, not only can our names be misused, but also those of others to whom we are linked, such as schools or football clubs. This third commandment is about the disturbing fact that we can – and do – misuse God's name.

The use and misuse of God's name involves far more than matters of swearing or blasphemy. It involves a number of things that relate to who God is. And for us to understand who God is, is going to require us to do some serious thinking.

The heart of the matter

Names are more than words

Names are not just collections of consonants and vowels. They are far more than that. They have meaning, conjure up associations of ideas and images, and have power and prestige. That power and prestige can even be transferred to a third person. I'm sure many of us can remember how we used the name of some friend in order to get into a party. Some of us may have attended a high-powered conference as a delegate for a company or an organization. At an even higher level are ambassadors, who serve in foreign countries as 'the Queen's representative'.

The fact that we know that authority and status can be transferred with a name is behind a lot of advertising. I have already mentioned, in discussing the tenth commandment, the hold that product names have over us. The attraction that many expensive brand names have is due to the fact that people believe that something of the power of the name is transmitted to the wearer.

In some cases, though, names have a meaning in themselves. For many of us in Britain now, personal names mean very little.

In fact, the naming of children today often seems a frivolous activity, with the poor infant being lumbered with the names of obscure flowers, entire football teams or pieces of fruit.

For some people, and for many in other cultures, naming is still important and significant because of what the name means. Nelson Mandela wrote:

> Apart from life, a strong constitution and abiding connection to the Thembu royal house, the only thing my father bestowed upon me at birth was a name, Rolihlahla. In Xhosa, Rolihlahla literally means 'pulling the branch off the tree', but its colloquial meaning more accurately would be 'trouble maker'. I do not believe that names are destiny or that my father somehow divined my future, but in later years friends and relatives would ascribe to my birth name the many storms I have caused and weathered.[1]

Certainly, for the people of Bible times, naming a person was a serious event. Some of the names are physically descriptive. We are told in Genesis 25 when Isaac's wife Rebekah had twins, the first-born was red and covered in hair, while the second came out holding his brother's heel. As a result they called the first one 'Esau', which means 'hairy', and the other 'Jacob', which means 'he grasps the heel'. Other children in the Bible were given names that didn't describe them physically but which spoke about what God had done, or was going to do. For example, when Hannah, a barren woman who had prayed to God for a child, was blessed with a son, she called him Samuel, meaning 'God heard me'. The prophets Isaiah and Hosea both gave their children names that referred to what

---

[1] Nelson Mandela, *Long Walk to Freedom* (Little, Brown and Company, 1994), p. 3.

God was going to do. The best example of all is the name Jesus: this is the Greek form of the Hebrew 'Joshua', which means 'the LORD saves'.

The name of someone in biblical times was more than just a word that identified a person. It signified something about a person and communicated something of what they stood for; to use a name was to say who that person was. God's name was no different.

The privilege of knowing the name of God

I would love to have been in the Garden of Eden just after Adam had been given the job of naming all the animals (Genesis 2:20). It must have been a fascinating exercise and I wonder how he came up with all the names. It's hard enough naming a single pet, let alone countless species. Behind this charming picture lies, however, a very important point. Humanity had been given dominion over living things and the first act of this dominion was for Adam to give names to the animals and birds. It established the fact that Adam – one who names – was above the creatures that he named. Yet there was one being that Adam did not give a name to. That being was God.

God does not let human beings name him. Why not? One reason is that God is above us, and in the Bible the inferior does not name the superior. Another reason, and it is probably related, is the fact that no human being could name God properly. We wouldn't have a clue what to call him. Any name of God would have to refer to who God was, and would have to be in some way descriptive of him; that would be far too much for us. For one thing, we cannot understand God enough to name him and for another, our language is inadequate for us to even try. It is said that when Ludwig Wittgenstein, the famous twentieth-century philosopher, came to discuss the nature of God in lectures, he would bring a cup of steaming coffee into the room. He would then ask volunteers to describe the smell of coffee, a task that always proved impossible without saying something meaningless like, 'It has a coffee-like smell'! Wittgenstein would then make the point that if we haven't got the ability to describe accurately what coffee smells like, how on earth can we hope to describe God?

Clearly, if we were trying to name or describe God ourselves, Wittgenstein's point would be valid: we would face an impossible task. Yet thankfully this is not the case, because we read in the Bible that God has revealed both himself and his name to us. We don't have to stretch our brains trying to imagine what he is like and making up some name that we hope might do him justice. God has told us who he is and has given us his name. It is vital for us to understand that what Christianity says about God comes not from vague and fuzzy human speculations, but directly from God himself. Throughout the pages of the Bible we read that God is not a *something*, but a *someone*; a loving, personal God who cares for us and who has chosen to make himself known to humanity.

In fact when God did reveal his name, he did it in a very personal way. In Exodus 3 we read how Moses, having fled from Egypt where the Israelites were in slavery, was looking after his father-in-law's sheep in the wilderness when suddenly he came across a bush that, although it was covered in flames, was not burning. From the bush, Moses heard God call him by name. God announced that he was going to liberate his people who were in slavery, and told Moses to go back to the ruler of Egypt and bring the Israelites out of captivity. When Moses, evidently unenthusiastic about his mission, protested that he wasn't up to the task, God promised that he would go with him. Moses, still reluctant, then raised another objection. 'Suppose I go to the Israelites,' he told God, 'and say to them, "The God of your fathers has sent me to you," and they ask me, "What is his name?" Then what shall I tell them?' The answer is both powerful and mysterious. 'God said to Moses, "I AM WHO I AM. This is what you are to say to the Israelites: 'I AM has sent me to you' "' (Exodus 3:14, NIV).

Two verses later God uses a name for himself, YHWH, which is a form of I AM and which, for reasons I will explain later, is translated in most English Bibles as 'The LORD'. This word, effectively the personal name of God, occurs some 6,800 times in the Old Testament. Each time, it refers back to this great promise, I AM WHO I AM.

But what does 'I AM WHO I AM' mean? It is in fact an incredibly deep statement about God. It means something like 'I am the Living One' or 'I am the One who exists' or 'I am the One who will be who I will be'. Behind these words lies the concept of a being who is quite unlike anyone – or anything – else. God's name of I AM suggests that he is a being who is independent of everything else that exists and someone who cannot be contained. With that comes the idea of God being absolutely trustworthy and unchangeable; when he makes up his mind to do something he will do it. Furthermore, it suggests that rather than being some remote, philosophical abstraction or a vague force, God is the one who *is* someone. Who that 'someone' is, the rest of the Bible spells out, so that by the end of it we realize that God has said to us, 'I AM your Creator, Saviour, Sustainer, Leader, Protector, Healer, Helper, Judge and Comforter.'

Now in revealing his personal name, God reveals his identity to us. And in doing that he has made himself vulnerable, because for us to know someone's name is to have a hold on them. It is quite extraordinary that God should do this, because by revealing his name to us he leaves himself open to us misusing his name. Of course, when we read about Jesus and the cross we see that, in order to help us, God went further than this. It wasn't just his name he left open for us to abuse, but the life of his own Son.

In Old Testament times, people appreciated that knowing the name of God as 'I AM' was a great privilege. In fact they treated the name with such high regard that they tried to avoid using it in speech or in prayer, just in case it was misused. When the scribes came to write out the name of God, on this safety-first principle they never wrote it out in full, but only the four consonants. And when they did come to write the Hebrew letters 'YHWH' they would wash, put on new clothes, use a new quill, write the name and then throw the quill away. When they came to read the word aloud, rather than pronounce it they substituted the word 'the LORD'. In fact so reverently did they handle this word, that we are not now completely certain what it sounded like. Although our ancestors guessed that the name was 'Jehovah', scholars now think that 'Yahweh' was more likely; most English Bibles stick with 'the LORD'. In case you are worried, its exact pronunciation is not important for us as Christians because Jesus has told us that we can address God as 'Father'. Actually, in many ways, the word 'Jesus' has taken the place of the mysterious YHWH.

However strange and ritualistic to us, the point behind not using God's name at all was a very valid one. It was to ensure that, at all costs, this commandment to treat God's name with reverence was kept. I think it would be misunderstanding these people if we felt that their motive was fear, as if God's name was some sort of unexploded bomb that had to be handled with care. I think it was rather that they knew there was a great honour and a joyful privilege in knowing the name of God. After all, the fact that God had made himself known to his people was at the centre of their existence as individuals and as a nation. They were God's people and he was their God.

Jesus and the name of God

The coming of Jesus brought in a whole new era of knowing about God better, as in Jesus God reveals himself fully. In fact, through Jesus, God now invites us to be on first name terms with him.

The names that Jesus bears point to what he does for us. As we have seen, the name 'Jesus' means 'the LORD saves', but Jesus is also called Immanuel (Matthew 1:23), which means 'God with us'. Together ('God for us' and 'God with us') they sum up all who Jesus was and is. The result is that the awesome gulf between humanity and God that had existed since Adam and Eve, is now bridged. That is why Jesus is also called a mediator (1 Timothy 2:5).

In God coming to us in Jesus, there is a closeness and an intimacy that it would be hard to exaggerate. A young girl was crying in her bedroom one night and her mother came in and asked her why she was so upset. 'Mummy,' she answered, 'I'm scared because I feel all alone.'

'You're not alone, darling,' said her mother. 'God's here with you.'

'But Mummy I don't want a God I can't see. I want a God with skin on.'

Jesus is, if you like, the God with skin on. He is the God who was touched and held, who was addressed and questioned, who ate and drank, and who finally was tortured and strung up. You see, when God wants to be near us, he doesn't issue some prayer formula or a series of rules for us to follow. Instead, he comes himself as a person to whom we can relate personally. As someone has said, 'Christianity is not a religion but a relationship.'

Jesus himself models how we are now to treat God's name. As an observant Jew he would have known all the rules about how God's name was to be carefully revered. Despite this, he introduced a new name for God that shocked those around him. Using the word that a young child might call his father, Jesus referred to God as 'Abba'. His use of this term, similar to our 'Daddy', displays the intimacy and confidence of a child with a parent. Yet Jesus never played down God's majesty or holiness, or signalled in any way that God's name should be treated with any less honour than it had been.

Jesus makes this plain at the very start of the model prayer that he gives his disciples as an example of how to pray. We call it the Lord's Prayer and in a modern translation it begins, 'Our Father in heaven, may your name be honoured' (Matthew 6:8, NLT). In those two phrases, Jesus perfectly balances an intimate familiarity with God with a profound sense of the honour and respect that is due to God. In Jesus, God has become accessible instead of remote. He is not just a lord, he is now also our Father in heaven. Yet these new privileges give us even more reason to honour God's name.

Respect: an endangered attitude?

In our twenty-first-century Western world, God is not treated with respect. The names of God and Jesus are used lightly, or abused everywhere. I suspect much of this is not a deliberate attempt at attacking God, it is just part of the tide of disrespect for any authority figure that has flooded over almost every area of our culture. No one – and nothing – is respected now, and God is just one more target to mock. Institutions and organizations that were once looked up to and highly esteemed are now treated with scorn or cynicism. Parliament is no longer respected as it once was: we barely blink when we hear of politicians' indiscretions. Any senior police officer will tell you that attitudes towards the police today are very different from the respectful feelings they used to command. The most vital skill for many schoolteachers these days is not an ability to teach but to be able to exercise classroom control. Sadly, even when church leaders call for attention on certain matters, their words command little attention and even less obedience. Even the monarchy does not have the respect that it did.

Now there are complex reasons for all this, but the fact is that no one seems to get automatic respect any more. It is quite worrying. What is more than worrying – in fact it is profoundly disturbing – is that respect has even been withdrawn from God himself.

Treat God with reverence

My wife's name is 'Killy'. That name is, for me, most precious. Were I to hear someone pouring scorn on her name, abusing it, treating it flippantly or using it when they were annoyed or angry, it would hurt me very much. The reason is, of course, that Killy is the human being I love and respect more than any other. Such abuse would show that they didn't really know her, that they didn't have regard for her, and that they did not respect her.

My reaction can be predicted: I would be angry and try and put them right. My wife deserves respect. I am sure that I am not alone in having such attitudes and responses. Now, if this is true in our relationships to other human beings, how much more should it be true for how we relate to Almighty God?

Let me give you two reasons why you should respect God's name.

Respect God's name because of his actions

God deserves respect because of what he has done and continues to do. The Bible tells us that God is the creator of the universe, and that he continues to sustain it moment by moment. If God stopped his actions for even a fraction of a second, then in that brief moment of time everything – all the stars, all the cells in our bodies, every atom and molecule – would vanish into nothingness. There would just be nothing; nothing at all. When we think of that, we should realize that God is worthy of the highest respect and honour that we can manage.

God makes a similar point, only using pictorial language, in the book of Job. Job has suffered greatly; everything and almost everyone he has loved and enjoyed has been taken away from him. Although Job keeps his faith in God, eventually he comes to the point where he complains to God about the unfairness of his suffering. He demands answers. God's reply comes with thunder:

> Who is this that questions my wisdom with such ignorant words? Brace yourself, because I have some questions for you, and you must answer them.
>
> Where were you when I laid the foundations of the earth? Tell me, if you know so much. Do you know how its dimensions were

> determined and who did the surveying? What supports its foundations, and who laid its cornerstone as the morning stars sang together and all the angels shouted for joy? (Job 38:2–7, NLT)

In the two chapters that follow, God challenges Job with more and more questions. Their effect is to make Job realize both how great God is and how small he himself is. It is a lesson we badly need to learn today.

God's name should be honoured because he is powerful. We have learned to revere power when we can measure it in volts, horsepower or tons of TNT equivalent. No one, unless they are very naïve or stupid, tries to play with a high voltage electric cable, or go for a swim in a sea of storm-driven waves. We have a wise fear of what will happen to us. Yet people play around with the name of God, and God is the one who is inconceivably more powerful than any force we can imagine.

Think of the power of the most common name, 'Mum'. The children are in their bedroom playing and all of a sudden there is screaming and crying. What happens next? One of them will come running out and cry, 'Mum, Mum, he just keeps hitting me!' And Mum says, 'You go and tell your brother that I said to stop fighting.' Then the child will run back, and what's the first thing you hear? 'Mum said . . .' The child has gained power. How? By using Mum's name. How much more power exists in God's name.

In the Bible, we are told there is power in God's name. Not power in any magical sense, but because behind the name stands the one who is all-powerful, all-seeing and all-knowing. God is the one who started the entire creation, who holds it all together and who will, one day, reshape it. God has power over all things: over the laws of nature, over life and over death.

God's name has power and should be revered. Calling on his name brings salvation: 'everyone who calls on the name of the Lord will be saved' (Acts 2:21). In God's name evil is rebuked, in his name healing is given, in his name acts of service are done and in his name people are commissioned and sent out for service. His name should be treated with reverence. One day it will be. In the future, we are told, at his name 'every knee should bow . . . and every tongue confess that Jesus Christ is Lord' (Philippians 2:10, NIV).

There are lessons here for all of us, not just with regard to blasphemy or swearing. In the film *Leap of Faith*, Steve Martin plays a travelling revivalist preacher, touring round America with a large tent and all the trappings. He offers healings, encounters with God and life-changing miracles. The man is actually a fraud and the film cynically portrays the whole thing as a money-making sham with everything staged and manipulated. At the end of the film, though, a real healing of a young boy on crutches occurs. The preacher is left bewildered and frightened, and the fear of God falls upon him and his team.

God is a powerful God. To misuse his name is dangerous. The Bible and commonsense agree: those who play with God's name, in attempts to use him for their own benefit, are playing with fire. And they are likely to get more than their fingers burned.

Respect God's name because of his character

It is not just God's awesome power that should make us cautious about misusing his name; it is also his character. We worship God not just because he is powerful (after all, a dictator may have power), but because God is perfect and holy. What we find admirable in other people (their love, wisdom and thoughtfulness) we find in God to an unlimited extent. People may sometimes be kind, truthful and holy, but God is always love, truth and holiness.

All human beings are, to a greater or lesser extent, sinful. If our names are misused then we may well deserve it. There may even be some truth in some of the things that are said about us. But with God there can never be any grounds for misusing his name. God is free from sin and full of everything that is good and right.

To misuse God's name is foolish because of his mighty power; it is also immoral because of his perfect character.

How to honour God's name

Let me now give you four ways in which we can honour God's name.

Don't swear

If you are anything like me, the first thing you think about when you think of this commandment is swearing. In my dear friend Dr R. T. Kendall's book on the Commandments, *Just Grace*, he points out that in the ninth edition of *The Concise Oxford Dictionary* (published in 1995) the entry under the word 'Jesus' is as follows:

> **Jesus**: *Colloquial interjection.* An exclamation of surprise, dismay, etc. [name of founder of Christian religion d. *c.* AD 30.]

In other words, 'Jesus' is to be understood first as a common expletive and only then as the name of the founder of Christianity. As outrageous as that is, it is a sign of the times. If a film has sexual swear words in it, the British Board of Film Classification will require it to be given a '15' certificate, but if it has blasphemies in it, it can be given a PG rating. In this environment, I think the majority of us have just become numb to the way that God's name is so widely abused in our society.

Let me suggest some ways in which we can counter this. First, we can watch our own language and make sure that we don't use God's name in a way that is dishonouring. Second, we can be prepared to take people to task for it. There are imaginative and sensitive ways that we can make others aware of the language they are using. In fact in most cases people do not realize that what they are saying is offensive. For instance, if I hear someone reply to a question with 'God knows!' I often respond with something like 'Yes, he does actually'. If people say 'Jesus!' as a swear word I will often ask 'Who?' or 'So you know my best friend do you?' It may even be that their realization that you take God and Jesus seriously may open the door to a very interesting conversation. Third, we can let our voice be heard about the misuse of God's name in the media, especially on radio and television. A letter or a phone call is treated with quite some weight in these media organizations, and if you see or hear something that offends you, then let them know. The names and addresses of some media organizations are at the back of the book. You might point out that we are only demanding equal treatment with Muslims; after all, no scriptwriter would use the word Muhammad as a swear word!

Decide today not to use the name of God in an irreverent, frivolous and disrespectful way. If you would not call yourself a Christian, then on behalf of those of us who would, can I ask you to do us a favour and respect our God's name? Having read what I have written above, you will see why we find it hurtful.

Don't name-drop with God

This commandment addresses far more than open blasphemy, and there are ways in which even those who would never dream of swearing can break this commandment.

One subtle temptation is to name-drop with God. Now name-dropping is perhaps one of the commonest human traits. We let people know, either openly or in a more understated way, that we know X as a friend and we imply that he or she values our friendship. X may be a politician, a film star, a sports personality, a novelist or even, if we are desperate, a preacher. There are the blatant name-droppers, who openly and unashamedly make us know who they recently saw or talked with, and there are the more subtle kind who somehow always manage to let it slip out that they know important people. By name-dropping what we are doing is boosting ourselves by hanging on to the coat tails of someone else's reputation. By borrowing glory from them, who we are – and what we say – becomes far more important. Now when we do this with human personalities we merely make ourselves look foolish and expose our insecurity, but when we do it with God we run far greater risks.

Misusing God's name this way has been distressingly common at a national level. In history there have been far too many 'holy crusades', 'sacred struggles' and 'wars in defence of Christian values'. God has been used to justify apartheid in South Africa, death camps in Nazi Germany, and under such titles as 'our mission to bring civilization' any number of greedy imperialistic ventures have been undertaken. We need to be wary of thinking that such things are in the past: God's name has been invoked on both sides in Northern Ireland. To invoke God or Christianity to enable us to oppress, intimidate, hurt or exploit others surely involves a breach of this commandment. Those who do this will have to give an account of their claims. Our leaders would do well to learn from President Lincoln's wisdom. Shortly after the fall of Atlanta during the American Civil War, a woman exclaimed to President Lincoln at a White House function, 'Oh, Mr President, I feel sure that God is on our side . . . don't you?'

'Ma'am,' replied Lincoln solemnly, 'I am more concerned that we should be on God's side.'

This sort of abuse can also occur with us as individuals and even within churches. We can use God's name to make us look good or to further our own projects. We name-drop God to give ourselves the ultimate credibility, sometimes allowing God's name to confidently underwrite something that is no more than a hunch or wish of ours. We can do it on a personal level and justify the end result with such words as 'The Lord showed me that . . .' The problem is that sometimes statements like this may be true; God *may* have spoken to us as an individual or to us as a church. But he may not, and there is often a temptation to bring him in to justify some plan that we have (especially when it needs a helping hand).

Please do not misunderstand me: I am not saying that God does not speak today. That would contradict the Bible and does not honour his name. I believe that God speaks to the church, he speaks to me as an individual about my life and work, and I believe he speaks through other Christians too. Yet I do not think that we should immediately believe everything that is claimed as being from God. Both as individuals and churches we must realize the seriousness of claiming that God has given us something specific for a situation or person. This is particularly so when the vision or prophetic word is likely to have significant implications for the person concerned.

The apostle Paul is helpful in this area. In his first letter to the church at Corinth he distinguishes clearly between what is his own advice and what he knows is from God. So in 1 Corinthians 7:10 he says, 'To the married I give this command (not I but the Lord),' and then two verses later he says, 'To the rest I say this (I, not the Lord).' Elsewhere he emphasizes the need for discernment: 'Do not put out the Spirit's fire; do not treat prophecies with contempt. Test everything. Hold on to the good. Avoid every kind of evil' (1 Thessalonians 5:19–22, NIV).

Normally, when you take someone else's name and use it for your own ends, it is called forgery. When, either unconsciously or consciously, we attach God's name to something he has not said, it is as if we were writing a cheque and forging God's signature on the bottom. Because God makes promises, he is not pleased when we invent promises that he has not written and pass them off as his. We must beware of spiritual forgery.

Don't cheat God of his honour

Strangely, we can misuse God's name by not mentioning it at all. All too often, when we do something praiseworthy, we personally receive all the honour. This is sadly true even if it is in answer to prayer. Often God doesn't even make it into the credit list of our lives. If the temptation we considered previously was to say that God did something that he didn't, this is the opposite: it is the temptation to say that God didn't do something, when he did.

We need to honour God by crediting him with all that he

does. To do this requires the much-neglected virtue of humility. Humility means that when it comes to any sort of award ceremony we step back and wave God forward into the spotlight. After all, everything we have, we have been given by him. Even what we are inclined to think of as our own talents are nothing of the sort: they have been given to us – or more properly loaned to us – by God himself. Humility is to receive praise, and to pass it on to God untouched.

Again the apostle Paul can teach us a lot. Not long after the church at Corinth was founded, some men who considered themselves 'super-apostles' began to trouble it. By boasting of what they were and what they had done, they were able to exert a harmful influence. In 2 Corinthians Paul addresses this problem and actually boasts of his sufferings. At one point (2 Corinthians 12:1–7) Paul talks about 'a man I know' who had the most extraordinary vision of heaven, seeing things that 'no-one should tell of'. The odd thing is that a couple of times Paul lets slip that it was him, but because he is trying to be humble, he tells it as if it wasn't him. He goes on to say that actually he prefers 'to boast about my weaknesses, so that the power of Christ may work through me' (2 Corinthians 12:9, NLT). In some circles it is all too common to hear people boasting of the wonderful visions and experiences they have had, as if they had earned them. In contrast, Paul had a stunning vision, but then refused to talk about it and instead changed the topic to his own weaknesses! Paul was anxious that God should get the glory and in this he was honouring God's name, not his own.

How do we get attitudes like Paul's so that we give glory where glory is due? One way would be to lower our value of ourselves; to stand in front of the mirror and tell ourselves that we are worthless wretches and miserable worms. Don't laugh

– such techniques have been taught. No, I think the best solution is not to lower ourselves, but to elevate God. And we elevate God by worshipping him. The best antidote to the misuse of God's name is to ensure its proper use, and the best way of using God's name properly is through praise and prayer. This is not the place to talk in detail about how we worship God, but I believe that if our worship was more God-centred the temptation to break this commandment would be drastically reduced.

There is a danger today that our worship revolves around *us*, when its true focus should be God. I said earlier about how the temptation of name-dropping is that it makes us look good. We must be careful that something similar does not creep into our worship. Neither prayer nor worship is meant to exalt us. There is wisdom in the story of two people who were coming out of church and one asked the other how they had found the service. 'Oh,' came the reply, 'I didn't get anything out of the worship.'

'I'm sorry,' was the response. 'I didn't realize it was for you.'

Worship is for God's benefit not ours. Frequently, when listening to songs and prayers, I have wondered whether we have it all the wrong way round and are making ourselves the centre and expecting God to circle around us at our disposal. We must be careful to give glory to God alone.

In this matter of not cheating God, let me ask you to review those things that you are most proud of; the things that you count as your achievements. Are you giving God adequate credit for all he has done and is doing? Have you ever thanked God for them? Do you feel that in these areas you have given him the honour that's due to him? If not, why not do it now?

Can I also ask you to review your present spiritual life? When you pray are your prayers God-centred? Or are they self-centred? Believe me, these are hard questions for all of us, but if we are going to take this command seriously we need to respond to them. We honour God by crediting God with all that he does and is. By stealing glory for ourselves we break this commandment.

Don't live an inconsistent life

Finally, we can dishonour God's name without ever speaking a word. In fact, our words can be excellent: they can be free from swearing or any name-dropping of God, yet we can still dishonour God if the lives we live do not match up to the words we speak. We need to live lives that show that the words we say are true. Now that's difficult, but it is essential. One reason, I believe, why the church's reputation has suffered lies here. Too many people have heard 'religious' people say one thing and then seen them do another.

When Jesus ascended to heaven his followers on earth became his body and continued his work and witness. Very soon they became known by his name, as 'Christians'. Interestingly, it does not seem this was a name that they gave themselves. Instead, outsiders – who saw how central Jesus Christ was to what these people did and said – decided that *Christ*ian was a good term for them. His followers bore his name then, and they still do.

Now as Christians who carry this name, we are called to live lives that are worthy of the name of Jesus. It is as if we go through life with his name marked on us. Often Paul encourages us to be worthy; of some false believers he says, 'They claim to know God, but by their actions they deny him' (Titus 1:16, NIV). We are urged not to bring disrepute on the family name by our behaviour. We must always ask ourselves whether there is a gap between our beliefs and our actions.

In closing, there is one more thing that I feel needs to be said. It is that the whole issue of names is at the heart of our relationship with God. In Jesus, as I said earlier, we can be on first-name terms with God. Jesus in turn tells us that God cares for us so much that he knows every detail of who we are. Yet this is just the beginning of the relationship, for the amazing thing that happens when we begin to honour God's name is that he honours us back. The nearer we draw to him, the closer he comes to us. The more we call him by name, the more we hear him calling us by name. As we do this, we learn one of the most wonderful truths about God: you can never out-give him and you can never out-love him. To honour God's name is to put in process a chain of events that, one glorious day, will result in us seeing God face to face.

COMMANDMENT 2

You shall not make for yourself an idol in the form of anything in heaven above or on the earth beneath or in the waters below. You shall not bow down to them or worship them; for I, the LORD *your God, am a jealous God, punishing the children for the sin of the fathers to the third and fourth generation of those who hate me, but showing love to a thousand generations of those who love me and keep my commandments.*

(Exodus 20:4, NIV)

So what's the problem?

A confused world

Our voyage into the Ten Commandments has taken us a long way. We started by looking at coveting, lying, stealing, adultery and murder; topics that deal very much with how we relate to our neighbours and those around us. We then came to the command to honour our parents, with all its implications for family life. Then we examined those commandments that focus not on those we meet or are related to, but on God himself. At first it was indirect, as we looked at how we remember God and look after ourselves by keeping a Sabbath. Then, more directly, it was how we honour God's name. Now, as we come to the heart of the Commandments, we will be focusing more and more on who God is. When we examine the first commandment, we will face the awesome glory of the nature of the one true God. This second commandment deals with a vital and related issue: not so much who God is, but who God is not. Now of course who God is and who he isn't are two sides of the same coin, and both commandments need to be read together. But it is useful here to deal solely with the topic of idolatry – the giving of worship to things that are not God. There's a lot of it about.

There is now a confusion that has not existed for centuries about who (if anybody) we worship in this country. In fact you would probably have to go back over fifteen hundred years to find a similar turmoil in Britain. From Anglo-Saxon times until the present there have been many religious debates and disputes in British history. Some of these disputes were over vital matters and some of them were over trivial issues. But whether serious or stupid, they were all about Christianity, and the issues they dealt with were basically how we worship the God of the Bible. They were not about who or what we worshipped – that at least could be taken for granted. But not any more.

There is now an extraordinary bewilderment about whether we worship one god, many gods or no gods at all. The best definition for the national religious beliefs that anyone can come up with is the totally meaningless statement that in Britain we are 'post-Christian'. It is hard to map the present religious scene in Britain, and it would need another book to do it. Let me confine myself to making some brief observations.

Clearly there has been a decline in traditional or institutional Christianity in Britain. With some splendid exceptions, church attendance is in decline and knowledge of Christianity is very limited. A generation ago the idea of doing what I have been doing, teaching people about the Ten Commandments, would have been strange, because they were part of the fabric of our society and even if we didn't keep them we were familiar with them. Now it is a strange idea because most us don't have a clue what they are!

Yet it is not as though we have moved to being an agnostic or atheistic society; religion is alive and well in modern Britain. Two trends are important. The first is that Britain now has sizeable Muslim, Sikh and Hindu populations. These represent what we can call formal religions with their own traditions, structures and rituals.

A second phenomenon is the rise of what is generally summarized under the phrase 'New Age religion'. Akin to a spiritual shopping mall of a thousand beliefs, New Age is hard to classify. Apart from where it grades into Hinduism or Buddhism, New Age is a very informal belief; after all, one of its attractions is that you can do what you want. Whether it's meditation, feng shui, Gaia, reincarnation, astrology, crystals, tarot or rebirthing, it's all on offer today and you can pick and mix to suit yourself. You can believe what you want with New Age.

The arrival of other formal religions and the spread of New Age beliefs, in a situation where the church was weakened after a century of conflict over issues of philosophy, evolution and other matters, has produced a confused and misty religious landscape. In the spiritual haze of modern Britain, I think three linked features stand out.

The first is the widespread rejection of any sort of authority in the religious area. 'I'll believe what I want,' people say proudly. Curiously enough, they are often the same people who assure you, with an unshakeable confidence, 'Of course you can't believe that bit in the Bible.' When you ask why not, they say that they heard someone on the radio telling them they couldn't. Eighty-five per cent of the population might well say they 'believe in God', but if you asked them to describe the God that they believe in, the answers would be as varied and different as the people you asked. The fact that the Bible speaks with authority on such matters really does not make it – or Christians who believe it – popular.

A second feature is the preference for spiritual beliefs that are undemanding. Religion today is presented as some sort of lifestyle option, like keep-fit or gardening. It is simply the 'spiritual dimension' to life; if you need fulfilment, then you tack some spirituality on. Now Christianity, people protest, is narrow and oppressive because of the fact that it denies so much. Besides, it makes ethical demands; it says 'do this' and 'don't do that'. That is not popular. People ask what morality has got to do with being spiritual. Much religion today is something that we are supposed to *feel*; it is a matter of mood. And doing what is right can often get in the way of feeling spiritual. In the supermarket of New Age beliefs, the big sellers are the packets that have on them 'low in moral demands'.

A third feature of modern religion is the widespread belief in the sort of tolerance that wants nothing to be ruled out. 'It may not be for me,' people say, 'but we'd better not knock it.' This goes for beliefs and for morals. One of the few New Age commandments is 'Thou shall not say "thou shall not"'. Anything goes today; apart from bloodsports, fur coats and new bypasses. The thing that irritates such people about Christianity is not so much what it affirms, but what it denies. They can probably be persuaded to say that Jesus was good and wise and maybe a 'son of God', but to say that he is the only way to God is too narrow and restricting.

The upshot is that Christianity is not the flavour of the month. It is too inflexible, too dogmatic, too restrictive and too demanding. People want a religion that they can tailor to suit their circumstances. God should fit in with us, rather than us fitting in with him.

In fact, today we prefer to make God in our own image. For example, the Girl Guides Association has revised the words of the Guide promise from promising to 'do my duty to God' to 'do my duty to my God'. That new two-letter word covers a vast difference between the promises. Now, the thing that defines God is me; I can create a god as I would want him (or her, or it) to be.

The writer G. K. Chesterton said, 'When people stop believing in God they don't believe in nothing, they believe in anything.' Chesterton died in 1936. I think he would have been horrified to see how, within 70 years, British national religion had come to match his statement so closely. We now worship anything that suits us. The problem is that this 'anything' is idolatry.

Idolatry today

I think that one of the biggest dangers surrounding idolatry is the screen of preconceptions that prevents us from seeing what it really is. When we think of idols and idolatry, our minds conjure up pictures of statues in exotic Far Eastern temples. For most of us, bowing down to some carved piece of wood or stone seems illogical, unattractive and rather ridiculous. We smile at the thought. 'No,' we say. 'That's one commandment you will never see me breaking!'

This view is dangerous for several reasons. One is that it obscures the extent, variety and subtlety of the idolatry that we face today. Idolatry does not involve just bizarre ancient sculptures and carvings. It is as up to date as you and I; in fact, it is probably more so. The principle that every human being is prone to worship what is not God is, I believe, a universal one. Idolatry has always been there and it always will be there. The only thing that changes is the nature of the idols.

Idols do not have to be figures made of stone or precious metal; they do not have to be things that you can touch and hold at all. In fact, I suspect that some of the most powerful idols exist only in the mind. Human understanding is a workshop where idols are continually being crafted.

What is an idol? There are so many idols and they are so subtle that a simple definition is hard. Let me try to express it this way. Christians could make the following statements about God:

- *God* gives purpose, meaning and fulfilment to their lives.
- *God* governs the way they act.
- *God* is the focal point around which their existence hangs.
- *God* is often in their thoughts and they get enthusiastic about *God*.
- Thoughts of *God* comfort them when they are down.
- They read about *God*, they talk about *God*, they make friends with those who are also committed to *God*.
- They desire more of *God*.

You've got the picture? Now idolatry is where something – anything – takes the place of God in this central position. An idol is anything that you could put in place of the word *God* in statements like those above. Try it with 'money', 'possessions', 'careers', 'holidays', 'sport', 'music', 'sex' or almost anything else. That is what an idol is. An idol is what people live for. An idol is what fills our minds when we lie awake at night; idols are what we buy magazines about; idols are what we spend our time, money and energy on. Idolatry occurs when we hold any value, idea or activity higher than God.

The heart of the matter

Let me raise two questions. Why are we so prone to idolatry? Are idols that bad anyway? I believe that if we can answer these questions we will have come a long way to understanding what the problem of idolatry is.

The attraction of idolatry

Idolatry, it seems, is a universal feature of the human species. Yet why is it so attractive?

The first thing to say is that idols are not basically evil. In fact, the most dangerous idols are actually good things that have been twisted. Think of the things I just listed as being potential idols: money, possessions, careers, holidays, sport, music, sex. Not a single one of them is bad – they are all good, and all gifts of God. And as good things they retain their attraction for us. In fact, it is the very best things that make the most tempting idols.

Let me give an example of how this works with one very dangerous modern idol: nationalism. Now God made different peoples, ethnic groups and races. God obviously appreciates diversity and he delights in such differences. I have no doubt it is a good thing to celebrate our culture, to love our nation and to be proud of it. It can give worth, purpose and value to those involved and make us feel far more significant. Yet it is all too easy for those attitudes to slide over into something far nastier. If the race or the nation that we belong to starts to become the central feature in our lives, then we must be careful. Once we start saying that we are better than our neighbours, or that any means justifies us beating them in sport or business, then we are in trouble. It is not hard to see where nationalism can lead you: you only have to look at Hitler's Germany or Rwanda or the modern Balkans.

Sadly, even churches are not exempt from idolatry. Organs, music groups, fine preaching and correct theology are all good things, and there is no reason why we can't take pride in them. But it is all too easy for them to acquire a distorted prominence. When they do, we can start to hear contemptuous voices saying how inferior those churches are that lack these things. Now at this point, such things have ceased to be good, and they have started to become idols. When finally they become the focus of what we are and what we stand for as churches, then I feel that God tends to leave quietly by the back door. He will not share his worship with any idols.

The other attraction of idolatry is that idols are generally tame gods that you can keep at arm's length. For one thing, they make fewer moral demands on us than the real God. The one true God is so uncompromising that idols present something of an attractive alternative. For a start, they rarely insist that you give up adultery, lying or theft, but God does.

The classic example of the attractions of idolatry can be found in the Bible. Even as God was giving this commandment to Moses on Mount Sinai, the Israelites were breaking it. Why? Moses, we are told, had been up the mountain for some days and the people were frustrated and impatient with waiting for God. They wanted something instant and immediate. So Aaron melted down their jewellery, cast it into a golden calf and presented it to the people as a substitute focus for their worship. The attraction of idols is not that they are gods; it is that we know they are not gods. Idols offer the possibility to men and women of making their own controllable god: one they can deal with on their terms.

It is because we cannot picture God in our minds that we are tempted to create an idol. Down through history people have made symbols to represent the things they cannot see. People have argued that if images help us to worship God, then they have some value. The problem is that aids to worship can easily become objects of worship. God knows that any image we might use to portray him would depict him as less than he truly is. Eventually we would begin to conceive of him in ways that mirror the image we constructed. It is so nearly right – but it is wrong. To fill God's place with an image is like blotting the sun out and substituting a 45 watt bulb in its place.

It is not wise to underestimate the subtle attraction of idols. The story of King Solomon is very sobering. He was the wisest man of his day, a zealous and pious constructor of the temple and a man whom God had appeared to twice (see 1 Kings 3–10). Yet we read in 1 Kings 11 how in his old age he turned to the worship of foreign gods and incurred God's anger. If a man like Solomon can fall into idolatry, then you and I ought to be very careful.

The adultery of idolatry

'But so what?' I hear people say. Does it matter that the New Britain is awash with a thousand varieties of formal and informal religion? Does it matter that for many, football, shopping or films are what is at the heart of their lives?

With regard to these other religions and beliefs, I can imagine people saying: 'Well, isn't God big enough to handle this? Does God really mind whether he is called "Krishna", "Gaia" or "Great Light of the Cosmos"'? Can't he just say about such prayers and devotions, "Well, I know what they mean. They may have the wrong address on their prayers but I'll just redirect them to me"? And if people worship rocks, trees or crystals does it really matter? I mean, no one's perfect. Besides shouldn't the church (and God) be glad of any devotion, whatever form it may take?' I can hear people protest that surely God doesn't mind if our hobbies, causes and pursuits are the core of our lives? After all, he made these things. God can't seriously be threatened by someone's love of their garden, fishing or Manchester United?

To answer these questions I need to talk about something that may seem a very long way from religion and idolatry. I need to talk about adultery.

I love my wife Killy very, very much. We were married in 1983 and I am more in love with her today than when we married. But can you imagine how she would feel if, finding my wallet on my desk, she noticed a photo of another woman alongside the one that I have of her? Do you think that she would say, 'Well this is interesting, but my husband is entitled to his freedom and privacy so I won't ask any more'? Don't you think it far more likely that she would immediately find me and demand to know who this other woman was and what her picture was doing in my wallet? What do you imagine her reaction would be if she learned that I had developed a friendship with this woman outside of our marriage and that I turned to her when I felt especially in need of support, affection or encouragement? Do you think it would upset Killy? Do you really think that she would continue to believe me when I whispered in her ear that I loved her with all my heart? Could you blame her if she confronted me, tore the photograph into pieces and demanded that I never see the other woman again? Could you fault her for feeling jealous, hurt, betrayed and angry about having to share my love and devotion with another?

These are obviously absurd questions. You can't love a person and be tolerant of other loves. You can't love someone and be indifferent about them having an affair. Killy is my wife; she has every right to expect and insist that I keep myself for her, and her alone. And I want to live up to those expectations, because I love her, I need her and our relationship is the most important earthly thing I have. And the idea that there might be 'someone else' is terrible to both of us. Yet a scenario like this goes to the heart of the issue that is addressed in this commandment.

Surely though, you protest, this commandment is about idols? And besides, didn't we deal with adultery earlier? In fact, this commandment is about how we love God, a relationship for which the nearest parallel we have is marriage. In marriage, there is no room for any other person, precisely because a marriage is totally based on a unique and exclusive relationship between two people. That exclusivity is at the very heart of what a marriage is all about. And our relationship with God is to be similar.

The idea of using marriage as an image for how we relate to God is not mine. It is God's, and we find it used directly and indirectly several times in the Bible. There are many similarities between a relationship with God and a marriage.

Both are personal relationships that are bound by pledges of faithfulness and priority. In fact the concept of a covenant, a mutually binding treaty of one party to another, lies at the heart of both relationships. As the husband and wife make promises exclusively to each other, so God and his people make similar promises; he to protect and bless us and we to trust and obey him. A key element of any covenant, ancient or modern, is its restricted nature; it is *only* between the named parties. The exclusivity that is at the core of a marriage is also at the heart of our relationship with God. If you think about it, there cannot be any sort of heart-to-heart intimacy between two individuals unless all third parties are ruthlessly excluded.

Now idols are those things that tempt us away from our exclusive bond to God. They strike at the very foundation of this relationship with him by introducing 'someone else'. God is as uncompromising about the purity of his relationship with us as any partner in a marriage – in fact even more so. In the Bible, he uses strong language about what bringing any idols into this relationship means. It is adultery, unfaithfulness, a breaking of a sworn agreement, the very deepest breach of trust and devotion. In short, God wants sole rights to our worship.

Confronting idolatry today

I want now to look at how we combat idolatry. First, I want to give you some signposts on strategy and then I want to look at some specific areas where idolatry needs to be confronted today.

How to confront idolatry

Recognize a double danger. Engaging with idolatry is far from easy. Let me suggest that two opposite dangers exist.

The first danger is that of simply giving up. Faced with overwhelming pressure from our culture to worship such things as sex, power and possessions, we could just shrug our shoulders in defeat. It is all too much, we might say. The only hope, we conclude, is that we can preserve an idol-free hour in our churches on Sunday. This is wrong. If we realize how serious idolatry is, and how much of an affront it is to God, we cannot simply give in. Besides, for how long would our holy hour survive?

A second danger is subtler. It is to look at what the idolatry centres on and to reject that. Is sex being worshipped? Then the response is to be against sex. Is meditation being made a god? Then the response is to reject anything in our own worship that remotely smacks of being contemplative. Is sport becoming an idol? Then the response is to preach against it and to be suspicious of anyone in the congregation in trainers. Is being green replacing being godly? Then the response is to ostentatiously drive to church rather than walk.

Now of course, because what is at the heart of almost all idolatry is good, this results in a strategy that almost certainly hurts us more than it hurts idolatry. We reject what is good for us, simply because it has been abused by others. Taken to a logical conclusion, when we are faced – as we are today – with so many idols, the only strategy is to reject everything. Such an approach also has the habit of making Christians seem joyless and negative; they are always against something.

It is easy to find ourselves trapped between these two

positions of defeatism or unconditional rejection. Let me suggest a more profitable strategy.

Plant the flag for God! The theologian Dr Tom Wright talks about a discovery that he made which helps us address the question as to what we should do to confront idolatry. He tells that when the first Christians arrived in Britain and started to build places of worship, they chose to build them on sites that the pagans had used for worship. Why did they choose to build on top of places where there had been temples and shrines to pagan gods? Was it because there was something special about those places? No, it wasn't that. Rather, it was a conscious decision to say something about Christianity: that the call to us is to worship God in places where idols are worshipped. It is to plant the flag for God in hostile soil, to claim the good things of God for him, to proclaim that only under the loving and gracious gaze of God can everything be held in the right balance and with the right perspective.

I find this a very helpful concept. Instead of running away scared or looking around seeking what we can reject because it has been contaminated by idolaters, this gives us a better alternative. Of course, it's harder work, but then most good ideas are.

Some current confrontations

With these things in mind, I want us now to look at five areas where there is a struggle against idolatry going on. This is not an exhaustive list, nor are these five necessarily the worst issues. But they make good case studies and I believe that the principles that we see in them can be applied elsewhere.

Preserving the natural world. As I suggested earlier, as a rule the best things make the most tempting idols. It is when God's handiwork is at its best that we are most tempted to worship it, instead of its creator. Nowhere is this truer than in the area of the environment.

Until almost within living memory, humanity's attitude to the natural world was straightforward. Life was a hard struggle for existence against the elements, the seasons, and predators and pests great and small. For most people, nature was something that you battled against, because if you didn't, you starved. Only the rich had the luxury of contemplating the majesty of nature in the grandeur of the mountains; the poor were too busy bent over their ploughs to look up. The idea that we could do harm to the natural world did not enter many people's minds. After all, wasn't nature effectively infinite? Suddenly, in the past few decades, there has been a growing realization that our species is capable of doing permanent and lasting harm to the world. Indeed, as the ever-growing list of extinct species demonstrates, we have already done it. The result of this has been a great deal of interest in the environment – something which is good, right and long overdue.

Yet parallel to this concern has emerged a variety of views associated with the New Age movement in which the earth, living things and indeed Nature (always with a capital letter) are to be worshipped. Indeed some people, digging around in old mythologies, have revived terms such as *Mother Earth* or *Gaia* for the planet and have credited her (feminine deities are currently fashionable) with being the creator. People recite mantras to life, invoke the spirits of winds and atmospheric energies, and protest that all life, whether plant, animal or human, is of equal value. Some wild places have become sacred sites, mystical glades or focal points of spirit power.

Now actually, as Christians we have some sympathies with people who hold such ideas. They have rejected the atheistic view that there is nothing but cold, sterile biology, physics and chemistry in our world. So have we. They recognize in woods, animals and countryside something wonderful, something far greater than anything that time, chance and natural selection could produce. So do we. Where we must, sadly, part company is over what it all means. They see Nature as so wonderful that it is to be worshipped; we see it as the wonderful craftsmanship of God the Creator, who alone is to be worshipped. The splendour of the natural world is to us a mirror in which God's glory is reflected. The distinction is important; I know that Killy would think me very strange if I paid more attention to her reflection than to her.

So what should we do when, in this area of the environment, we see a good thing being turned into an idol? As I suggested earlier, the answer is not, I'm afraid, simply to scream 'Idolatry!' and run away with our eyes closed. The solution is that we need to 'plant a flag for God' in this area. To do that means first the hard work of thinking and praying through how we should treat the natural world, and then the even harder work of getting out there and doing it.

In fact there are an increasing number of Christians involved in conserving the environment and there are some remarkable projects underway in the name of God. At the back of this book I have given the address of an organization you could get involved in.

Incidentally, it turns out that the worship of Nature is not actually a very good basis for conservation at all. There are, after all, often hard decisions to be made. For example if rats threaten rare seabird colonies, can we take the life of the rats when they are a sacred part of Nature? If all life is holy, how dare we intervene at all? The Christian view of us holding a delegated responsibility for the natural world, and of being God's stewards, is actually a far safer one.

Sex. Whether in Soho's strip joints, the pages of *Playboy*, the office affair or at a teenagers' party, erotic love continues to entice us with the promise of bliss and escape. Although there is nothing new in this – after all, eroticism has always existed – it would probably be difficult to find a culture where it has had the grip that it currently has on us. In our discussion of the seventh commandment, I talked about the effect that the worship of sex has on our society, and there is no need to go over that again here. But here is a classic case of idolatry. How do we deal with it?

In fact the principles are similar to those I outlined before. Here too there is a temptation to adopt a simple solution and reject the good that is being abused. This has led in the past to attempts either to enforce celibacy or to deny, even in the right circumstances, the good of eroticism. Here problems arise. When sex is not talked about, sexuality soon becomes something to be wary of and kept away from. The trouble is that sexuality is too potent a force to be neutralized by simply pushing it below the surface of our lives. Out of sight, the clock on the bomb may still be ticking. Some people are so afraid of facing up to their problems in the area of sex that they try to pretend that they have no past or present struggles. This can be the recipe for future disaster. If this is you, I urge you to seek professional advice.

With sex, we need again to be those who 'plant the flag' for God. It will not be easy. The middle of a battlefield is never an easy place to plant any flag, and I have no doubt that both sides will misunderstand us when we try and set up God's ideal standards and claim this whole area of human life for him. We will need to be patient and gracious with those who are victims of the god of sex – an ever-increasing number of whom are cast aside, hurting people who need the healing of the God of life.

The body. The whole discussion on sexuality leads to another major god of our age – the perfect body. In this 'feel good' age, the second commandment could read 'Do not make "yourself" an idol.' 'How do I look?' has become a question that haunts both sexes, especially from adolescence upwards. We are surrounded by examples of those who are portrayed as being physically perfect: the super-thin supermodels, the lean and muscular footballers, the glamorous and immaculately groomed rich. In a million air-brushed and digitally manipulated glossy pictures, human perfection is laid out before us. 'Are you like this?' ask the advertisements. And depressed and guilty we stare at ourselves in the mirror and try to tug our waistlines in. We bow to what the scales say about us, and let their verdict determine how we feel about ourselves. It is idolatry.

On the idolatrous altar of the perfect body we pile up sacrifices; especially if we don't match up to the cruelly rigid criteria of beauty and looks. In order to try to live up to these impossible standards held up before us, we sacrifice wealth, time and health. We feel we must stave off age and its ravages at all costs, whether by beauty treatments or surgery. Women especially feel this enslaving compulsion to fit the mould – a mould more often than not created by men. The victims are everywhere. Low self-image is common among young people who feel that they just don't look right, and the numbers of people suffering from eating disorders like anorexia and bulimia have never been higher. If this is something you feel caught up in, or you are concerned about someone you know who is struggling with this, then I would urge you to seek professional help. Your local GP will be able to recommend people for you to talk to.

Yet when we look at this idolatry, we see again the pattern that we have seen before. Once again, it takes what God made good and fatally distorts it by making it everything. To state that one look or one physique is superior to another, denies the truth that we are all made in God's image. It also hides the fact that God made us all different and that he is far more concerned about who we are than what we look like. We could respond by being negative about health, fitness and beauty. But again, this will not do. We need to come up with another flag-planting alternative that affirms what is good about the body.

Such an alternative would, I suggest, point out a number of things. Yes, we would agree, healthy bodies are important and it is good to pursue bodily health for ourselves and for others. Our bodies shouldn't be mistreated, neglected or discarded; we are to take good care of what God has given us. However, we might gently want to point out that our bodies, even the fittest, are not going to last for ever; we are all finite and fragile. We would also want to state, very firmly, that we are all made in the image of God and given his breath of life. The God who created us, values each and every one of us, whatever we look like. In fact, God loves us all so much that he put the highest value on us: the life of his Son. We would do well to remind ourselves that beautiful bodies are fine, but what God seeks most of all is not outward good looks, but an inner, spiritual beauty. Only that is of eternal value.

Power. 'Power' is a word that makes us sit up and listen. On the international stage, there is weekly posturing by 'political powers' and there is always mention of such things as the regional 'balance of power'. The media talk about global military power and economic power. We talk about power in our offices, councils and governments. Cars and computers with ever greater power tempt us. We read of politicians and governments 'coming to power', when we had thought they were being 'elected to serve'. In today's world, power of every sort is important and is worshipped. Power has become an idol.

Here again, as with the natural world, sex and the body, we see the same pattern of the good gift mutated into the tempting idol. There is nothing wrong with power: used correctly and responsibly, much good can be done. God has given humanity power and we are called to exercise it for the sake of his world and his people. The trouble occurs when power turns into an idol and is pursued as an end in itself, so that it is desired just to control and influence others. This is so tempting that it is all too common for people who started off seeking power for all the right reasons to end up becoming corrupt and betraying their original principles simply in order to stay in power. They have been seduced into worshipping the idol of power. We see the same pattern repeated throughout history in every organization, from schools to offices to governments. Not even the church is immune from the idolatry of power. Power seems to become an idol very easily.

So how do we react? The temptation here is the same as before. We could just reject everything to do with power entirely. We could make it a point of principle that all Christians automatically refuse promotion and deliberately seek jobs at the bottom of whatever ladder they are perched on. It is a simple, satisfying and apparently spiritual solution. It is also wrong. Never having power is too easy an answer. If we opt out of society, we can hardly complain when things go wrong. We are told to be salt and light in society, and to be either means that we must be where we can have influence. There are numerous examples in both the Old and the New Testaments of men (Daniel, Ezra) and women (Esther) who used their power for good, even within corrupt systems.

In this whole area of power, we need again to plant a flag for God. I have no easy answers, but let me make some points. We need to watch our motives. If we want to gain (or keep) some position of authority and power, we must ask ourselves why we want this. The only really safe answer is, 'To serve God and to do good to others.' If we are in power, we need to have wise and honest friends who will tell us if they think that our authority is adversely affecting us. Another principle is to ensure that there are outside checks and balances on our power. It is so tempting to abuse power that we need to be accountable to others.

Above all, we need to have before us the example of Jesus. Here was a person with literally unlimited power (after all, he was God), who spent time doing the lowliest of jobs and finally died a shameful death for others. He sets *the* example of humility and selflessness. All the power that he wielded was entirely for others. Furthermore, we read that Jesus spent most of his time with those outside the structures of power; those who were stripped of respect and dignity. He had little time for the religious or political establishment.

We need to ask how our exercise of power at home, work or church matches up to that of Jesus. Do we have the same attitude as he did? Do we have the same concern for the poor and powerless as he did? We have no excuse for worshipping power when we have the greatest possible example of someone rejecting its attractions put in front of us. Jesus totally rejected the corruption and idolatry of power. So should we.

Possessions. I talked earlier of the greatest of all our modern-day temples of worship: the shopping centres. We are a nation whose favourite pastime of shopping is in order to amass yet more possessions. This is an ancient trait in our species; human beings have always accumulated things and been strangely obsessed by them. In fact, much of what we know about the ancient world is because people were so strongly linked to their possessions that they had them placed with them in their graves. We have never had a time when we have had so many things that cry out for us to possess them, whether they be cars, houses, computers, jewellery, gadgets or books.

Here again, the temptation is to react to this idol by a drastic outright rejection of all possessions. Throughout the history of Christianity there have been individuals or groups that have decided to renounce all ownership of private possessions. It is tempting and superficially 'spiritual', but it suffers from the same problems as the other drastic solutions to the other idols. It doesn't work and it isn't true to the Bible. It neglects the fact that creation is good.

In planting the flag here, let me sketch out some guidelines. We need to handle possessions, but we must hold lightly to them.

We need to be able to look around at all that we have (our house, our car, our videos, our music, our books and our best clothes) and say, 'Well God, if you asked me to, I could give them up.' If we can say that, we are on the right track. An even better practice is to get into the habit of giving things, even good things, away. Nothing insults idols quite so much as giving them away.

These are just some examples of where idolatry is being confronted. What you and I need to do is to look at our own lives and see where we need to challenge the idols. Where in your life do you need to plant the flag for God?

Remember the cost of idolatry

As we come to the end of looking at this commandment, I want to discuss the cost of idolatry.

It is worth remembering that the Ten Commandments are given for our benefit, not God's. He is against idolatry, not just because it robs him of his rightful worship but because it is hurtful to us. In this commandment, as in all the others, he has our own best interests at heart. This commandment reminds us that God is jealous of anything that would take his place. God is not jealous because he is like some wicked dictator who just wants to dominate us and stop us from enjoying ourselves. On the contrary, it is precisely because he so passionately loves us that he is so severe about stopping us being involved in anything that would hurt us. If God did not react like this in the face of such potential harm, it would show that he did not care what sort of mess we got ourselves into.

Idolatry is harmful in two ways. The first is that it cheats and destroys those who practise it, and the second is that it steals from us the most precious thing we can have: a knowledge of the living God.

Idolatry cheats and destroys the idolater

The whole basis of idolatry is that it is a lie. We take things that are not God and pretend that they are. The results are catastrophic. For a start, idols lie to us. Think of the examples we've just looked at:

- The idol of the natural world whispers that, if we serve it, it will show us truth and meaning and give us purpose in our lives. But it never does.
- The idol of sex murmurs to us that, if we serve it, it will give us a permanent state of ecstatic joy, delight and intimacy. But it never does.
- The idol of the body tells us that, if we serve it, it will make us the gods and goddesses that we want to look like. But it never does.
- The idol of power thunders at us that, if we serve it, it will give us the freedom to do whatever we want, whenever we want. But it never does.
- The idol of possessions announces that, if we serve it, it will make us fulfilled, complete and content. But it never does.

They all lie. They never – except for the briefest moment – ever deliver. Many years ago, an Old Testament prophet said the following: 'Those who make idols are disillusioned because the gods they make are false and lifeless' (Jeremiah 10:14, NIV). It is hard to argue with that summary of things. These idols promise the world but cannot deliver; that is hardly surprising, since the world is not theirs to give.

If this was all that idols did to us, then that would be bad enough. But it gets worse. Idols also enslave their followers. In an effort to find what the idols have promised, we get lured in ever deeper. Devotees of the idol of sex know it well: they spend their lives in a futile, dangerous and ever more draining hunt for sexual fulfilment. But that is a mirage, as real as the pot of gold at the rainbow's end. The idol of possessions exerts the same hold; you may 'shop until you drop' but even then you will still want more. Idolatry is as satisfying as drinking salt-water.

The reason why idols grip us in an ever-tighter embrace is simple. When we give to some part of the created world the worship that belongs to God the Creator, that idol acquires power over us. When we worship things, we offer them our service. We may think they serve us, but in fact it is totally the other way round – we serve them. And idols are cruel masters.

Some of the most profound words on idols are found in the Psalms, the worship book of God's people.

> For our God is in the heavens
> and he does as he wishes.
> Their idols are merely things of silver and gold,
> shaped by human hands.
> They cannot talk, though they have mouths,
> or see, though they have eyes!
> They cannot hear with their ears,
> or smell with their noses,
> or feel with their hands,
> or walk with their feet,
> or utter sounds with their throats!
> And those who make them are just like them,
> as are all who trust in them. (Psalm 115:3–8, NLT)

The psalm writer is making the point that the idols of men and women are not real, they are not living and they are not lasting. If you are in trouble, they are useless. They have feet, but they can't come to you; they have hands, but they can't lift a finger to help you; they have eyes, but don't see what's going on in your life; they have ears, but they don't hear your cries when you are lonely, frightened or in despair. They are useless.

What is more, the writer says, their makers become like them. It is hardly surprising that when people worship idols they become like them: more and more unreal, more and more untrue, more and more false, and more and more dead. The trouble with idolatry is that it makes us less than human.

Idolatry cheats us of the living God

You may not believe it possible, but there is still worse news about idolatry. It is this: idolatry hides the fact that God wants to be the centre of our lives. Around sixteen hundred years ago the wise Saint Augustine opened the account of his conversion with the following statement to God; '. . . you made us for yourself and our hearts find no peace until they rest in you.' What he was saying is that there is a 'God-shaped void' in our lives that only God can fill. Idols fatally obscure that fact.

There is a living God and he is one we must worship. Now, I must remind you that God is very different from idols. Above all, he is the living God, the one who is above everything, the one who cannot be controlled by us. 'I am who I am' is how he defined himself, and part of that is his total freedom and independence. Psalm 115 said of the true God, 'Our God is in the heavens, and he does as he wishes.' There is a fierce independence about God that we need to respect. If there is a danger that we ignore the true God by worshipping idols instead, there is also another danger – that of treating the true God as simply another, but bigger, idol. In coming to the real God, we are coming to someone who will never be at our beck and call.

C. S. Lewis alludes to this in his children's story *The Lion, the Witch, and the Wardrobe*, when Mr Beaver talks about Aslan, the great lion.

> 'Who is Aslan?' asked Susan.
>
> 'Aslan?' said Mr Beaver. 'Why, don't you know? He's the King. He's the Lord of the whole wood . . .'
>
> . . . 'Is he – quite safe? I shall feel rather nervous about meeting a lion.'
>
> 'That you will, dearie, and no mistake,' said Mrs Beaver; 'if there's anyone who can appear before Aslan without their knees knocking, they're either braver than most or else just silly.'
>
> 'Then he isn't safe?' said Lucy.
>
> 'Safe?' said Mr Beaver; 'don't you hear what Mrs Beaver tells you? Who said anything about safe? 'Course he isn't safe. But he's good. He's the King, I tell you.'[1]

Lewis's description of Aslan is, of course, that of Jesus. He is one who, while being good, is not 'safe'. Idols are 'safe' – that is why they are inadequate.

This idea that the living God is free, active and cannot be manipulated by us comes over again and again in the life of Jesus. There is an independence about Jesus that we can – and ought to – find disturbing. Jesus can never be controlled or made to say what we want him to say; he will never 'toe the party line' and he never marches to our tune. Yes, he keeps his

---

1 C. S. Lewis, *The Lion, the Witch and the Wardrobe*, first published 1950.

promises, but in his way and in his time. He wants us to pray to him, but we can't give him orders.

Now this has exhilarating consequences for those of us who are followers of Jesus. You see I made the point earlier that we become like the things we worship and that dead idols produce enslaved idolaters. But in contrast to the idols, God is alive and free; he does hear, does see, does feel, does speak and does know. The Bible tells us we were made in the image of God, therefore if we worship him we become more human, more like the people we were made to be. To worship God is to become liberated.

We all need to remember that the living God is free and active. Oddly enough, we need to remember this especially in our churches. One of the dangers in the Christian faith can be that we acquire a certain view of God and how he works, and cling on to it. These images or ideas are often formed through experiences or teaching. They are often good and right ideas, and were probably God-given. The trouble is that we let them set the agenda for how God must work again; we hold on to past experiences and just look for repeats. We look back to wonderful times in the life of a church and use them as the criteria for whether God is working today. If something doesn't fit the pattern, then we reject it. I travel a lot and meet many people who have made past experiences, past churches and past ways of doing things into idols. Some aspect of their faith rather than God himself has become the thing they really worship. Because of this idolatry, new and good things can be rejected. Now, of course, I am not saying that new things are always the best, or that novelty is a proof that God is working in a situation. What I am saying is that we need to remember we are dealing with a God who is living, who is more real and alive than we ever imagine. We must allow God to be God, and not treat him as a tame idol.

Keep yourself from idols

At the very end of a letter written as an elderly man, the apostle John wrote this, 'Dear children, keep yourself from idols' (1 John 5:21, NIV). It is advice we need to remember.

Let me ask you what the 'photos in your wallet' are that could gradually steal you away from a relationship with God. Are there any things to which you have been offering sacrifices, perhaps secretly? What do you talk about the most? What does that reveal about the things you have at the centre of your heart? How free are you to give things away or to give things up?

We must all confront these idols, because they will hold us captive if they are not confronted. And, I'm afraid to say, it will not just be us they enslave. Did you notice that this commandment talks about the children of those who bow down to idols? That is not because God is some vindictive God who wants to punish innocent people; it is because idolatry has repercussions that, unless God intervenes, roll on for years. Whole families, and generations, get taken into captivity. What the parents worship, the children will do too. It is clear the stakes are high.

There is room for only one woman's photo in my wallet: her name is Killy. There is only room for one Lord in my life: his name is Jesus. What about you? We may reject God's warning by neglecting this commandment. But as Jonah in the Bible learned the hard way, 'those who cling to worthless idols forfeit the grace that could be theirs' (Jonah 2:8, NIV).

Now let me conclude with an encouragement. One of the exciting things about times like these is that we suddenly find ourselves in the world of the Bible again. The atmosphere that Christianity was born and grew up in was full of idols and worship of other gods. With great skill and courage, churches in cities and towns around the Mediterranean confronted idols and called the people to worship Jesus as Lord – as the God who was not created by them or controlled by them.

It is this call that the world needs to hear again, and needs to see lived out again. The apostle Paul, when he wandered around the city of Athens just under 2,000 years ago, was 'greatly distressed to see the city full of idols'. He then proclaimed the gospel, and many 'turned from idols to serve the true and living God' (Acts 17).

God knows that the 'images' offered by the world are bankrupt. He knows that if we pursue them, in the end we will find ourselves disappointed, devastated and worthless. The false gods will only take, take and take. The true and living God gives, gives and gives again.

Now, as we come to the first commandment, it is this true and living God we must consider.

COMMANDMENT 1

You shall have no other gods before me.
(Exodus 20:3, NIV)

So what's the problem?

Finally, we have arrived at the very heart of the Commandments; the great rule that we are to have no other gods but the one true and living God. If the second commandment deals with idols, those make-believe gods, this concentrates exclusively on the true God.

Now it is this commandment that underpins all the others and is the reason for everything we have already looked at. As the sun lies at the centre of the solar system and has the planets orbiting around it, so all the other commandments revolve around this first one. God himself lies at the heart of the Commandments and holds them all in place. It is vital that we understand that the one true and living God himself is at the core of all these Commandments, for two reasons.

First of all, it reminds us that we cannot remove God from the Commandments. This is something that people often try to do. In fact, if you think about it, I could have written a book on the Ten Commandments following the pattern that I have adopted here, but without so far mentioning God at all. In it, I would have argued that not murdering, coveting or stealing was a good idea because it was the best way for a stable society to exist. I could have argued that not coveting leads to less stress, having a day off a week makes you feel better, and that not committing adultery keeps your marriage intact.

I would not have been lying; in fact, all these things are true. On this basis, I could have justified all the previous commandments without bringing God in at all. True, I would have to have done some fast footwork on the last one. But even there, I think I could have justified a 'no-idolatry policy' on plain commonsense grounds, probably by interpreting it to mean 'thou shalt not get things out of proportion'. Such a set of commandments would probably be very popular and might find wide support across the diverse religious and spiritual landscape of modern Britain. But this first commandment makes such an interpretation totally impossible. These are God's Commandments and his name and character are stamped through them.

Yet as sensible as these Commandments might be, they only really make sense when we see God as being behind each of them. Murder is wrong, primarily because it takes from another person what was given them by God – life itself. Bearing false witness or lying is wrong because God is a God of truth. Adultery is wrong because God is a God of faithfulness. And so on. For us to really understand these Commands, I want to argue that it is vital we understand the God who is behind them. God is the foundation on which all the Commandments stand. He is not some optional addition to them, as if they were available in two versions, one labelled *With God* and the other *Without God*. You cannot take the God of the Bible out of the Ten Commandments any more than you can take the steel frame out of a skyscraper. All the Commandments refer to

God, and it is only possible to obey them when we are in a proper relationship with the God who gave them.

I said that there were two reasons why the idea that God himself is at the centre of the Commandments is important. The second reason is that Christianity isn't just about obeying some rules for life. It is not about 'the best way to act', or having a 'moral code to guide us'. In fact, to think of the Christian life as being a matter of 'do's' and 'don'ts' is to miss the point. For some people it may even be a catastrophic mistake. To say that Christianity is only about keeping the Ten Commandments is like saying that driving is all about keeping the traffic regulations and the Highway Code. No one would say that. We all know that driving is something else: it is getting into a car, starting the engine and travelling. The traffic regulations and the Highway Code are vital, but they are not at all what driving is about. The Ten Commandments have a similar relationship to the Christian life: they are the guidelines for life; they are not the life itself. This is something that needs to be explained because many people think that this is exactly what Christianity is. They think of it as being about a code of rules to live by. It is not. Fundamentally, Christianity is about getting and staying in a right relationship with God. And that is why this first commandment is so important. It puts God first.

The heart of the matter

Who is God?

'Very well,' someone might agree, 'God is behind all the Commandments. But who is this God? After all, there are many different gods around. Why should we take account of this one?'

Actually, God declares who he is at the very start of the Commandments. We mislead ourselves if we start the Commandments by simply saying, 'Number one: You shall have no other gods before me.' The Commandments really start with the two previous verses: 'And God spoke all these words: "I am the LORD your God, who brought you out of Egypt, out of the land of slavery. You shall have no other gods before me"' (Exodus 20:1–3, NIV).

The way the Commandments are set out is very similar to a legal or treaty agreement. They start, like most legal documents have done ever since, with the name of the one who makes the agreement. It is not quite '*I, John Smith, the undersigned, do hereby* . . .' but it is not far from it. In this brief introductory sentence, the one who makes the treaty with its Commandments sets out who he is. In it, God defines himself.

When we read these opening words carefully, we can find in them direct or indirect mentions of four descriptions of God. He is *God*, the maker of all things; he is *the LORD*, the one who reveals himself to humanity; he is *King*, the one who is our God; and he is *Redeemer*, the one who saves his people. Using these four pointers as guides I want to sketch out briefly what the Bible tells us about the one who gave the Ten Commandments to us.

The one who creates and sustains – God

'*And God spoke all these words* . . .' The one who gave the Commandments is the God who created and sustains the universe. The Bible opens with the declaration that God is the maker of the cosmos, of all living things and of us. There is no suggestion in the Bible that God *had* to make the universe. No one can make God do anything. So if he didn't have to make it, it must have been because he wanted to, because he chose to, because that's the kind of God he is. God is the one behind all the breathtaking beauty and astounding intricacy of the world we see. He is the one who is both powerful enough to create vast star systems and delicate enough to make a butterfly's wing. All the rhythms of days and seasons, all the cycles of life with their complex interdependency that we will never get to the bottom of, are God's handiwork.

God has not finished being God either. The Bible is plain that he continues to work in the universe by sustaining it and keeping it going. What we see as the 'laws of nature' are simply a description of God's normal working patterns. In everything that happens, from the sun shining to flowers blossoming, we see God's powerful but gentle hand.

Jesus, as God made flesh, was also a creator. Without being flippant, we can say that he took after his Father in this respect. We see this in the miracles where, for example, he turned water into wine, multiplied fish and bread and stilled storms. He did things that only a creator God could do. Perhaps we could say, though, that Jesus' main work was not so much in the area of creation but in the area of 're-creation'. In a world where God's good creation had been damaged Jesus brought a healing and restoring touch: the blind had sight given them, the paralysed were given working legs, and even the dead were raised. Now in heaven, Jesus continues that work. He creates new things and he restores and renews things that are damaged and broken by sin. And one day, we are promised, he will return in power and restore this ravaged world and make a new creation.

Now such a view should fill us with awe and reverence, and it ought to move us to worship. It should encourage us to treat these Commandments seriously. They are not the product of some human 'Working Party on Ethics'; they are a statement of God himself. It should also inspire us with confidence in them. These Commandments are indeed 'the maker's instructions', and we would be well advised to follow them. We need to be sure that the only god we have is this God.

The one who reveals himself – LORD

'*I am the LORD your God . . .*' In this opening to the Commandments, God states that he is *the LORD*. Now we looked at that strange expression 'the LORD' when we discussed the third commandment. Just to remind you, I said it represented an attempt by our English translators to represent the personal name of God that is written in Hebrew as YHWH but which was probably pronounced 'Yahweh'. This four-letter name means something like 'the one who brings into being all that is'. Behind this term lies the vital truth that God is not simply a maker or creator; he is also one who reveals himself to people.

The idea that God has revealed himself is critical. If God had not spoken to us frail and finite people we could never have found out about him. He would have remained a distant mystery, someone – or something – who could only be speculated about. But we see throughout the Bible how God spoke repeatedly to humanity, and how he has revealed to us who he is and what his character is like. In giving his name, with its links to the great statement that he is the 'I AM', God is allowing himself to be found by us. As God reveals in the Bible that his name is 'the LORD' or Yahweh, he also lets us know that this is his covenant name. It is this name under which he makes – and keeps – his promises to the human race.

In the Old Testament we see how the LORD revealed himself

to people in many ways: through words, visions, actions and by rare, brief and mysterious appearances. There is a distance between humanity and God, a distance caused not just by him being the eternal, infinite God but also by him being holy and us being sinful. In Jesus, though, God reveals himself fully to us. We see in Jesus as much of God as we can take in. God is no longer elusive, appearing only rarely to the very holiest of people; he stands before us in the flesh.

I was once faced with an incredibly hostile school assembly. To try to break the icy atmosphere, I began my talk by introducing myself as a Christian and asking if anyone had any questions about God. A hand shot up at the back and one of the obvious 'characters' of the final year asked sneeringly, 'Have you ever seen God?' I said, 'If I had lived 100 years ago in London, I would have seen Queen Victoria – the longest ruling monarch this country has ever had. If I had lived 400 years ago in Windsor, I would have seen Henry VIII, one of the most immoral monarchs this country has ever had. If I had lived 2,000 years ago in Palestine I would have seen Jesus Christ. But I wasn't around 2,000 years ago, so I didn't see him, but many people were around then. And they did see Jesus, so they did see God.'

In Jesus, we see what God is really like. Perhaps you've seen the film *The Wizard of Oz*? If you have you will remember the part where Dorothy and her friends follow the yellow brick road and eventually get to the Emerald City to see the great Wizard. There they get ushered in for an audience with him and find themselves standing in front of a huge and awesome face from which comes a booming voice. Just then the yappy dog Toto nips behind a curtain and reveals the real Wizard: an old man who projects his face onto a big screen and speaks through a microphone. The whole thing is a fraud and a big disappointment. It's important to realize that the God of the Bible isn't like that. In Jesus he meets us face to face and openly. There is no projection or screen, no booming voice or curtain. We see God as he wants us to see him.

Not only was Jesus like 'the LORD' of the Old Testament in revealing God to his people, he was also like him in making promises to them. In fact, he announced a new covenant, one that was to centre on his death on the cross and which was to be commemorated by a shared meal of bread and wine.

Jesus' role in showing who God is did not end with his death, resurrection and return to heaven. Jesus said he would never leave his people and promised that when he had gone back to heaven God would send his Holy Spirit to stand alongside believers instead of him. True to that promise, God still comes to his people – now no longer a nation but instead spread worldwide as the church – in the Holy Spirit. The Spirit reveals to us his love and his care, speaks to us his truth and helps us to pray and to know him.

The God who gave these Commandments is not a distant, aloof God. He is a God who has revealed himself to us, most fully in Jesus. He is a God who has done all he can to come down alongside us, to show us who he is, and make it as easy as he can for us to enter into relationship with him.

The one who rules humanity and history – King

'*Your God.*' It would be easy to overlook this little expression, 'I am the LORD *your God*'. To do that would be to lose a great truth, because this phrase points to the bond or agreement that already existed between Yahweh and the people of Israel. They are his people and he is their God. This is the language of a king and his subjects, and much of the setting and the structure of the Commandments is similar to the sort of treaty that kings made.

That God is King is a theme that occurs throughout the Bible. God, it declares, is King over humanity. He is King over individuals in that he sets laws for us, and he is King over nations in that he orders their rise and fall. He is also King over history in that he makes all its tangled events work out to serve his purposes. These Commandments were given that God himself might be King over the nation of Israel and that they would be his people. As we read in the Bible, we see that this idea was rejected by the nation of Israel and they decided they would rather have a human and visible king than a divine but invisible one. After a brief time under King David, these earthly kings failed but the hope remained; one day the Messiah, the godly King, would sit on David's throne.

When Jesus came, he came as that true and long hoped for King of Israel. His kingship, though, was not the sort that his contemporaries wanted. Jesus avoided any open and direct claims to being King and spoke instead of a kingdom of God that was far from the political notion favoured by the nationalists. However, those who observed him with open minds saw in his words and miracles undeniable evidence that he was indeed the Messiah King. Yet he was rejected, and under the Roman Governor's ironic (but prophetic) placard, 'This is the King of the Jews', he was crucified. Three days later, he rose from the grave and appeared to his disciples. Within weeks, the message was spreading out from Jerusalem: Jesus was risen and had given his followers power in the Holy Spirit. The words they were using for Jesus in the message were significant ones; he was Christ (the Greek for 'Messiah') and he was Lord, a title of respect that was used for emperors and kings.

The kingship of Jesus is not yet fulfilled; he is now the hidden king over a world that still rebels against him. That will not last for ever. The Bible is full of promises about the future and how, on a day unknown, Jesus will return in unspeakable glory and majesty to be the crowned ruler of this world. As he does, history as we know it will end and the kingdom of God will triumph. King Jesus will exercise a final and full act of judgement, and all those who have turned to him will live with him for ever. All evil, along with all those who practised it, will be eternally destroyed. In the new heaven and earth that the King will bring in, eternal wholeness, joy and life will replace all the pain, mourning and dying of this present age.

The God who is King gave the Ten Commandments, and if we are to be the King's people then we must follow them. Yet because of the fact that he is the King, and because he will triumph one day, we also know that to keep his Commandments is the best possible investment for our future.

The one who saves his people – Redeemer

'. . . *who brought you out of Egypt, out of the land of slavery.*' Finally, in this brief introduction to the Ten Commandments, God reminds his people that he has acted on their behalf. He is not just God the creator, God the LORD and God their King, he is the God who has taken them out of Egypt and brought them out of slavery there. Thankfully, we are unfamiliar with concepts and language of slavery today, but there is a word that was used to describe such a release. It was the word 'redeem' and the New Shorter Oxford Dictionary gives, as one of its meanings, the following: 'Free (a person) from captivity or punishment, especially by paying a ransom'. God was saying to the Israelites, 'I, Yahweh, am your redeemer. I have set you free, I have brought you out of slavery.'

This is another great theme of the Bible: God is our redeemer, rescuer and deliverer. Almost as soon as humanity had fallen into sin and rebelled, God announced that there would be a deliverer. The entire history of the Old Testament is that of God working out his purposes to create a people of his own from whom the great deliverer could come. He called Abraham and made promises to him, brought his descendants out of Egypt and put them in the Promised Land. Then through wars, famines and exile, under judges, prophets and kings, God taught his people that he was the one and that he would accept no rivals. God also taught them that he was holy and that the only way a sinful humanity could come to him was by rigorously and repeatedly obeying a system of animal sacrifices. Throughout these centuries of discipline and learning, God continued to show that he was a loving redeemer, constantly reaching out to rescue his people and forgive them.

Finally, just over 2,000 years ago, a baby was born into a family of the kingly line of David, in David's own city. The child was given the name Joshua, which as we saw when we looked at the third commandment means 'the Lord saves'. This child, Jesus, grew up to start his ministry acclaimed as 'the Lamb of God that takes away the sin of the world'. Throughout his ministry of preaching and healing, he made a number of references (often misunderstood by those around him) to his death. He would, he said, 'give his life as a ransom for many', have to 'drink the cup' of God's judgement and wrath and be 'the good shepherd who lays down his life for the sheep'. Finally, on the night of his betrayal, Jesus spelled out the meaning of his imminent death to his followers. Using the language of sacrifice, he told his followers that the broken bread and poured wine of the Last Supper represented his body and his blood.

The next day after a series of hasty, sham trials, Jesus was executed on a cross. What happened there is something so momentous that it is difficult for our minds to comprehend. Somehow, in dying on the cross, the totally innocent Jesus took upon himself the guilt and sin of other human beings. There are many pictures for what happened there. Some of them come from the New Testament (he 'became sin for us', 'made peace for us', 'paid a price', 'made atonement for sin' and 'was the slain lamb'). Other images have come from 20 centuries of imaginative preaching. For instance we might think of Jesus on the cross as becoming the lightning rod upon which the energy of God's judgement is expended, or think of him hanging there as a ladder between heaven and earth. Others have come up with stories from war, sailing or similar situations, where someone sacrifices himself or herself for the good of others. If you have seen the film *Saving Private Ryan* you will be aware of how its theme is that of a man being saved from death by the sacrificial death of another.

I rather like this rural picture I was once given. A country fox, I was told, gets rid of its fleas as follows. It collects bits of wool from hedgerows and fences and makes them into a ball in its mouth. It then walks into a stream slowly, causing the fleas to scramble up its body. As the fox goes deeper into the water, the fleas climb towards its neck and face until the fox lowers its head under the water and all that remains above the water is the ball of wool. The fleas climb onto the wool, the fox lets go and the fleas float off down the river, leaving behind a clean fox. Jesus, in some way, acts like that ball of wool; he acts as the focus for evil, absorbing the sin of the world so that we can be clean.

Now all these images are inadequate in one way or another. The death of Jesus on the cross is too big for any images. But the fact is this: on the cross Jesus became one of us and took our place. In that awful death lies our forgiveness, our freedom and our hope. Through it those of us who were guilty rebels are now able, if we choose, to become the sons and daughters of God.

It is no accident that God referred back to the way he had saved his people from Egypt before giving them the Commandments. He wanted to remind them that he was their redeemer. We have a far greater privilege than they had. The Israelites knew merely that God had redeemed them out of Egypt. We know that, in Jesus, he has redeemed us from hell.

The one who is more than we can imagine

This is just a thumbnail sketch of some of the things we know about God from the picture he paints of himself in the Bible and that he hints at the very start of the Ten Commandments. It is just a tiny fraction of what could be said.

One night Saint Augustine had a dream in which he saw a little boy on a beach. The child was at the water's edge, scooping up the ocean in a thimble and pouring the water out onto the sand. In his dream Augustine heard an angel tell him that this boy would have emptied out the ocean long before anyone could possibly have exhausted what could be said about God.

All other gods are finite and will fail; they are not worth worshipping for a moment. Only the true and living God, God the creator, God the LORD, God the King and God the redeemer, is truly worthy of worship, and he is worth worshipping for eternity.

Getting right with God

The Commandments, then, are fundamentally about ensuring that we are in a right relationship with God and that we stay in it. As I come to the close of this book I want to spend some time focusing on just how we do that.

We need to recognize God

Sometimes after a war or a power struggle in some country, we read that our government has 'recognized' the new leadership. We need to do that with God.

First, we need to recognize *who God is.* Many of us have an inadequate understanding of who God is. I have tried to explain something of the nature and character of the God who speaks to us in these commands. He is not an unknown mystery, some unfathomable being, or some make-him-up-yourself deity. He is the God who reveals himself clearly in order that we might know that we can trust him. Can I challenge you to think over what you know of him? Maybe you now realize that you have had some inadequate idea of who God is and that it needs changing. Perhaps you need to admit, for the first time in your life, that God really does exist.

Second, we need to recognize *God's concern for us.* The Bible tells the story of a God who cares for men and women even though they have rebelled against him. He cares for them so much that he has personally and painfully intervened in history in order to pay the price for their wrongdoings. He wants us to get into a right relationship with him. God desires us. He wants us to be friends with him, for us to know him in this life and throughout eternity, and for us to have abundant life. In short, he loves us.

Third, we need to recognize *God's demands.* It is God who has given us these commands. He has given them to us because he made us, he knows what we are like and he knows the best way for us to live. They are not given to become a weight around our neck, but to give us boundaries within which we can live safely.

Fourth, we need to recognize that *God wants the fullest possible relationship with us.* He wants first place in our lives, and he wants to rule over every area of who we are and what we are. There's sometimes a danger of thinking that God is just interested in the spiritual side of us. This is not the case. On a plane journey to the Atlanta Olympics a journalist asked President Clinton what his favourite event was. Without hesitation he said, 'The Decathlon.' He went on to explain that this event, with its ten different sections, was so like life, because there were separate disciplines which all had to be concentrated on with equal determination. Now many people compartmentalize their lives. You hear people say that they are only able to cope in life because they live their life in separate compartments, such as work, home, family, friends, pleasure, hopes and loyalties. These things can often be in watertight compartments that are kept entirely separate from one another.

The God of the Bible won't put up with being kept in a little compartment marked 'spiritual'. He isn't a one-day-a-week or a special occasion God. In this first commandment, God spells out what he expects, which is everything. Let's face it, he deserves nothing less than that. God is *God.* He is not applying for a job or bargaining for a position. Giving God the number one spot in our lives is not us doing him a favour; it is simply us recognizing the position that is rightfully his.

We need to review our lives

Having recognized all that God is and all that he demands of us, we need to review our lives. Imagine your life is like a car. Where is God? Is he actually in the car? Good. If so, whereabouts is he? It might be that you feel he is there, but you really try to hide him, in which case it's as if he's in the boot. It might be he is in the back seat, or he is in the passenger seat trying to direct things, but not fully in control. Or is it the case that he is, perhaps, as he should be, in the driving seat? But if he is in the driving seat, are you behind him trying to do some back-seat driving, trying to tell him how to drive and where to go? Jesus will settle for no other place but one in which he takes full control. That's what we mean when we call him Lord.

In the light of this, it is worth taking some time to do some stocktaking of our life as one of God's people. Let me remind you about some of the issues that we have looked at in this book.

Coveting. What is it that we aspire to? Who sets our desires? Do we desire what God desires or are we getting caught up in chasing after the things of this world? Do we trust him to provide all we need?

False testimony. Does the fact that God hears every word we say give us any cause to be ashamed? Are we truth tellers? Could we say that the words we use are always right? Is this an area of life in which we feel we have God and his standards at the centre?

Stealing. Are there things that we have acquired through dishonest means? Are all our dealings in order and above board? Does our life speak of the honesty of God? Do we put God first in our finances?

Adultery. In our relationships with members of the opposite sex, is there ambiguity or secrecy? If we are married, are we faithful to our partner in all our actions, thoughts and desires? Is our sexuality something we feel God is glorified by?

Murder. Are there people who we refuse to forgive? Are our relationships, at work and at home, healthy and free from malice and resentment? Are we prone to violence or harming another person in any way?

Honouring parents. Does our family life, whatever shape that is, honour God? Is there respect and gratitude, commitment and care? If some of the people we work with or mix with could see us in our home environment, would they be surprised by how we treat those closest to us? Is God the head of our family?

Day of rest. Do we take regular time off each week? Do we trust God enough to take a whole day off? Do we use that time wisely? Is there anything we do with our time that we are ashamed of in front of God?

The name of God. Do we live consistently? Do we swear? Do we ever justify our ideas by saying that God is behind them? Do we bring honour to the name of God?

Idols. Are there things that have us in their grasp, such as money, sex or power, for example? Do we ever find ourselves controlled by desires we feel powerless to resist? Do we have divided loyalties? Does anything else claim number one spot in our life?

I don't know about you, but I barely get past the first of these before being challenged about what God wants for my life. None of us can keep the Ten Commandments. In fact there is only one person who has ever kept them, and his name is Jesus. It is because he was able to live a life which pleased God in every way that he was able to pay the price for our lives which fall short in so many ways. Falling short of what God requires of us is called sin – something we are all guilty of and, what's worse, unable to do anything about.

Fortunately, we are not left simply under the judgement of God. We may be those who have broken the Commandments, but God has intervened in Jesus to help us.

We need to respond to God

It is quite amazing that God, rather than leaving us in the dark to work out how best to live, gives us instructions so that we can be the people we were made to be. It is even more amazing that he has provided a way to rescue us when we fail to keep those instructions. Far from despairing of us, God himself comes and pays the penalty for our rebellion from him and his ways. Jesus, the only one who ever lived by the Maker's instructions, chose to take our place. We are told in the Bible that 'God made him who had no sin to be sin for us, so that in him we might become the righteousness of God' (2 Corinthians 5:21, NIV). In him, a great exchange takes place. He gets what we deserve, and we get what we don't deserve: forgiveness, a new start, the promise of eternal life with God for ever.

God does this because of his love for each one of us, not because we earn it or have to show ourselves worthy of it. We do, however, have to accept it. Admitting our wrongdoing, we must say 'yes' to him and all that he has done for us. In grateful response to him we must now seek to put him first in everything. As he knows how weak we are, he fills us with his Holy Spirit so that we are able to do what he asks of us. It is only in the strength that the Holy Spirit gives that we can live lives that honour him.

God has saved us in Christ. The first thing we need to do is accept it with gratitude. The second thing we need to do is to work at relating properly to God as a result. It's easy to think that, even if we are forgiven, we are no more than God's servants. In fact he wants us to be his friends and children of God. So it isn't that he just wants us to do the right things; he wants us to have a right relationship with him.

What should characterize our relationship with God? Let me suggest that, as in any friendship, time is needed. One of the ways we keep God at the centre of our lives is to give him time. There is no better habit to get into than spending regular time with God. I would encourage you to carve out time, as busy as your schedule is, every day if possible (if not, then two or three times during the week) and set this time aside just to be face to face with him. During my face-to-face times with God I try to spend a proportion of the time in each of the following areas:

Praise. Give time to praising God, as a response to all he has done. This is one of the best antidotes to this generation's biggest problem, which is our obsession with ourselves. When we turn to God and put him at the centre of our lives, we take the focus off ourselves and put it onto him. Focus on him – worshipping and thanking him for all he has done.

The Bible. Read his word and listen to what he says. This takes the focus off listening to both our own words and all the advice and opinions in the world around us. Jesus himself said, 'People need more than bread for their life; they must feed on every word of God' (Matthew 4:4, NLT). In this day and age we have more access to the Bible than any other time, we have more study aids, more to help us get into it. There is very little to excuse how little we know of God's word. A very godly man called John Henry Newman once said, 'I read the newspaper to know what people are doing and I read the Bible to know what people ought to be doing.'

Confession. We must lay our lives open to him, asking him to show us where we haven't put him at the centre, as well as times when we have lived in ways which have harmed our relationship, and ask for his forgiveness.

Prayer. We bring our needs and concerns to him and ask him to establish his ways in the world. Again this serves to help us take our hands off the things that it is so tempting to hold on to, and give them over to God.

These four things – praise, reading the Bible, saying sorry, praying for ourselves and others – have been the main elements of time spent with God by Christians for 2,000 years.

However, I need to say that being face to face with God isn't just an individual thing, it also involves others. The Bible leaves me in no doubt that God wants me to meet with other people who love his name. Attending church is not some optional extra that is only for Christians who are particularly sociable. Church is where we can meet with others who are seeking to live their lives completely for God, so that we can worship him together, learn more about him, remember his death with bread and wine, and seek together to serve the world about us, as well as celebrating his life among us. God made us for relationships. When we are close to others who are seeking to put him first in their own lives, then we receive encouragement to live for him. In such an environment of trust we can be open about how difficult it is sometimes. We all have blind spots, and other people can point out areas of our lives that we aren't aware of, that are displeasing God. We can then receive support and advice.

It is more than likely that you know that the church isn't everything it should be. Perhaps you have had negative experiences of a local church or of Christians. But God is committed to his church, for the church is his people, and we must be too. If you are going to obey this first commandment, you must get involved in a church.

I want to conclude practically, by encouraging you to pray the following prayer. In some churches this prayer is prayed by the whole congregation at the beginning of each new year. It is a radical prayer of commitment to God, giving him everything and trusting him with all we are and all we have, from this day on. It is not a prayer that can be prayed lightly or flippantly. It is a prayer that changes our lives.

Holy God,

I am no longer my own, but yours. Put me to what you will, rank me with whom you will; put me to doing, put me to suffering; let me be employed by you or laid aside for you, exalted for you or brought low for you; let me be full, let me be empty; let me have all things, let me have nothing; I freely and heartily yield all things to your pleasure and disposal.

And now, O glorious and blessed God, Father, Son and Holy Spirit, you are mine and I am yours. So be it. And the covenant which I have made on earth, let it be ratified in heaven. Amen.

To pray this is only possible because we know that the God we pray to knows us and loves us. Therefore, we can trust his promises and give ourselves to obeying his commands, relying on his endless forgiveness, grace and strength.

> See, I set before you today life and prosperity, death and destruction. For I command you today to love the Lord your God, to walk in his ways, and to keep his commands, decrees and laws; then you will live and increase, and the Lord your God will bless you. (Deuteronomy 30:15, NIV)

Bibliography

Bass, Dorothy, 'Keeping Sabbath' in *Practising Our Faith* (San Francisco: Jossey-Bass, 1997).

Bloomfield, Harold H. with Leonard Felder, *Making Peace With Your Parents* (New York: Ballantine Books, 1996).

Carson, D. A., R. T. France, J. A. Motyer and G. J. Wenham (eds), *New Bible Commentary* (Leicester: IVP, 1994).

Cole, R. A., *Exodus* (Leicester: IVP, 1973).

Craigie, P. C., 'The Ten Commandments' in Walter A. Elwell (ed.), *Evangelical Dictionary of Theology* (London: Marshall Pickering, 1985).

Cray, Graham, *Postmodern Culture and Youth Discipleship* (Cambridge: Grove Books, 1999).

Edwards, Brian H., *The Ten Commandments for Today* (Bromley: Day One Publications, 1996).

Felder, Leonard, *The Ten Challenges* (New York: Harmony Books, 1997).

Field, David, *God's Good Life: The Ten Commandments for the 21st Century* (Leicester: IVP, 1992).

Ford, David F., *The Shape of Living* (London: HarperCollins, 1997).

Harrelson, Walter, 'Ten Commandments', in Bruce M. Metzger and Michael D. Coogan (eds), *The Oxford Companion to the Bible* (Oxford: Oxford University Press, 1993).

Horton, Michael S., *The Law of Perfect Freedom* (Chicago: Moody Press, 1999).

Kaiser, W., 'Exodus' in *Expositor's Bible Commentary* (Michigan: Zondervan, 1990).

Kendall, R. T., *Just Grace* (London: SPCK, 2000).

Kline, M. G., 'Ten Commandments' in *The Illustrated Bible Dictionary*, 1st ed. (Leicester: IVP, 1980).

MacDonald, Gordon, *Ordering Your Private World* (Crowborough: Highland, 1987).

McCarthy, John, *Some Other Rainbow* (London: BCA, 1993).

Mehl, Ron, *The Ten(der) Commandments* (Oregon: Multnomah Publishers, 1998).

Schlessinger, Laura, *The Ten Commandments* (New York: HarperCollins, 1998).

Sider, Ronald J., *Rich Christians in an Age of Hunger* (London: Hodder & Stoughton, 1990).

Sine, Tom, *Mustard Seed Versus McWorld* (London: Monarch, 1990).

Storkey, Elaine, *The Search for Intimacy* (London: Hodder & Stoughton, 1995).

Volf, Miroslav, *Exclusion and Embrace* (Nashville: Abingdon, 1996).

Wright, N. T., *Following Jesus* (London: SPCK 1993).

Wright, N. T., *New Tasks for a Renewed Church* (London: Hodder & Stoughton, 1992).

Useful Addresses

Write to your MP:

House of Commons
London
SW1A 0AA
Tel: 020 7219 3000

Bereavement

Cruse Bereavement Line
Helpline for bereaved people and those caring for bereaved people.
Tel: 020 8332 7227

Child Death Helpline
Telephone helpline for anyone affected by the death of a child.
Tel: 0800 282 986 – free call

Children

Childline

Helpline for children and young people or issues concerned with them.

Tel: 0800 11 11 – free call

NSPCC

For anyone concerned about a child at risk of abuse. Staffed by social work counsellors.

Tel: 0800 800 500 – free call

Drugs

National Drugs Helpline

Helpline for drug users, their families, friends and carers.

Tel: 0800 77 66 00 – free call

Domestic violence

Refuge

24-hour crisis line providing practical advice and emotional support for women experiencing domestic violence.

Tel: 0990 99 54 43

Environment

A Rocha International

Christians in conservation, working in a number of different countries.

A Rocha Trust
3 Hooper Street
Cambridge CB1 2NZ
Tel/fax: 01387-710286
E-mail: a_rocha@compuserve.com

Housing

Shelter
Helpline for anyone facing a housing emergency.
Tel: 0800 446 441 – free call

Money

National Debtline
Help for anyone in debt or concerned they may fall into debt.
Tel: 0645 500 511 – local call rate

Older people

Seniorline
Information service for senior citizens, their relatives, carers and friends.
Tel: 0800 65 00 65 – free call

Age Concern
Telephone service for older people, their families, and people working with them.
Tel: 020 8679 8000

Post-abortion counselling

CARE Centres Network, a department of CARE, supports and resources independent crisis pregnancy centres across Britain and provides a national helpline – CARE confidential on 0800 028 2228 – for anyone experiencing an unplanned pregnancy or difficulties following an abortion.

For further details please contact

CCN
1 Winton Square
Basingstoke
Hants
RG21 8EN
Tel: 01256 477300

or look at the CARE website, www.care.org.uk

Life
Helpline offering post-abortion counselling and support during pregnancy.
Tel: 01926 311511 (9am–9pm Monday to Saturday)

Life
Life House
Newbold Terrace
Leamington Spa
Warwickshire
CV32 4EA
Tel: 01926 421 587
www.likeuk.org

Rape and sexual abuse

Helpline for women and girls who have been raped or sexually assaulted.
Tel: 020 7837 1600

Samaritans

Confidential, emotional support for anyone in a crisis.
Tel: 0345 90 90 90 – local call rate

Broadcasters

BBC TV
BBC Television Centre
Wood Lane
London W12 7RJ
Tel: 020 8743 8000
E-mail: vlc@bbc.co.uk

BBC Radio 1–5
BBC Radio
Broadcasting House
Portland Place
London W1A 1AA
Tel: 020 7580 4468
E-mail: vlc@bbc.co.uk

ITV Network Centre
200 Gray's Inn Road
London
WC1X 8HF
Tel: 020 7843 8000
E-mail: info@itv.co.uk

Channel 4
Television Corporation
124 Horseferry Road
London
SW1P 2TX
Tel: 020 7396 4444
E-mail: viewer_enqs@channel4.co.uk

Channel 5
Channel 5 Broadcasting Ltd
22 Long Acre
London
Tel: 020 7550 5555
E-mail: dutyoffice@channel5.co.uk

British Sky Broadcasting Ltd [SKY]
6 Centaurs Business Park
Grant Way
Isleworth
TW7 5QD
Tel: 020 7705 3000
E-mail: feedback@sky.co.uk

Independent Television Commission ITC
33 Foley Street
London
W1P 7LB
Tel: 020 7255 3000
E-mail: publicaffairs@itc.org.uk
Regulates all commercially funded TV: ITV, Channel 4 and 5, cable, satellite and digital.

Radio Authority
Holbrook House
14 Great Queen Street
Holborn
London
WC2B 5DG
Tel: 020 7430 2724
E-mail: info@radioauthority.org.uk

The British Standards Commission
7 The Sanctuary
London
SW1P 3JS
Tel: 020 7233 0544
E-mail: bsc@bsc.org.uk

Contact Details

If you would like to know more about the ministry of J. John, or order books and resources, please contact:

The Philo Trust
141 High Street
Rickmansworth
WD3 1AR
admin@philotrust.com

or visit the website at www.philotrust.com

The Philo Trust is the charity which supports the ministry of J. John. The word Philo is Greek for brotherly love.

The Philo Trust was launched as a registered charity in 1980. Since then it has enabled J. John to lead nearly 200 missions throughout the UK and overseas, developing many innovative approaches to communicating the message of Christianity.

J. John is also a prolific writer, currently having 26 titles in print in 13 languages.

God's Priorities

Living the Lord's Prayer in the 21st Century

by J. John

Prayer shapes our lives. Through prayer we come to know the all-powerful God and who he is. Through prayer we allow God to direct our lives. The need to pray seems to be built into the heart of all human beings. So it was natural for Jesus' followers to ask him to teach them how to pray.

This book has been written for four groups of people:

- those who have just made a decision to follow Jesus
- those who have come back to faith after a time away from God
- those who know the Lord's Prayer but who feel they want to get to know and use it better
- those who are searching for God and feel that this prayer is a good way to start